ANNALS OF LIFE INSURANCE MEDICINE

1962 VOLUME 1

EDITOR:
SWISS REINSURANCE COMPANY ZURICH

WITH 22 FIGURES

SPRINGER-VERLAG
BERLIN · GÖTTINGEN · HEIDELBERG

Preface

The year in which this first number of "Annals of Life Insurance Medicine" goes to press happens to be the Fiftieth Anniversary of the Swiss Reinsurance Company's activity in the field of underwriting and reassuring those risks which later became known as "substandard lives".

In retrospect, it is a far cry from the old days when life assurance proposals were either accepted or rejected on medical grounds to the modern principles and methods of rating substandard cases both medically and actuarially. It can be assumed that in the course of the last few decades solutions, or at least approximate solutions sufficiently accurate for practical purposes, have been found to most of the numerous and often rather tricky actuarial problems relating to substandard policies, adequate premiums and reserves. No Life Assurer to-day however can fail to recognize that actuarial skill may only be applied to substandard life risks on the basis of medical assessment. Even the lay underwriter certainly realizes that the medical and statistical problems inherent in the underwriting of substandard risks are infinitely more complex than any actuarial consequences of a calculated or assumed extramortality.

It is primarily this basic fact which has stimulated the Swiss Reinsurance Company's plans to intensify and develop its research work in the field of the medical assessment of substandard lives. This research work is actually the sequel to long years of studies already completed in this field, the following-up of data collected on a large portfolio of substandard lives and of papers published on various occasions on both actuarial and medical problems. Any project which aims at contributing substantially to the modern science of medical underwriting can do so only if the many people preoccupied with these problems throughout the world join forces to the ultimate benefit of those most in need of life assurance.

It gives me therefore particular satisfaction to see that many a well-known name in Life Insurance Medicine is already backing these "Annals". May the circle of those interested in this paper, and particularly of those willing to contribute actively, widen in the years to come. The Swiss Reinsurance Company will at all times be glad to assist the Editorial Board to achieve its goal.

Max E. Eisenring, D. Sc.

Contents

Aims of the Annals of Life Insurance Medicine

At first sight it may seem venturesome to consider initiating a new publication at a time when the unprecedented flood of scientific printed matter continues to swell. Is there at this stage still a genuine demand for new publications?

On the one hand we have an inundation of medical papers with which the individual can no longer keep abreast. The reader can do no more than devote close concentration to a limited selection of interesting periodicals, of which there are a number of excellent ones available. However, from the viewpoint of insurance medicine such literature fails us in that it usually adheres to a purely clinical viewpoint.

On the other hand we now have a number of well-documented publications dealing with insurance medicine. We have in mind more particularly the reports on important national and international conferences, especially the publications by North American companies. However, the nature of such reports rarely permits the inclusion of long treatises. In general it is difficult to put into print detailed works of intermediate scope which are more extensive than articles in periodicals but less so than lengthy monographs.

We believe the problems of insurance medical statistics and their interpretation are insufficiently discussed at conferences on insurance medicine. Epidemiology and Prophylaxis continue to be the neglected "poor relations", despite their great importance in preserving and extending the life expectation of Man.

Instead of the limited regional thinking which is customary today in this field, it would surely be of interest and benefit to many for all of its aspects to be assembled, reviewed and reported on a global scale. The continually growing ramifications of political and economic interdependencies throughout the world demand an ever broader basis of operation.

The aim of our "Annals of Life Insurance Medicine" is to close or at least bridge these gaps.

In our publication, which is to be of considerable scope in most issues, the intention is to discuss current problems in insurance medicine. To render this specialist field more easily comprehensible, it seems to us that a close association with actuarial mathematics and insurance statistics is essential. In particular, statistical problems deriving from public health reports, mortality studies and clinical observations, are to be considered.

Two most important elements in this work of insurance medicine are the epidemiologic and prophylactic developments which currently play such a decisive part in the long-term prognosis of human life. That they will have an increasingly significant influence on life expectancy in the future is certain. We intend to study and report on these topics in detail.

It is proposed to draw upon articles from all parts of the world, not only for the sake of academic interest, but also with the practical desire to obtain other, new perspectives. To this end we have the valuable assistance of the world-wide organization of the Swiss Reinsurance Company, the sponsor of our publication.

An Editorial Committee and, in particular, an Editorial Board, have been formed for the purpose of preparing this publication, which will appear as a brochure issued at irregular intervals. These Editors include prominent physicians and insurance medical officers, representatives of a great variety of specialist branches, actuaries, statisticians and scientists from all parts of the world. We hope that with the valuable support of all these representatives from the world of science, we shall come close to achieving our aim.

The Editorial Committee:
Eugene V. Higgins,
Heinrich Jecklin,
Ernst Tanner,
Harry E. Ungerleider.

The Investigation of Mortality

H. WIESLER

Foreword

"Stat sua cuique dies" (Virgil)

Although our knowledge of the human life span provides the technical basis of every form of life assurance, the methods of investigating mortality have received only summary and theoretical treatment in most of the text books on actuarial science. The present paper will therefore provide actuaries with an introduction to these methods.

The paper, however, is also addressed to demographers, biologists and physicians. It is hoped that it will serve to sharpen their critical judgment of numerical data and warn them against the calculation and application of rudimentary index figures of limited significance. Although in subjects like physics and chemistry the use of statistics is regarded as entirely natural, the application of such methods to medical problems is far from being an established practice. It would be very gratifying if this paper were to succeed in affording the medical profession a better understanding of the statistics of mortality and causes of death, for the value of these figures largely depends upon their accurate collaboration. Such collaboration on their part would relieve official statisticians of the need to query entries in so many death certificates (over 15% of all deaths in Switzerland) and would also enable them to evaluate the data on the concomitant causes of death.

In deference to the last group of readers, I have kept the mathematical side of my explanations as simple as possible and, more particularly, avoided the infinitesimal calculus. I do not think that this will result in any substantial loss in the exposition and solution of the most important problems.

Indeed it is of the greatest importance in statistics to know the origins of the numerical data and whether they are subject to any systematic errors; the conclusions of mathematics are only as good as the figures upon which they are based.

This paper does not deal with the theory of graduation of life tables and their application in actuarial science or with matematical and statistical testing methods, for there is already an extensive literature on these subjects.

Zurich, June, 1962

H. WIESLER

Contents

Introduction

In dealing with living creatures, it seems, at first sight, futile to attempt to measure or calculate their length of life. In this sphere chance alone seems to operate: death befalls one man in the prime of life but allows another to exceed his allotted span. From the earliest times, men have regarded death as symbolic of the random and indiscriminate element of existence, and they have given expression to this idea in innumerable pictures ranging from early man's cave drawings to Holbein's "Dance of Death". And yet 'death, which may to many seem subject to no order at all, is actually a truly admirable exhibition of the most excellent order and its power is governed by the most stringent rules.' (J. P. Süssmilch).

Generally speaking, we take the investigation of mortality to mean those statistical methods which enable us to express mortality in numerical terms. Essentially this involves establishing certain index figures (crude, life table and standardized death rates) and constructing mortality tables. These methods, which are usually perfectly adequate for practical purposes, require only an elementary knowledge of mathematics. In most cases it is much more difficult to collect the data properly than to evaluate the figures once they are obtained. Hence, before proceeding to a discussion of methodology, we will explain in greater detail the definitions we use. Prior to this, however, we shall take a brief look at the history of the investigation of mortality.

1. The investigation of mortality — historical aspects

Amongst the peoples of prehistory and the ancient world, all the events befalling man were thought to be determined by natural forces, gods and demons. To learn what the future held in store, man devised astrology, augury, palmistry and other occult sciences. The Sumerians, the earliest of civilized peoples, devoted much time and thought to astrology. Diodoros* wrote: "They (the Chaldeans) have made observations of the stars for a long time and have studied the motions and forces of the individual stars with greater precision than any other men. It is for this reason that they can foretell so much of the future. They have devoted

* Diodoros, II, 30.

the greatest pains to studying the motions of the fives stars called the planets." All the astronomical lore accumulated in Mesopotamia, together with its astrological interpretation, the names of the stars and the division of the sky into the twelve sections of the zodiac, was imparted to the other peoples of the Near East and then passed on, mainly through the Hittites, to the Greeks and so to the Romans. Although Cicero, Horace and Propertius ridiculed the astrologists who were consulted by the populace in the Circus Maximus, still many educated men like Caesar and Augustus believed in the influence of the stars. During classical times the gods were still thought to govern nature and the fates of men. In Greek mythology fate was often personified as a supreme deity to whom all creation was subject, sometimes identified with Zeus himself, sometimes distinguished from him and called Moira, as in Homer. Later it was imagined that there were several Fates; these were called the Parcae by the Romans: Clotho, who spun the thread of life, Lachesis, who measured it, and Atropos, who cut it.

Although number systems had been developed in Mesopotamia and Egypt at an early stage of their cultures and Babylonian and Greek mathematics had reached a high standard, and although many statistical observations had been made of various natural phenomena and detailed statistical records kept of the population, particularly in the Roman Empire, there are virtually no clues suggesting that any attempt had been made to obtain concrete data of the human life span by rational, scientific means. The few clues we have are provided by the references of Herodotos to the average age of the Egyptian kings (II, 142) and to the life span of the Ethiopians (III, 23) and the Persians (III, 22)*. Servius Tullius introduced a kind of registration of civil status amongst the Romans. This was done by depositing a piece of gold in the temple of the goddess Libitina, the consort of Orcus. We know from occasional references of various writers that these registrations were also applied. For example, Ulpianus

* The King of the Ethiopians asked the envoys of the Persian King Cambyses "what their king ate and what the greatest age was that a Persian man attained. They replied that the king ate bread and explained to him the nature of the wheat. They also told him that 80 years was the greatest age a man attained. Thereupon the king retorted that he was not surprised that they lived so few years when they ate such rubbish, and that they would not live even as long as that if they did not drink themselves back to health, this being an allusion to the Ichthyophagi and their wine, for only in this were they (the Ethiopians) inferior to the Persians".

"When the Ichthyophagi in turn asked the king how long they lived and inquired about their manner of life, they learnt that most of them (i.e. the Ethiopians) lived to 120 years, and some of them even longer."

The number of 120 years is also mentioned in Genesis (VI, 3) as the span of life allotted to man by Jehovah; Moses also died at the age of 120 years (Deuteronomy XXXIV, 7).

In the palace of Sennacherib on the site of ancient Nineveh, lists of kings were found according to which the 10 'ancient kings' of the Sumerians had ruled for the fantastic time of 432,000 years. Thereupon followed the flood and then 23 more kings are said to have reigned for a total of 24,510 years, 3 months and $3^1/_2$ days. These figures are derived from the Babylonian priest Berossus. It has been suggested that these are not years in our sense of the word. I cannot agree, for it was the Sumerians who invented the calendar; it seems to me more likely that what we have here is a heroization of the kings, accomplished, amongst other means, by attributing to them extreme longevity.

(170—228 A. D.) calculated the average expectation of life for various age groups*.

In the 14th century Europe was ravaged by appalling plagues. The "Black Death" claimed its victims indiscriminately and the survivors were filled with dread and fear by the unpredictable and irresistible march of events. And as it was beyond mortal power to check this terrible disease, people turned in their despair to astrology and number mysticism. Ancient astrology was revived and its methods improved. The secrets of life and death were sought in arithmancies like those contained in the Arabian handbook of astrology entitled "Picatrix". Horoscopes were also cast which often entailed abstruse calculations, thus earning for the learned astrologer the name of "Mathematicus". Over the different periods of human life the stellar gods held sway, and since there were seven planets known at that time, man's life was divided into seven ages. Seven was in any case a number of great significance in the number mysticism of those days**.

One result of these speculations about life and death was that records of births and deaths were introduced in the 16th century. The Council of Trent (1545—1563) had decreed that a register of baptisms and a register of marriages should be kept in each parish. In 1614 Pope Paul V made registers of deaths compulsory. In England the first parish registers were introduced in 1583 in Worsop and Melton-on-Hill. The parish registers of London came to have a special importance, for it was in extracts from these "Bills of Mortality" that JOHN GRAUNT first began to seek the operation of some law where hitherto chance alone had seemed to be at work***.

* Ad legem Falcidiam, 35, 2. — The values are:

Age (years)	Expectation of life years	Age (years)	Expectation of life years
Birth to 20	30	44 to 45	15
20 to 25	27	45 to 46	14
25 to 30	25	46 to 47	13
30 to 35	22	47 to 48	12
35 to 40	20	48 to 49	11
40 to 41	19	49 to 50	10
41 to 42	18	50 to 55	9
42 to 43	17	55 to 60	7
43 to 44	16	60 and up	5

There is some question whether these figures are for expectation of life or for the present value of an annuity of 1. They were still in use in northern Italy until the 18th century.

** Cf. Daniel, 4., 16 and 17: "let seven times pass over him. This matter is by the decree of the watchers and the demand of the holy ones."

*** JOHN GRAUNT was born in London in 1620. He was first a draper and then became Commissioner for London's Water Supply. He had no previous mathematical knowledge but possessed a great flair for natural science. A second edition of his work had to be printed in the following year and on the strength of this he was made a member of the Royal Society. GRAUNT died in 1674 in London.

In 1662 he presented to the Royal Society a treatise entitled: "Natural and Political Observations mentioned in a following Index, and made upon the Bills of Mortality, with reference to the Government, Religion, Trade, Growth, Ayre, Diseases and the several changes of the said City". His treatise contained a table which may, with some reservations, be called the first life table. Presented in a modern manner it reads:

Age	Number of living	Age group	Number of dead in the age group opposite	
0	100	0—6	36	
6	64	6—16	24	The seven ages of man
16	40	16—26	15	
26	25	26—36	9	
36	16	36—46	6	
46	10	46—56	4	
56	6	56—66	3	
66	3	66—76	2	
76	1	76—86	1	
86	0			

By modern standards this first life table is very crude. For the years 1629—1636 and 1647—1658 the "Bills" recorded a total of 229,250 deaths, of which 15,757 persons were described as being "aged". As no differentiation was made between the dead in regard to age, GRAUNT made an arbitrary division in which he was guided by the mystical idea of the seven ages of man. Nevertheless, GRAUNT's table is the first known attempt to evaluate statistical data in this field. He also found that a numerical balance was maintained between the two sexes, that more boys were born than girls, and that the frequency of suicides depended on district, season, occupation and sex. So great was the interest of his contemporaries in publications of this kind that GRAUNT's essay went through seven editions. The brothers CHRISTIAN and LUDWIG HUYGENS used it to calculate the probable and average life span of man.

The prejudices inseparable from the philosophical outlook of the age and still inherent in GRAUNT's Table were meanwhile beginning to disappear, and man's approach to knowledge underwent a radical change. Experience and experiment took the place of metaphysical speculation as the instruments of research, technology ousted magic, and the exact sciences were born. Closely associated with this revolution are the names FRANCIS BACON (1561—1626), GALILEO GALILEI (1564—1642), JOHANNES KEPLER (1571—1630), ISAAC NEWTON (1643—1727) and WILLIAM HARVEY (1578—1657).

About this time there lived in Breslau a learned professor of theology by the name of CASPAR NEUMANN (1648—1715) who also had an encyclopaedic knowledge of natural science. He wished to take the methods his contemporaries had employed so successfully with the motions of heavenly bodies and the phenomena of nature and apply them to the processes of human life and death.

From the registers of births and deaths in the town of Breslau he drew up statistics with which, he believed, a great deal of superstition would be all the better refuted by experience. His figures proved that the dreaded influence of the planets on the deaths of men was quite without foundation.

Towards the end of the 17th century, the Royal Society in London resolved to measure the human life span in various places by a 'mathematical invention and by means of arithmetic'. CASPAR NEUMANN, probably through the good offices of Leibniz, was asked to lend his tables and the work to be performed on them was entrusted to the astronomer EDMUND HALLEY. In the "London Philosophical Transactions" for 1693 his treatise appeared under the title: "An estimate of the degrees of the Mortality of Mankind, drawn from curious Tables of the Births and Funerals of the City of Breslaw; with an attempt to ascertain the price of Annuities upon Lives". The life table given by HALLEY covering the years 1687 to 1691 is as follows*:

Age	Number dying within one year	Expectation of life, years
0	28*	33.50
5	3	41.55
10	1	39.99
20	1	33.61
30	1.5	27.35
40	2	21.78
50	3	16.81
60	4	12.09
70	8	7.53
80	17	5.74

* This calculation is based on an interpolation of the figures given to HALLEY.

This treatise earned for HALLEY the reputation of being the "inventor" of the life table because he was the first consciously to conceive the notion of a given population dying in certain proportions at different ages, i.e. the survivorship function.

However, his method was not free from error, for he supposed that the population of Breslau remained unchanged. Such an assumption may have been closer to the truth in the case of an inland town like Breslau than for a commercial centre like London with its floating foreign population. All the same, NEUMANN's death registers record 1174 deaths for an average of 1238 births.

On comparing HALLEY's life table with later tables, we find that it tallies approximately with the mortality trend of the German population in the years 1871—1880.

In the years that followed, little fresh light was thrown on the problem of investigating mortality. HALLEY's work did not always get the attention it deserved; it even provoked mistrust. The Dutchman, NICOLAS STRUYCK (1687 to 1769), professor of mathematics, cosmography and astronomy at Amsterdam, was

* including stillbirths.

the first to show (in a treatise published in 1740) that the mortality of women differed from that of men throughout their lives. He also found that there was a difference between the mortality of persons living on private incomes and that of the rest of the population. Another Dutchman (WILLEM KERSSEBOOM, 1691 to 1771) constructed a life table based on data concerning groups of Dutch annuitants, and the Frenchman DEPARCIEUX (1703—1768) constructed a similar table on the figures concerning the tontines* of the French state. They both avoided the errors made by HALLEY. In Sweden the astronomer PER WILHELM WARGENTIN (1717—1783) constructed the first national mortality table.

In 1741 there finally appeared a work which was a milestone in the history of investigation of mortality. It was entitled 'The Divine Ordinance manifested in the Changes of the Human Race through Birth, Death and Propagation' by JOHANN PETER SÜSSMILCH, provost at Cölln (on the Spree) and a member of the Royal Academy of Sciences. The fourth edition appeared in 1788 (after the death of the author) and, including the notes, comprised more than 2,000 printed pages. Although this work contained virtually nothing new, it was the first to associate the investigation of mortality with the ideas of politics and political economy, and it treated its subject with unrivalled exhaustiveness. LEONHARD EULER, who was a member of the Royal Academy of Sciences in Berlin at the same time as SÜSSMILCH, undertook to revise a chapter himself for the second edition. To seek the divine ordinance in all the phenomena of life was a task that was congenial to this man with his deeply religious mind and predilection for Christian apologetics. SÜSSMILCH himself wrote: (Part 2, fourth edition, pp 286 ff) 'Here an ordinance is apparent which can and must be rightly called the greatest, the most beautiful and the most perfect. Here we find general rules in obedience to which the life span of all men on earth is most exactly determined. When a thousand die, the number among them aged 20, 50, 60 and 80 is usually the same everywhere. Climate and variety of diet appear to have almost no effect in changing the proportion of those dying at each age to the total number of deaths. Only the way of life, its moral circumstances, vice and virtue, soft living and hard work causes a small difference between the numbers dying in the country and in the big towns.'

SÜSSMILCH also inveighed against the superstitious fear of the climacteric years. 'It is and old and commonly held belief that every seventh year is a step or rock where many a life meets with disaster. The sixty-third year, being a multiplication of two supposedly sacred numbers, 7 and 9, is thought to be especially dangerous. There are in fact many persons — even intelligent people — who allow themselves to be frightened by this belief, and whose peace of mind is restored only when this alleged mountain is surmounted.'

* The tontines were loans (usually from the state but also from private persons) in which the subscribers were promised an annuity representing a certain unchanged rate of interest on the loan. As annuitants died in the course of the years the survivors obtained a proportionately higher annuity, i.e. they inherited from the others.

Sometimes SÜSSMILCH gave his own observations, but he primarily collected the statistical data of his age. His tables were of great importance in German insurance until well into the 19th century.

SÜSSMILCH's point of view was that of a politician and still more of a theologian who wanted to demonstrate in his work the 'divine ordinance' in the deaths of men. His contemporaries, the great mathematicians ABRAHAM DE MOIVRE (1667—1754), DANIEL BERNOULLI (1700—1782) and HEINRICH LAMBERT (1728—1777), approached this problem in an entirely different spirit. For them it was simply a problem to solve in mathematics. ABRAHAM DE MOIVRE was the first (1725) to work out a mathematical formula for mortality trends so as to obtain easier rules of arithmetic in his computations of annuities. According to this formula

$$l_x = 86 - x$$

the number living at successive ages would be in an arithmetic progression. DANIEL BERNOULLI published in the "Histoire de l'Académie royale des sciences" for 1760 a treatise with the title "Essai d'une nouvelle analyse de la mortalité causée par la petite Vérole et les avantages de l'Inoculation pour la prévenir". In this he solved the problem of how many more persons would remain alive if there were no smallpox, and for this purpose he used the infinitesimal calculus for the first time.

LAMBERT, who was also a member of the Royal Academy of Sciences, was the first to draw the curve of survival. An investigation of mortality had been made in London for the years 1728—1757 but the numbers of survivors had only been given at decennial intervals. LAMBERT made an approximate calculation of the numbers living at the exact ages in between. LAMBERT was also the first either to introduce the following important concepts or to give them an accurate scientific definition: force of mortality, expectation of life, probable lifetime.

At the end of the 18th and the beginning of the 19th centuries the mathematical sciences received a powerful impetus from EULER, the BERNOULLIS, NEWTON, LEIBNIZ, D'ALEMBERT, LAGRANGE, LAPLACE, GAUSS and others. The age of religion and philosophy, D'ALEMBERT averred in his introduction to the 'Encyclopedia', had been succeeded by the age of science. As to the problem of causality in nature, the doctrine of determinism became established which argued that all natural events are strictly determined and predictable by a supreme mind. The following famous passage from LAPLACE stated this doctrine with admirable precision: "Une intelligence, qui pour un instant donné connaîtrait toutes les forces dont la nature est animée, et la situation respective des êtres qui la composent, si d'ailleurs elle était assez vaste pour soumettre ces données à l'analyse, embrasserait dans la même formule les mouvements des plus grands corps de l'Univers et ceux du plus léger atome: rien ne serait incertain pour elle, et l'avenir comme le passé, serait présent à ses yeux."

This was the philosophy with which LUDWIG MOSER, doctor of philosophy and medicine, professor of physics at the University of Königsberg, approached the problem of investigating mortality. In 1839, almost a century after SÜSSMILCH's book, he published his own treatise on the subject entitled. 'The Laws governing Length of Life, together with Investigations into the Duration and Fertility of Marriages, the Mortality from Diseases, the Ratio of the Sexes at Birth, the Influence of the Weather etc.' He drew a comparison between the law governing human deaths and the law controlling the free fall of a body. 'If we wish to obtain a more general understanding of the phenomenon of gravity, to extend the laws governing it to everywhere on earth and to define these laws numerically for each place, then we must make several observations of a similar kind so as to determine, as mathematicians say, the constants of the formula. The same is true of mortality. The number of deaths up to a certain age, provided it does not exceed thirty years from birth, is proportional to the fourth root of this age. For complete exactitude the law requires more than one observation, e.g. how many of a given number of persons aged 20 die in one year.' Today we should express his law as follows:

$$l_x = l_0 - a \sqrt[4]{x} = l_0 - a\, x^{1/4}.$$

For ages over 30 he gives the formula

$$l_x = l_0 - a\, x^{1/4} - b\, x^{9/4} - c\, x^{17/4}$$

where x = age, l_x = number of living at age x; *a*, *b* and *c* are constants.

Like MOSER, THEODOR WITTSTEIN also sought to reproduce the pattern of mortality by means of a mathematical natural law in his paper: 'The Mathematical Law of Human Mortality' (1882). He writes: 'However, the ideal goal of investigations of this kind is to be able to construct with certainty a complete life table from the observations of a few age groups, just as the astronomer can calculate the entire orbit of a heavenly body from a few observations.'

During the 18th and 19th centuries a number of great minds attempted to find the "law" of human mortality. In addition to those already mentioned, there were also: the English physicist THOMAS YOUNG, the astronomer LITTROW, the mathematician GAUSS, the Englishmen GOMPERTZ, MAKEHAM and EDMONDS, the Germans LAZARUS, AMTHOR, GROSSE, SCHEFFLER and SELLING, the Scandinavians OPPERMANN and THIELE and the Frenchmen DUVILLARD, LAURENT and QUIQUET.

Of the many attempts made, however, only the formulas of GOMPERTZ and MAKEHAM have stood the test of time. MAKEHAM's formula is

$$l_x = k\, s^x\, g^{c^x}$$

and gives the mortality from the age of about 25 or 30 with fair accuracy. Where s = 1 the formula can be stated in GOMPERTZ's

$$l_x = k\, g^{c^x}.$$

Methods of investigating mortality were further refined by the two demographers KNAPP and LEXIS (1836—1914). In his theory of dispersion the latter developed a method making it possible to ascertain whether the relative frequencies of death observed could be considered probabilities of the same kind as those dealt with in the probability calculus.

LEXIS was aware that life contingencies did not obey the laws of classical physics but that these values, deduced from a very large number of observations, are only a statistical representation of natural events. However, it was only in recent times, with the coming of modern physics, that this view could gain ground. The strict determinism described above, in which LAPLACE's daemon could predict all natural events, had to be discarded, and today we know that the pattern of life, sickness and mortality is not governed by laws like those of classical physics.

Today investigations into mortality are the business of statistical offices and insurance companies. The former give us the national life tables, which reveal a somewhat different pattern from the insurance companies' mortality tables because insured persons have undergone a certain selection from the health point of view. Today the investigation of mortality is no longer an end in itself; it serves the needs of industry and of government, which is concerned with social legislation and insurance of every kind. Accurate statistics on causes of death throw an explanatory light on the general decline in the death-rate and on the progress achieved in public health and medicine.

References

BRAUN, H.: Geschichte der Lebensversicherung und Lebensversicherungstechnik. Nürnberg 1925.

— Urkunden und Materialien zur Geschichte der Lebensversicherung und der Lebensversicherungstechnik. Veröffentlichungen des Deutschen Vereins für Versicherungs-Wissenschaft, Fascicle 58, Berlin 1937.

— Die Ansichten vom Leben und Sterben im Wandel der Zeiten. Veröffentlichungen des Deutschen Vereins für Versicherungs-Wissenschaft, Fascicle 60, Berlin 1937.

— Von der makrophysikalischen Auffassung des Sterbegeschehens zur quantentheoretischen Auffassung. Zeitschrift für die gesamte Versicherungs-Wissenschaft, Vol. 38, Berlin 1938.

EISENRING, M. E.: Bemerkungen zu den Sterbetafeln von J. H. Lambert. Mitteilungen der Vereinigung schweizerischer Versicherungsmathematiker, Vol. 48 (1948).

KING, G., and BÉGAULT, A.: Text-Book de l'Institut des Actuaires de Londres. Brussels and Paris 1894.

KNAPP, G. F.: Theorie des Bevölkerungswechsels. Braunschweig 1874.

LINDER, A.: Methoden zur Berechnung von Volkssterbetafeln. Bern 1934.

LOEWY, A.: Johann Heinrich Lamberts Bedeutung für die Grundlagen des Versicherungswesens. Festschrift für Alfred Manes, Berlin 1927.

LOREY, W.: Über die Lambertsche Sterbeformel. Blätter für Versicherungsmathematik, 3. Vol., 11. Fascicle, Berlin 1936.

— Johann Heinrich Lambert, 26. August 1728 bis 25. September 1777. Sitzungsberichte der Berliner Mathematischen Gesellschaft, XXVIII, Berlin 1929.

ROSIN, A.: Lebensversicherung und ihre geistesgeschichtlichen Grundlagen. Eine kultursoziologische Studie zum englischen 18. Jahrhundert. Kölner anglistische Arbeiten, 16. Vol., Leipzig 1932 pub. Bernhard Tauchnitz.

SPIESS, O.: Leonhard Euler. Ein Beitrag zur Geistesgeschichte des XVIII. Jahrhunderts. In the collection „Die Schweiz im deutschen Geistesleben". Frauenfeld and Leipzig 1929 pub. Huber & Co.

WESTERGAARD, H.: Die Lehre von der Mortalität und Morbidität. Jena 1901.

— Contribution to the History of Statistics. London 1932.

WIESLER, H.: Über die Grundlagen der Lebensversicherungsmathematik. Mitteilungen der Vereinigung schweizerischer Versicherungsmathematiker. Vol. 44 (1944).
— Die Statistik im Altertum. Zürich 1958.
WITTSTEIN, TH.: Das mathematische Gesetz der menschlichen Sterblichkeit. 2. Edition, Hannover 1883.
ZWINGGI, E.: Leben und Sterben in mathematischer Darstellung. Mitteilungen der Vereinigung schweizerischer Versicherungsmathematiker. Vol. 42 (1942).

2. Basic considerations in investigating mortality

2.0 Distinction between de facto and de jure populations

In censuses the population can be divided into two classes: the *de facto* population and the *de jure* population.

The *de facto population* comprises all those persons who are physically found in an area at the census date regardless of their usual residences; that is to say, it includes foreigners and any other persons who are there by chance whereas residents who are temporarily absent are not included. Because of its simplicity this distinction was employed for a long time, and it is still employed today, particularly in the underdeveloped countries. Recently, however, it has been replaced in most of the civilized countries by the *de jure* enumeration, which gives a much more valid picture. This method assigns the population to the respective areas of usual residence; thus persons who find themselves in a country or a community by chance are not enumerated in the de jure population, while those who are temporarily absent, but normally resident in the community, are enumerated*. The distinction between the de facto population and the de jure population is of particular importance when it is desired to compare the figures.

Needless to say, the same question also arises in connection with the registration of births, deaths and marriages etc. In such cases must one consider the place where the event occurred or the place where the person is normally resident? For example, should the question be framed to elicit the place where the child was born or the usual residence of the mother, the place where the deceased died or his usual residence?

Here again, the older school of statistics wanted to know simply where the event occurred because this was much simpler. However, the defects of such a method will become apparent when it is remembered how many persons enter

* In Switzerland the de jure population is used as a basis for all censuses, the only exceptions being the censuses of 1870 and 1880. As the figures given below show, there may be substantial differences between the results of the two methods:

	1941	1950
De facto population	4,279,455**	4,723,163
De jure population	4,265,703	4,714,992
Difference	13,752	8,171

** Including 10,800 military internees.

town hospitals or maternity homes from surrounding rural areas*. Today the ruling in Switzerland is that, in principle, each death is registered in the community where the deceased was legally resident. Where, however, the deceased has spent more than six months in a hospital or a sanatorium, the place of death is taken to be the place of usual residence**.

2.1. *Distinction between urban and rural*

A distinction of this kind becomes necessary not only in the analysis of general mortality but more particularly in determining the incidence of various causes of death. Unfortunately there is no unanimity as to a basis of distinction between urban and rural; some statisticians base their distinction on the extent to which an area is built up, others refer to the social or economic structure. The simplest and also the most usual method is a purely statistical distinction according to the population. But here again there is no uniformity as the following two examples show:

In Switzerland		In the USA
100,000 and over:	large towns	Cities of 100,000 or more
30,000—100,000:	medium towns	„ „ 25,000 to 100,000
10,000— 30,000:	small towns	„ „ 10,000 to 25,000
less than 10,000:	country	„ „ 2,500 to 10,000
		country less than 2,500

As already mentioned, such a distinction is based on a purely arbitrary classification of population figures. Individual towns of 30,000 inhabitants may be found which are still rural in appearance while there are villages with a population of only 5,000 which have an urban character.

It is more difficult still to draw up rules where various connected communities of a similar character are combined to form a conurbation. In some states the functional connections between the town and its suburbs — the town as the place

* In the *USA*. 14.8% of the deceased in 1940 were not normally resident where they died. In towns with populations from 10,000 to 100,000 more than 23% of all registered deaths were non-residents. In the same towns 36.8% of births were the children of mothers who were not usually resident there.

In 1954 the figures for the *City of Zurich* were as follows:

Total births in Zurich	8,069
Births to non-residents in Zurich	2,386
Births to residents in Zurich occurring elsewhere	118
Births to residents in Zurich	5,801

** This is, of course, a debatable convention. There is no doubt that the period of six months was too short considering the former methods of treating tuberculosis. On the other hand this period served to eliminate the many cases of persons who succumbed to the fatal influences of a place while staying there only temporarily.

of work for the suburban population, commuting etc. — are taken as a basis; other states use purely formal (statistical) data such as the extent to which an area is built up*.

2.2. *The definition of death, stillbirth*

Although the definition of death is clear and unequivocal, the statistical definition of stillbirth causes serious difficulty. In the course of time various definitions have been given. They aim at a precise distinction between live birth, abortion or miscarriage. The definitions proposed by the World Health Organization and the United Nations Organization are as follows: **

Live birth is the complete expulsion or extraction from its mother of a product of conception, irrespective of the duration of pregnancy, which, after such separation, breathes or shows any other evidence of life, such as beating of the heart, pulsation of the umbilical cord, or definite movement of voluntary muscles, whether or not the umbilical cord has been cut or the placenta is attached; each product of such a birth is considered live-born.

Foetal death is death prior to the complete expulsion or extraction from its mother of a product of conception, irrespective of the duration of pregnancy; the death is indicated by the fact that after such separation the foetus does not breathe or show any other evidence of life, such as beating of the heart, pulsation of the umbilical cord, or definite movement of voluntary muscles.

These definitions have now been adopted by various countries (including the USA).

In Switzerland the following definition is given:

A child is deemed to be stillborn and notifiable according to the provisions of the Civil Code if, after completely emerging from the womb (head, body and limbs) it does not breathe, its heart does not beat and the body is more than 30 cm long.

When reporting the causes of a stillbirth, the physician must indicate whether this was due to a disease or anomalies in the mother or the growing body of the child, or to other factors such as Rhesus incompatibility etc.

Even where objective standards have been established, data concerning stillbirths is still largely influenced by subjective and ideological factors, and this must be remembered when comparing different regions.

2.3 *The nomenclature of causes of death*

The sorting of deaths according to cause is probably the most difficult problem in mortality statistics. Here we are no longer concerned with formal data such as the place of death, civil status, sex, age etc. but with characteristics which are a reflection of the state of scientific knowledge, classifications which depend on the training and diagnostic ability of the physician, and frequently with the

* In Switzerland communities are considered to form part of an urban agglomeration if more than 30% of the working population work in the town and the proportion of the population engaged in agriculture is less than 20%.

** *United Nations.* Statistical Office. Principles for a Vital Statistics System; Recommendations for the Improvement and Standardization of Vital Statistics. 1953.

effects of subjective judgment, for which allowances must be made. Moreover, the classification can be made from a variety of standpoints. The anatomist, for instance, will start from the part of the body affected while the pathologist will be primarily interested in the nature of the morbid process. The clinician will view the case from both points of view and also take the aetiology of the disease into account.

WILLIAM FARR and MARC D'ESPINE were the first to attempt an *international nomenclature* of causes of death in 1853, but it was not until 1893 that a final version was submitted to the International Congress of Statisticians in Brussels by JACQUES BERTILLON. Every 10 years this nomenclature has been revised so as to keep abreast of medical progress. The present international nomenclature was revised by recognized experts on behalf of the World Health Organization and is used in most countries in Europe, North and South America and Australia. It comprises a joint index for the statistics of morbidity and causes of death and, in this respect, is different from the older international indexes. In addition to the detailed nomenclature with four-figure subcategories, there is a medium list with 150 items and a shorter version of each containing 50 items for mortality statistics and for the morbidity statistics of social insurance.* (Copies of each of these lists appear as appendices to this book.) The list is divided into major groups in the following order: First come the diseases due to a specific infectious agent, followed by the categories for neoplasms and the allergic, endocrine, metabolic and nutritional diseases. Most of the remaining diseases are classified according to their location with special divisions for mental diseases, complications of pregnancy and birth, characteristic diseases of childhood, senile decay, and morbid conditions and syndromes which are not readily definable. The last section consists of a double classification of injuries and external damage.

Until recently *Switzerland* took an independent line in classifying the causes of death. Nor was the system used a bad one; PRINZING said that Switzerland's statistics of causes of death took the first place in the world.** The system was introduced by the Federal Law on Civil Status of December 24, 1874, which came into force on January 1, 1876. This prescribed that the death register should contain the cause of death, certified whenever possible by a physician. However, little reliance could be placed on the data forthcoming as a result of this regulation; the doctors were of opinion that the registration of the cause of death constituted a breach of professional secrecy and held that this was a great fault in the system. In consequence they were very reticent in their reports. To remedy this state of affairs a confidential death card, intended only for statistical purposes, was introduced in 1901. In this way neither the registrar nor any other persons became cognizant of the cause of death. Professional secrecy was

---

* Manual of the International Statistical Classification of Diseases, Injuries, and Causes of Death; 7th revision of the International Lists of Diseases and Causes of Death, adopted 1955, Geneva, 1957.

** PRINZING, F.: Handbuch der medizinischen Statistik, 2nd edition. Jena 1931.

preserved by means of this anonymous death card, and this measure has been largely instrumental in making Swiss statistics of causes of death among the best in the world.

In order to embody the latest additions to scientific knowledge, the Swiss nomenclature of causes of death has been revised every ten years for the last thirty years. Care has always been taken to ensure that, as far as possible, comparisons with earlier Swiss nomenclatures as well as with the international system should remain possible. It may perhaps be asked why Switzerland has not simply adopted the international nomenclature. This was not feasible because in a number of groups, e.g. tumours and accidents, Swiss specifications are more detailed than those of the international system. It would therefore be a retrograde step for Switzerland to adopt this scheme and, what is more important, indispensable comparisons with earlier records would be rendered much more difficult.

The new detailed International List (1948 and 1958) proved unsuitable for the *German Federal Republic* particularly where the statistics of causes of death were concerned. Its classification is so detailed that, in practice, it is frequently impossible to assign a death to the correct category on the basis of the data available concerning its cause. With the International System as a model, the German Federal Office of Statistics therefore elaborated a taxonomy of about 380 items constructed on the decimal system. In addition the medium and two short international lists are also used.

2.4. Tumours — nomenclature

In order to obtain an optimal, international classification of the various forms of cancer which would make it possible to compare statistics collected at different times and places, the TNM system was devised. This permits the stages of tumour growth to be clinically classified on an international basis and was accepted by the IX International Radiological Congress at Munich in 1959. The system is described below.

In the TNM system T = tumour, N = noduli lymphatici, M = distant metastases. The state of the disease is expressed by means of a formula (indicative of the growth of the tumour and the metastatic condition) in which the following clinical data are given:

1. Primary tumour (T)

T_1 = Small primary tumour, strictly limited to the organ of origin,

T_2 = Relatively large primary tumour which has progressed beyond its point of origin but has not yet crossed the boundaries of the organ,

T_3 = Primary tumour which has crossed the boundaries of the organ and grown into the surrounding part,

T_4 = Primary tumour which has encroached broadly on the surrounding part,

2. Metastases (N and M)

Na = No lymph nodes palpable,
Nb = Mobile lymph nodes palpable,
Nc = Fixed lymph nodes palpable,
M = Distant metastases.

The TM system is used only when it is clinically impossible to demonstrate the presence of regional metastases for topographical and anatomical reasons.

The T system is employed for tumours which are non-metastasizing but frequently relapse and give evidence of infiltrative growth, i.e. the so-called semi-malignant tumours. Where distant metastases are found but the primary tumour cannot be located, the formula is T_0M.*

2.5 Certification of death and rules for classification

Definition of the underlying cause of death

It is a relatively simple matter to classify the causes of death for statistical purposes when there is only a single cause. Frequently, however, death is due to a combination of two or more diseases. Such cases are of growing frequency today because the recession of infectious diseases and the increasing proportion of old persons in the population have led to a greater number of deaths in which a variety of chronic diseases are implicated. In registering such cases it has always been the statistical practice to single out one of the causes. In the past this cause has been known by a number of names, e.g. "cause of death", "primary cause of death", "principal cause of death", "original cause of death", "basic disease". It can be defined as follows:

a) the disease or injury which initiated the condition resulting directly in death, or

b) the circumstances of the accident or violence causing the fatal issue.

In order to standardize both the terminology and the procedure for singling out the causes of death, the Sixth International Revision Conference drew up the following rules for classification. However, these rules cannot be applied unless the international death certificate proposed by the same conference (or a similar document) is also used.

Form of the death certificate

We reproduce on the following page the section of the *international death certificate* referring to the causes of death.

---

* For details see: Schinz and Wellauer, Das TNM-System bei den wichtigsten Krebslokalisationen und dessen Ausbau, in „Fortschritte auf dem Gebiete der Röntgenstrahlen und der Nuklearmedizin", Vol. 19, No. 1/1959, George Thieme, Stuttgart. — Schinz, Das TNM-System bei den wichtigsten Krebslokalisationen und dessen Ausbau, in „Krebsforschung und Krebsbekämpfung", Vol. III, Urban & Schwarzenberg, Munich and Berlin.

International form of medical certificate of cause of death

Cause of Death		Approximate interval between onset and death
I Disease or condition directly leading to death*	a) . . . . due to (or as a consequence of)	. . . .
Antecedent causes Morbid conditions, if any, giving rise to the above cause, stating the underlying condition last	b) . . . . due to (or as a consequence of) c)	. . . .
II *Other significant conditions* contributing to the death, but not related to the disease or condition causing it	. . . .	. . . .

* This does not mean the mode of dying, e.g., heart failure, asthenia, etc. It means the disease, injury, or complication which caused death.

As may be seen, this certificate comprises two sections: In Section I the cause leading directly to death is entered under a); under b) and c) the antecedent diseases and conditions are stated which led to the cause given above. An entry under b) and c) is superfluous when the disease reported under a) gives an adequate description of the train of events. Section II is for any other significant conditions which have adversely affected the development of the morbid process and thus contributed to the death without being related to the disease or condition leading directly to it.

The physician who makes out the death certificate is responsible for reporting the cause of death; he is better placed than anybody else to decide which disease or condition led directly to death.*

Rules for singling out the original cause of death (underlying cause) for statistical classification

As already mentioned, the World Health Organization advises its members to construct their primary statistics by singling out the underlying cause in accordance with the "International Statistical Classification of Diseases, Injuries and Causes of Death". No difficulty arises if only *one* cause of death is given. If

* In recent years the number of deaths occurring in Switzerland without medical attendance has been about 2% of the total. This figure varies from district to district and is, of course, higher in the mountains than in the lowlands. It is largely dependent on the number of practitioners in a given area.

In the USA the proportion of inadequately certified or unknown causes of death decreased from 3.92% in 1900 to 0.2% in 1940. Here again the figure varies widely from district to district. In 1940, for instance, it was only 0.01% in Rhode Island whereas in New Mexico it was 20%. The number of children under 1 year of age whose cause of death is unknown is particularly high.

an injury is involved, either the circumstances under which the injury was inflicted or the type of injury will be noted.

In all cases where more than one cause of death is given in the certificate of death, the cause to be registered is selected according to the following.

General rule. The cause to be selected is the underlying cause which initiated the train of events leading to death. In a properly completed international death certificate the diseases entered under Ia), b) and c) should be arranged so that the original cause (underlying cause) is given last.

Example: a) Uremia
b) Ischuria
c) Hypertrophy of the prostate
The cause to go on record is hypertrophy of the prostate.

Example: a) Lung abscess
b) Lobar pneumonia
The cause to go on record is lobar pneumonia.

In selecting the underlying cause the information supplied by the certifying physician must be accepted as correct since it embodies his opinion as to the diseases leading to death and the relations between them. Exceptions are made only when it may be assumed that the certificate of death has been incorrectly completed since the entries are improbable, inaccurate, inappropriate, incomplete or ambiguous*, as in the following cases:

Example: a) Diphtheria
b) Acute myocarditis
Enter as diphtheria because it is clear that the above-mentioned sequence has been reversed.

Example: a) Lung metastases
b) Cerebral carcinoma
c) Lung abscess
Enter as malignant cerebral tumour.

Example: a) Cor pulmonale
b) Esophageal varices, liver cirrhosis and chronic bronchitis
Enter as chronic bronchitis. The train of events "cor pulmonale following upon chronic bronchitis" has precedence over "esophageal varices following upon liver cirrhosis".

Example: a) Bronchopneumonia
b) Senility
Enter as bronchopneumonia. Vague declarations such as senility and the like are best avoided wherever possible.

* The Statistical Office of the USA has published a special "Manual of Joint Causes of Death" (4th Edition 1939). For each number of the International Index of Causes of Death, this manual indicates which other numbers are to be selected as causes of death if they appear concomitantly.

Since in recent years some countries have adopted the *Swiss method of notification* with an anonymous death card, some further details of this system may be of interest.

At the top of the card in use there is a strip where the registrar enters the year and number of the death register, the name of the deceased as well as his or her year of birth and place of residence. He then forwards the card complete with these particulars to the physician. The latter enters the cause of death, detaches the top of the form with the name of the deceased and then returns the anonymous card to the registrar in a sealed envelope. The registrar checks that the card has been received by means of the number of the death register marked on the envelope and then forwards it unopened to the Federal Office of Statistics. Here the particulars of the causes of death are checked by a physician and any doubtful points clarified with the doctor treating the case. After the data on the card have been evaluated by mechanical means, it is filed away and cannot be produced even in courts of law. In this way the professional secrecy of the physician is preserved in every respect.

As in the international certificate of death, the physician is required to enter on the Swiss certificate not only the primary cause but also the secondary disease and the concomitant disease or conditions.

Physicians are instructed to adhere strictly to the terms of the nomenclature of causes of death when making out death certificates. General designations such as pneumonia, diabetes, angina, icterus etc. or heart disease, kidney disease and the like are not sufficient. Instead it must be clearly stated what specific kind of disease is involved. Entries such as apoplexy, cardiac crisis, paralysis of the heart, dropsy, edema and similar expressions are to be avoided, for they are usually only the consequences of an underlying disease. In the case of tumours the type and the primary location should be noted wherever possible. Thus terms like neoplasm, malignant tumour or intestinal tumour should not be used but in their place specific designations such as cerebral glioma, carcinoma of the colon, stomach carcinoma, melanoma of the face etc. Instead of simply "carcinoma of the abdomen", explicit terms such as "carcinoma of the bladder, of the uterus, of the cervix, of the ovaries" etc. should be employed. Secondary localisations should be expressly designated as such. In cases of endocarditis, bronchitis, nephritis, articular rheumatism etc. it should be stated whether the condition is acute or chronic, in heart impairments, hydrocephalus etc. whether congenital or acquired. In heart disease a distinction should be made wherever possible between cardiopathies of arteriosclerotic and those of rheumatic origin.

Also to be avoided are such inadequate topographical descriptions as ear, throat, nose, arm, leg, abdomen, pelvis etc. Expressions like these complicate statistical work and lead to false conclusions. Information as to the anatomical site, the tissue or the organ, the seat or starting point of the disorder or neoplasm is also of interest to statisticians evaluating data on causes of death.

In the case of violent death, it should be stated whether it is the consequence of suicide, accident or a culpable act by a third party. Designations such as shot-wound in the head, cerebral injury, fractured skull, fractured pelvis, fall from window etc. are insufficient for statistical classification. Instead the type, cause and antecedent circumstances of the event leading to death should be briefly described. To permit comparison with the international nomenclature, a designation of the victim at the time of the accident (e.g. pedestrian, driver etc.) and also a description of the circumstances of the accident (car collision, fall from bicycle etc.) are required in addition to particulars of bodily injury.

If death occurred as the result of an operation or other therapeutic procedure, it is of interest for statistical purposes to have more particulars of the circumstances. In view of the strictly confidential treatment of the particulars given on the death card there is no reason to suppress any facts which are of importance in clarifying the cause of death.

The value of mortality statistics is largely dependent upon the accuracy with which deaths are classified by cause in accordance with the rules set forth above. Such statistics can present an entirely different picture depending upon the mode of classification selected, as the following examples will show. In 1957 Belgium reported 24 deaths from diabetes mellitus per 100,000 inhabitants, whereas West Berlin had only 6.1 in spite of the unfavourable age structure of the population there. This discrepancy is explained by the fact that in Belgium diabetes mellitus is specified as the cause of death where diabetic patients die from arteriosclerosis, whereas in West Berlin such deaths go on record as being due to arteriosclerosis. When the USA went over to the International Index of Causes of Death there were such serious changes in regard to diabetes mellitus that it is debatable whether a valid comparison with figures for previous years is now possible. According to the investigations of HERBERT H. MARKS* 193 (= 52%) of the 372 deaths recorded from January to April 1949 at the "Metropolitan Life" as due to diabetes mellitus would, by the new rules, be classifiable under headings other than diabetes mellitus; of these 193, 176 would be classified as dying from disease of the cardiovascular system (142 from heart attacks). Of the 848 reported deaths from diabetes mellitus in New York City from January to March 1949, 504 (59%) would, according to the new rules, be registered as deaths due to other causes, 459 being attributable to diseases of the cardiovascular-renal system (378 from heart disease).

The example of diabetes is perhaps better suited than any other to show the importance attaching to the details of the primary and secondary diseases given on the death certificate. Both the primary disease and the concomitant cause of death must be taken into account in assessing this disease, for there is no sharp

---

* Proceedings of the American Diabetes Association, Vol. I. 9, 1949. Cf. also: HASSO HÄRLEN, Die Problematik der Auswahl der Todesursachen bei mehrfachen Krankheitsangaben. „Lebensversicherungsmedizin", 5. No. 4 October, 1953.

and readily distinguishable transition from the primary to the secondary disease and vice-versa. In Switzerland the position is illustrated below*:

Deaths from diabetes mellitus, Switzerland

Annual average	Males			Females		
	Primary disease	Secondary disease	Together	Primary disease	Secondary disease	Together
1935/38	239	186	425	389	222	611
1940/44	180	205	385	305	275	580
1949/52	200	255	455	412	332	744
1954/56	237	296	533	450	451	901

Taking the figures as a whole, there are nearly twice as many cases of diabetes mellitus as would appear from the data on the primary disease alone. Today at least 1,400 persons die every year who certainly suffered to a greater or lesser degree from diabetes mellitus. Doubts are raised by the fact that these figures show 50% more women dying from this disease than men. Such doubts are justified, for as is well known, women consult the doctor more often than men, so that among the latter fewer of the mild cases are confirmed. Examination of the figures as a whole also shows that since 1935/38 there has been a substantial shift from the primary disease to the secondary disease.

In view of the importance of data on primary and secondary diseases, the statistical offices and the World Health Organization have for years been urging the medical profession to state the most precise details on death certificates. These efforts have been attended with such success in Switzerland that today one or two secondary diseases are specified in addition to the primary disease on threequarters of all certificates. On the other hand, the evaluations made of this data have so far been somewhat modest both in Switzerland and elsewhere.**

3. Simple index figures

3.0. General observations

It will be obvious that any pronouncement about mortality is based on the *absolute* figures; they show whether the incidence of something is great, small or non-existent, or whether any other feature is significant or not. But to know whether something is of greater or lesser incidence, we must refer to the *relative* figures. We must know the purpose of the investigation before we can say to what the absolute figures must be referred. For example, the number of motorists

* OTT, W.: Bevölkerungsbewegung in der Schweiz 1949—1956/57, Text page 211, „Statistische Quellenwerke der Schweiz“, Fascicle 275. Eidgenössisches Statistisches Amt, Bern 1959.

** In addition to the USA and England, Hesse has also made investigations into the statistics of joint causes of death. See Heft 89 der Beiträge zur Statistik Hessens und Statistische Berichte des Hessischen Statistischen Landesamtes, A IV., p. 54/55 (Tuberkulose aller Formen und Diabetes mellitus in Verbindung mit Haupt- und Nebenkrankheiten in Hessen 1954 und 1955).

meeting with fatal accidents in a town can be referred to the total population of the town (every nth inhabitant meets with a fatal car accident), to the number of adult inhabitants, to the population of the town and its environs, to the number of car drivers in the town (every nth car driver in this town meets with a fatal accident), and to the total number of fatal accidents (every nth victim of a fatal accident was a car driver) etc.

In computing such *relative frequencies*, we go by the principle of probabilities, i.e. *we divide the number of cases occurring by the number of possible cases.* However, we must beware of calling such a relative frequency simply a "probability". According to the theory of probability, this would be correct only if certain requirements were fulfilled*.

By relating these two figures we obtain a true fraction. But since most people find it difficult to think of indivisible units in terms of fractions and the usual fractions often cannot be readily visualized, the quotients are generally turned into decimal fractions. Thus the number of events is not related to the actual number of cases under observation but to a decimal multiple of this number, say 100 or 1000. For example, instead of saying there were 7,637 cases of cancer in 47,372 deaths, we say that 16 in 100 or 16% died of cancer. However, against the clarity of data in per cent and per mil must be counterposed the disadvantage that it is no longer apparent how large the numerator or the denominator of the fraction was. It should therefore be a rule only to speak of per cent and per mille when the denominator (number of cases observed) comprises at least 100 or 1000 units respectively.

In addition to their use in calculating relative frequencies and probabilities, we may establish other more or less meaningful relations between the figures. Examples are the density of population, births per marriage, and the sex ratio of births. In the latter case it is customary to relate the number of male births not to the total number of births but only to the number of female births.

It may often be very difficult to determine the number to which reference is to be made. We have already mentioned the difference between the de facto and de jure population and between the place of the occurrence and the place of residence (cf. section 2.1). Further difficulty arises in computing what is called occupational mortality, i.e. mortality among persons engaged in a particular occupation. Here account must be taken of migrations to and from the population, changes of occupation etc. Frequently the number to which the figures are related must be defined somewhat arbitrarily. Thus, to take an example, the frequency of births is determined simply by relating the births to the number of women of a certain age group (and not to the women capable of bearing children). A further example is that of determining the limits of the observed

* Cf. Wiesler, H.: Über die Grundlagen der Lebensversicherungsmathematik. Mitteilungen der Vereinigung schweizerischer Versicherungsmathematiker. Vol. 44 (1944).

Also: Der Begriff der Wahrscheinlichkeit in Mathematik und Statistik. Schweiz. Zeitschrift für Volkswirtschaft und Statistik 82 (1946).

population (population exposed to risk) in computing the mortality statistics for hospitals and sanatoria which serve a large and heterogeneous area.

To be able to express the mortality in a given group of persons in a single index figure, we usually use either the death-rate, or the expectation of life. By death-rate we generally mean the *number of deaths occurring during a given period (usually a year) in a given population, related to the actual number of the population in the middle of the observation period,* usually expressed in per mil. Three kinds of death-rate are in common use: The crude or general death-rate, the standardized or adjusted death-rate, and the life table death-rate, which is also called the death-rate of the stationary population. The use made of these three death-rates, both in private and official statistics, is in inverse proportion to their correctness. If a section is devoted below to the standardized and crude death-rate, this is not done with the purpose of recommending its use but rather in order to show its deficiencies.

3.1. The crude or general death-rate

This index figure is defined as follows:

$$\text{Crude death-rate} = \frac{\text{Number of deaths of all ages}}{\text{Number of living of all ages}} \times 1000.$$

As already noted, the number of living is taken to be the population in the middle of the period under observation, i.e. the population on July 1 if the observation period is a calendar year.

In the following we shall use an old but simple example for computing the crude (and later the standardized) death-rate which clearly illustrates the ambiguity of this index figure.

From English statistics — see table I on page 27 — the crude death-rate as defined above is

$$\frac{2{,}070}{100{,}000} = 20.7‰ \quad \text{for clergymen}$$

$$\frac{1{,}274}{100{,}000} = 12.7‰ \quad \text{for railwaymen.}$$

From these crude death-rates it might be concluded that clergymen have a higher mortality than railwaymen. If, however, the mortality is computed for each separate age group (i.e. the specific death-rate), it will be seen that the opposite is true [cf. columns (4) and (7) of the Table I]. As might be imagined, the railwaymen, being exposed to more rigorous living conditions, have a higher mortality at every age, and it is only because the population of clergymen consists predominantly of older men, and the population of railwaymen largely of younger ones, that the former have a higher general death-rate than the latter.

The crude death-rate is thus only suitable for purposes of comparison where the two groups compared have the same structure in regard to age and sex.*

The crude death-rate, which is often simply called the death-rate because of its widespread application, should, at best, be used simply to obtain a rough guide or an approximate estimate and be clearly referred to as the "crude death-rate". Wherever possible, the specific death-rate according to age should be used in its place, even if this is only possible for fairly large age groups. Needless to say, the smaller the age groups, the easier it is to eliminate the disturbing influence of a different age structure.

Table I. *Example for computing the crude and standardized death-rates*

Age group in years	Clergymen			Railwaymen			Standardized number of dead	
	Living	Dead	Death-rate in ‰	Living	Dead	Death-rate in ‰	Clergymen	Railwaymen
(1)	(2)	(3)	(4) = (3) ÷ (2)	(5)	(6)	(7) = (6) ÷ (5)	(8) = (5) × (4)	(9) = (2) × (7)
25—34	17,318	38	2.2	35,727	147	4.1	79	71
35—44	23,313	74	3.2	26,845	133	5.0	86	117
45—54	23,368	178	7.6	20,474	219	10.7	156	250
55—64	18,257	400	21.9	11,591	290	25.0	254	456
65—74	12,202	616	50.5	4,308	285	66.2	218	808
over 75	5,542	764	137.9	1,055	200	189.6	145	1,051
All ages	100,000	2070	20.7	100,000	1,274	12.7	938	2,753

3.2. The standardized or adjusted death-rate

To offset the difference of age structure, we choose one and the same age composition, i.e. a standard population, for the groups of persons to be compared. This standard population may be one of the series to be compared, or their average or an entirely separate series. By means of the given specific death-rates we then calculate, for each age group, the number of deaths to be expected in this standard population and relate this number to the standard population. Thus

$$\text{Standardized death-rate} = \frac{\text{Standardized number of dead, all ages}}{\text{Standardized population, all ages}} \times 1{,}000.$$

Example: Let us assume in the above example (Table I), that the two occupational groups were of the same composition in regard to age. Taking the age structure of the railwaymen as the standard, we should have 938 (column 8 as the product of columns 5 and 4) as the expected number of deaths for the clergymen, and the standardized death-rate for this class would accordingly be $\frac{938}{100{,}000} = 9.4$‰. Similarly, if the age composition of the clergymen is taken as

* A large number of men in a population has the same effect on the crude death-rate as a large number of older persons because the specific death-rate for the male sex is in general higher. However, the influence of sex is not so great as that of age structure.

the standard, the expected number of deaths among the railwaymen would be 2,753 and the death-rate 27.5‰. The following ratios are thus obtained:

Standardized death-rate	Clergymen	Railwaymen	$\frac{\text{Clergymen}}{\text{Railwaymen}}$
with clergymen as standard population	20.7	27.5	$\frac{20.7}{27.5} = 0.75$
with railwaymen as standard population	9.38	12.7	$\frac{9.4}{12.7} = 0.74$

As may be seen, the standardized death-rates vary according to the standard population; after all, they are simply the average of the relative frequencies of death of the various age groups weighted with the standard population, and the standard death-rates can thus be influenced by the way these weights are selected.

In order to remedy this arbitrariness in selecting the standard population, the International Statistical Institute made an early attempt to find a standard basis. In 1891 M. W. OGLE suggested the average of 7 European countries as a standard population, JOSEF KÖRÖSI recommended the population of Sweden as it was in 1890, and in 1917 the International Statistical Institute fixed a standard population based on the population of 19 European countries; however, this standard was not used by the United States at all and by England for only a short time. Today no more is heard of it. Where death-rates are to be standardized, this is done either on the basis of an average population (e.g. the whole of Switzerland for single cantons) or, in the case of chronological comparisons, the first of the groups to be compared is chosen.

The standardized death-rate is not so immediately understandable as the crude death-rate; it cannot, for it no longer presents the relative number of the deaths occurring during a specified time in the population observed. Its observed population is a fictitious one. *Thus standardized death-rates should never be interpreted in isolation; the ratios between such figures, however, may yield reliable information.*

Where the cause of death is not markedly dependent on age, i.e. it does not change greatly in the course of time with increasing age, the crude death-rate may also be useful for purposes of comparison. In such a case standardization will make hardly any difference to the results, as the following example shows*:

Deaths from tuberculosis per 1,000 inhabitants in the Canton of Basle-Town

Annual average	Crude	Standardized
1931/35	1.02	1.02
1936/40	0.75	0.75
1941/45	0.69	0.66
1946/50	0.47	0.44

* „Wirtschaft und Verwaltung", Statistisches Amt des Kantons Basel-Stadt, Fascicle 3. Basel 1953.

Indirect method of adjusting the crude death-rate

Let it be supposed that the age distribution of the deaths occurring in the two groups to be compared is not known, but that the age distribution of the living in these groups [columns (3) and (4) in the table II] is known, and also the specific death-rate of the different age groups in the universe or standard population [column (2)].

We first compute the *expected* deaths in the two populations to be compared on the assumption that the mortality conditions of the basic population apply to both and obtain the figures 3,601 and 6,196 respectively [columns (5) and (6) of the table II]. We now divide the *actual* 2,574 deaths observed in group A and 7,929 in group B by the expected deaths and thus obtain the mortality ratios

$$\text{for group A} \quad . \quad . \quad . \quad \frac{2{,}574}{3{,}601} = 0.71480,$$

$$\text{for group B} \quad . \quad . \quad . \quad \frac{7{,}929}{6{,}196} = 1.27970.$$

We now multiply these ratios by the crude death-rate of the standard population 0.00855 and obtain as a result the standardized death-rates 0.00611 and 0.01094 respectively or 6.11‰ and 10.94‰.

Table II. *Example of the standardization of death-rates. Indirect method* (England and Wales, census 1931, deaths from 1930—1932, male population)

Age	Death-rates of the standard population	*Group A* (Agricultural labourers)	*Group B* (Labourers, general[1])	Expected deaths	
				Group A	Group B
(1)	(2)	(3)	(4)	(5) = (2) × (3)	(6) = (2) × (4)
20—24	0.00315	77,085	93,665	243	295
25—34	0.00339	111,361	192,064	378	651
35—44	0.00554	76,904	147,067	426	815
45—54	0.01111	76,602	143,238	851	1,591
55—64	0.02364	72,058	120,289	1,703	2,844
Total	0.00855[2]	414,010	696,323	3,601	6,196

3.3. *The death-rate of the stationary population or life table death-rate*

The disadvantages of the crude and the standardized death-rates lie in the imperfection of the weights. The standard population used for standardizing is an arbitrarily selected, fictitious and rigid weighting factor. Arbitrarily selected because, as we have seen, there is no uniformity; fictitious because it represents a population different from that being compared; and rigid because it remains the same for the whole period of comparison and does not reflect the changes occurring in the age structure of a population as a result of changes in mortality. But, it may be asked, are not these the very defects from which the crude death-rate is free? The weights with which the individual age-specific rates are provided

[1] This group includes all occupied and retired males.
[2] This is the crude death-rate for the whole group from 20—64 years.

are in each case the actual population itself; thus they are neither arbitrary, fictitious nor rigid since they change every year with the age structure. However, changes in the age structure are due not only to mortality but also to births and migration to and from the population; but these two components must not be allowed to affect an index intended to measure mortality alone. The ideal population, then, is one which is neither arbitrarily selected, fictitious nor rigid, nor influenced by elements having nothing to do with mortality. Such weights are provided by the *stationary population*, i.e. the population which increases by the same number of births as it decreases by deaths, a population, in other words, which is always of the same size and whose age structure is represented by the number surviving to each age in the life table.

We start with a hypothetical population of l_x persons, all born at the same time and thus all of exact age x. After one year this population has decreased to l_{x+1} persons, after two years to l_{x+2} etc. This series $l_x, l_{x+1}, l_{x+2}, \ldots$ represents the *number surviving to each age* (or in terms of deaths, the *number dying between ages x and x+1*). From these further functions may be derived:

$d_x = l_x - l_{x+1}$ Number of deaths between ages x and $x+1$,

$p_x = \frac{l_{x+1}}{l_x}$ Probability that a person aged x will attain age $x+1$ (probability of surviving one year),

$q_x = 1 - p_x = \frac{d_x}{l_x}$ Probability that a person aged x will die between x and $x+1$ (probability of dying within one year),

$m_x = \frac{d_x}{\frac{l_x + l_{x+1}}{2}} = \frac{2\,q_x}{2 - q_x}$ central death-rate.

According to the general definition of the death-rate given at the beginning, the *life table death-rate* is equal to the total number of deaths at all ages ($\Sigma\, d_x = l_0$) relative to the mean number of all living at these ages, i. e. expressed in a formula:

$$\text{Life table death-rate} = \frac{\Sigma\, d_x}{\sum \frac{l_x + l_{x+1}}{2}} \times 1000$$

$$= \frac{l_0}{\frac{l_0}{2} + l_1 + l_2 + l_3 + \cdots} \times 1000 = \frac{\Sigma\, l_x' \times m_x}{\Sigma\, l_x'} \times 1000 \quad .$$

For simplicity let us denote the mean number of living as $l_x' = \frac{l_x + l_{x+1}}{2}$; it will then be clear from the preceding equation that the life table death-rate is the average of the single central death-rates weighted with the mean mortality table population. But these weights are derived from the single m_x and q_x respectively. The life table death-rate therefore depends on the mortality alone. Of the three death-rates discussed, it is the best for purposes of comparison; it alone gives the correct ratio between the mortalities of different groups of the population.

But over and above this the life table death-rate has a further significance, since

$$\frac{1}{\text{life table death-rate}} = \frac{\frac{l_0}{2}+l_1+l_2+l_3+\cdots}{l_0} = \frac{l_0+l_1+l_2+l_3+\cdots}{l_0} - \frac{1}{2} = \mathring{e}_0 .$$

$\mathring{e}_0$ is the number of years which a person aged 0 has to live on an average. The *mean length of life (or expectation of life) of a person aged 0 is thus the reciprocal of the life table death-rate.* Further we can write

$$\mathring{e}_0 - \frac{1}{2} = e_0 = \frac{l_1+l_2+l_3+\cdots}{l_0} = \frac{0\,d_0+1\,d_1+2\,d_2+3\,d_3+\cdots}{d_0+d_1+d_2+d_3+\cdots} .$$

In this formula the numbers 0, 1, 2, 3 ... are the ages and the deaths d_0, d_1, d_2, ... the weights; the average expectation of life is thus identical with the *average age at death from the mortality table.* Another advantage of the life table death-rate, apart from its absolute correctness, is its immediately apparent meaning, for it also gives the average length of life or the average age at death, a popularly understood measure.

3.4. *Specific death-rates*

If the number of the dead is classified according to various categories (age, marital status, cause of death etc.) and related to the population exposed to risk, such indices are called *specific rates, particular death-rates or limited death-rates.*

All these figures have the character of relative frequencies, i.e. the denominator indicates the number of events that could happen and the numerator the number actually occurring.

One of the most frequently used is the classification of deaths according to their various causes. In this connection it must be remembered when defining the limits of the group exposed to risk that, for instance, only women can be counted in the case of women's diseases and only infants in the case of infants' diseases.

One of the most commonly used death-rates is the *infant mortality rate.* It is defined as follows:

$$\text{Infant mortality rate} = \frac{\text{Number of children dying during a specified period below one year of age}}{\text{Total of live births during this period}}$$

As will be seen, the denominator used here is not the number of children aged 0*, since substantial errors are incurred in enumerating this group. The infant mortality rate thus defined is not identical with q_0, i.e. the probability of death of a child aged 0 (cf. section 4). The children dying at an age of less than one year and during a specified calendar year did not all have their birthdays in the same calendar year, some of them being born in the preceding calendar year.

* In statistics, where the number of completed years is usually taken as a basis, children aged 0 means those who are less than one year old.

Thus, if there is a marked fall in the birth-rate, the infant mortality death-rate will be too high because some of the deaths among the children born in the preceding year will be related to the smaller number of births taking place this year. If the number of births rises, then the mortality rate will be too low. To obtain a correct figure for the infant mortality rate the number of deaths is related not to the total number of births of the year under observation but only to a portion of them and also to a portion of the births of the preceding year. In Switzerland investigations showed that, for the years 1940—48, about 18% of the infants dying in a specific calendar year were born in the preceding year and that thus only about 82% were born in the calendar year itself. This ratio is approximately correct for both sexes. At times when there are marked fluctuations in the birth-rate, it is advisable to use these ratios* thus obtaining:

$$\frac{\text{Probability that a child aged}}{\text{0 will die within one year}} = \frac{\text{Children aged 0 dying during year of observation}}{\text{82\% of the births during the year of observation plus 18\% of births of preceding year.}}$$

Example: Switzerland

	1941	1940
Live births	71,926	64,115
Died under one year	2,959	2,960

$$\text{Infant mortality rate} = \frac{2{,}959}{71{,}926} = 41.1‰$$

$$\frac{\text{Probability that a child aged}}{\text{0 will die within one year (1941)}} = \frac{2{,}959}{0.82 \times 71{,}926 + 0.18 \times 64{,}115} = \frac{2{,}959}{70{,}520} = 42.0‰.$$

The greatest errors in ascertaining the infant mortality rate do not occur in the calculation but as a result of the different ideas prevailing as to what constitutes a stillbirth (cf. section 2.2). In many countries, too, there is a substantial underregistration of births. For example, until 1940, 8% too few births were enumerated in the USA.

3.5. Ratios

These figures indicate (usually in per cent or per mil) how many of the total number of observations are accounted for by a particular type. An example of this is the

$$\text{Death ratio} = \frac{\text{Deaths in a particular class, from a specific cause etc.}}{\text{Total number of deaths}}.$$

* For a long time the Registrar Generals for England and Wales used the ratio of 70% for the year of observation and 30% for the preceding year, these figures being based on 1914—18. In the „Statistik des Deutschen Reiches" Vol. 246, p. 67—69, and Vol. 256, p. 65—67 investigations are reported for the years 1910 and 1911 covering 20 and 14 states respectively and yielding ratios of 72% and 28% for males and 71% and 29% for females. These figures are also used for the USA mortality tables. — The "Institut National de la Statistique et des Études Economiques" in France has, since 1948, related the number of children dying at age 0 to 1/3 of the births of the preceding year and 2/3 of the year of observation.

It will be noted that deaths appear in both the numerator and the denominator. Such ratios (quotas) have two important disadvantages:

1. A real change in mortality for a specific cause, class etc. leaves the death ratio unaffected if the mortality for other causes changes proportionately. 2. A change in the death ratio can indicate an increase or decrease in the mortality due to the cause investigated but also an opposite change in the mortality due to the other causes.

Example: Switzerland, male population, 1956.

Age group years	Living population	Total deaths	Deaths by accident	Accident ratio %	Accident death-rate ‰
(1)	(2)	(3)	(4)	(5) = (4) + (3)	(6) = (4) + (2)
15—30	505,110	837	418	50	0.83
60 and over	313,434	18,124	614	3	1.96

The drop in the accident ratio from 50% to 3% might lead to the fallacious conclusion that the risk of dying from an accident is less at the higher ages. Actually the contrary is true, as may be seen from column (6), and the drop in the accident ratio from one age group to the other is due merely to the fact that the other causes of death increase.

3.6. *Other important rates and ratios in demography*

$$\text{Fatality rate} = \frac{\text{Number of deaths from a specific disease}}{\text{Number of cases of this disease}}$$

$$\text{Morbidity rate} = \frac{\text{Number of cases of disease}}{\text{Number of population exposed to the disease}}$$

$$\text{Crude birth rate} = \frac{\text{Live births during a specified period}}{\text{Total population at the middle of this period}}$$

$$\text{Specific birth rate} = \frac{\text{Live births during a specified period}}{\text{Total of female population at middle of this period}}$$

$$\text{Stillbirth rate} = \frac{\text{Stillbirths during a specified period}}{\text{Total of live births during this period}}$$

Index figures

When making comparisons between figures of the same kind in a series it is frequently difficult, if the figures are fairly large, to ascertain quickly whether any changes have taken place in the series. To facilitate such comparisons, all the figures are reduced to a common denominator. The first number in the series is usually taken as a denominator and all the others are divided by this number. The results are multiplied by 100 (or 1,000) and called the "index figures".

Example

Annual average	Of 100,000 living at age 1–74 there died of tuberculosis annually*	Index (1911/15 = 100)
1911/15	265.1	100
1916/20	206.2	78
1921/25	115.3	43
1926/30	93.2	35
1931/35	68.4	26
1936/40	51.3	19
1941/45	42.7	16

4. The life table

4.0. Concept

The most complete insight into mortality conditions is afforded by the life table. It forms the technical basis of all life assurance. The construction of life tables has a long history (see Section 1) and actuaries have devoted a great deal of work to their adjustment in order to obtain smooth functions (graduation). The essential character of the life table can be simply explained as follows: Let us take a *population all of exact age x,* i.e. all having the same birthday; l_x (l=life) is the international designation for this population. During one year a number of persons in this population will die; these are designated d_x *(d* for death), and the total l_x has diminished at the end of the year to l_{x+1}, i.e. to the persons who are now $x+1$ years old. That is to say, $d_x = l_x - l_{x+1}$. This process is repeated every year until the original population has completely died out and we have the series

$$l_0, l_1, \ldots, l_x, l_{x+1}, \ldots, l_\omega,$$

this being the series of numbers surviving to each successive age (ω is the highest age occurring). It shows how a population of living persons is thinned out by death.

It might be thought that the simplest way of obtaining concrete data for the series l_x would be to take all the births in a particular year (a generation) and find out how many people remained alive from year to year. In the first place, this is hardly practicable, for it would be extremely difficult to keep a particular generation under observation with so many migrations to and from it; secondly, such data would hardly be meaningful for most of the purposes for which a life table is required because there has been a marked change in mortality in recent decades. The mortality which applied, say, to ten-year-olds 20 years ago no longer holds good for ten-year-olds today. For this reason the computation of life tables is not usually based on one generation but on a population all living at the same time, i.e. during a specified period, or instead of so-called *generation life tables* we compute so-called *period life tables* or *current life tables.* We shall now see how a period life table is constructed from empirical data, the results of censuses and the deaths reported to registrars.

* USA, white men; observations of the Metropolitan Life Insurance Company. Standardized figures.

4.1. Construction

Defining the limits of groups

In order to draw valid conclusions from statistics, it is usually essential to make a great number of observations or experiments; for this reason the features of regularity appearing in a statistical series are often referred to somewhat vaguely as the "law of large numbers". Statistical populations or universes are formed by assembling all the elements to be observed into groups of the greatest possible homogeneity according to clearly defined criteria. Thus we speak of groups of persons and mean by that a number of persons who are lumped together according to one or more specific features, e.g. according to age, year of death, sex, occupation, domicile etc. The larger the number of common features required, the smaller the group becomes. The following five groups have become particularly important in the measurement of mortality: the *two main groups of the living and the three main groups of deaths.* The definition of these groups can be made clear with the aid of the method of graphic representation developed by WILHELM LEXIS*. His method is not concerned with geometrical relations but simply with a diagrammatic representation of the information**.

In a rectangular system of co-ordinates the x-axis is called the age axis and the y-axis the birth or time axis, i.e. age is entered on one axis and birthday or observation period on the other (cf. Fig. 1 and 2). Each individual has his "*birth point*" G on the time axis according to his birthday; his "*life-line*" continues to the age and time when he passes out of observation by death. In Fig. 1 three life-lines are plotted: one person was born at point $g_1 + 1/2$ and died

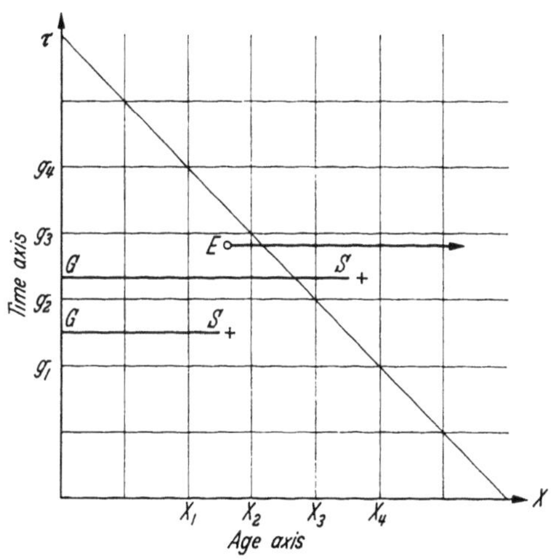

Fig. 1. *Lexis'* diagram showing three life-lines

* LEXIS, WILHELM: Abhandlungen zur Theorie der Bevölkerungs- und Moralstatistik. Jena 1903.

** For the creation of what is known as the formal branch of pop. stat. we are indebted to BECKER, KNAPP, LEXIS, ZEUNER, MAYER, BÖCKH, BERTILLON etc.

at age $x_1 + 1/2$. The point S is called the *„death-point“*. The other person came into the world at the point of time between g_2 and g_3 and died at the age between x_3 and x_4. If a person does not come under observation until later, his appearance is marked by *"entry point"* E. For instance, Fig. 1 contains the life-line of a person who was born between g_2 and g_3 but did not come under observation until age $x_1 + 1/2$.

Generally speaking, a vertical in this diagram divides the death-points of lives dying before or after reaching a specified age x, a horizontal the death-points of lives born before or after a specified date g, and a diagonal the death points of lives dying before or after a specified date of observation τ.

If we now imagine the life-line being plotted for each person, then clearly there will be as many people alive at the time of enumeration τ as there are life-lines cutting the diagonal starting at τ, while there will be as many deaths as there are death-points S below this diagonal.

We can now arrange — and this greatly simplifies what follows — for the three variables x, g, τ *to be whole numbers.* Thus

$$g, g+1, g+2, \ldots = \text{years of birth},$$
$$\tau, \tau+1, \tau+2, \ldots = \text{years of observation}.$$

The (approximate) age can be calculated from the equation

$$x = \tau - g.$$

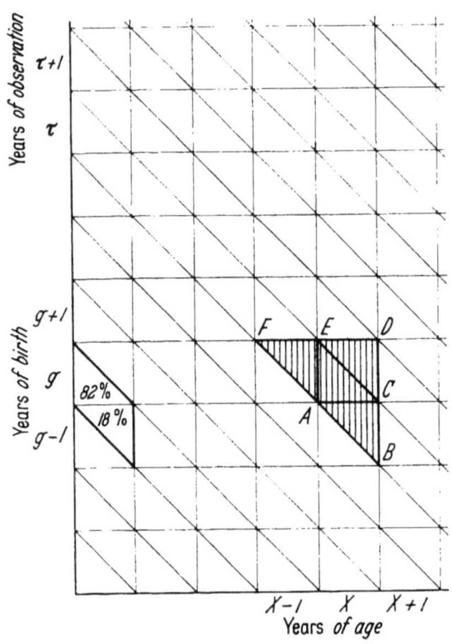

Fig. 2. *Lexis'* diagram showing the demarcation of the groups of the living and the deaths

In the case of continuous elements in observation, e.g. the population (B), lives (L), exposed to risk (R), number of policies etc. the indices x, g, τ indicate that reference is made to the group *at the beginning* of the period in question, i.e.

L_x = living at the beginning of age x, ${}^{\tau}B$ = population at the beginning of the year τ.

The straight lines in Fig. 2 are always plotted with an interval of one year in between. It is assumed that the time runs from January 1 to December 31. The indication $x/x+1$ etc. used below does not refer to the average value of these entities but means that the observation covers the two years x and $x+1$.

The following statistical *groups* can now be defined (Cf. Fig. 2):

First group of deaths = ACDE = ${}^{\tau/\tau+1}_{g}T_x$ = persons who were born in the year g and died at age x; they are distributed over two years of observation τ and $\tau+1$.

Second group of deaths = ACEF = ${}^{\tau}_{g}T_{x-1/x}$ = number of persons born in a specified year g and dying in the year of observation τ; these deaths occur over a period of two years of age, viz. $x-1$ and x.

Third group of deaths = ABCE = ${}_{g-1/g}^{\tau}T_x$ = number of persons aged x dying in a specified year of observation τ; clearly, they were born in years $g-1$ and g.

All these main or square groups can be bisected by a diagonal into subgroups (also called elementary, triangular or basic groups) which cover intervals of one year. The most important are:

First subgroup of deaths = ACE = ${}^{\tau}_{g}T_x$ persons who were born in year g and died in year τ at age x.

Second subgroup of deaths = CDE = ${}^{\tau+1}_{g}T_x$ = persons who were born in year g and died in year $\tau+1$ at age x.

First group of the living = $\overline{\text{AE}}$ = ${}^{\tau}_{g}L_x$ = *coevals*, i.e. persons at the beginning of age x or all persons whose life-line intersects the line $\overline{\text{AE}}$. Clearly, they reach this age in the course of the year of observation.

Second group of the living = $\overline{\text{CE}}$ = ${}^{\tau+1}_{g}B_x$ = *contemporaries*, i.e. all persons counted at a specified point of time; they were born in year g and are aged x.

Of the two groups of the living the first is the most important; however, it cannot be measured directly because this would entail keeping the persons born in a particular year under observation for a whole year. This group can, however, be obtained with the aid of the second group of the living, which can be enumerated. The procedure is as follows:

$$ {}^{\tau}_{g}L_x = \overline{\text{CE}} + \text{ACE} = {}^{\tau+1}_{g}B_x + {}^{\tau}_{g}T_x \ . $$

As mentioned in the foregoing, such an observation or enumeration should be made at the turn of the year. Where this is not the case (as, for instance, in Switzerland, where the censuses take place on December 1), the population at the end of the year should be estimated on the basis of the figures obtained in the census.

Theoretically, the best method of obtaining the *probability of death* is that perfected by BECKER and ZEUNER. This consists in establishing the ratio between the first group of deaths and the first group of the living as follows:

$$\text{Probability of dying within one year} = \frac{\text{First group of deaths*}}{\text{First group of the living}}$$

or in symbols:

$$q_x = \frac{\text{ACDE}}{\text{AE}} = \frac{\text{ACDE}}{\text{CE}+\text{ACE}} = \frac{{}^{\tau/\tau+1}_{g}T_x}{{}^{\tau}_{g}L_x} = \frac{{}^{\tau/\tau+1}_{g}T_x}{{}^{\tau+1}_{g}B_x + {}^{\tau}_{g}T_x}\,. \tag{4.1.1}$$

This method, which is called the *year of birth method*, yields the probability of death directly. It is difficult to use in practice, however, because it requires knowledge of the subgroups of death ACE, and it is exceptional for this to be obtainable from the population statistics.

This difficulty can be circumvented by using the following method, known as the *year of death method*. This involves establishing the ratio between the third group of deaths ABCE and the second groups of the living $\overline{\text{AB}}$ and $\overline{\text{CE}}$ which form its limits. These deaths refer to births in two separate years and occurred at age x in the course of year τ. This is the group which is customarily published in mortality statistics. If, at the same time, the number of the population at the end (or beginning) of each year of observation is known, then the *central rate of mortality* is

$$\frac{{}_{g-1/g}^{\;\tau}T_x}{\frac{1}{2}\left({}_{g-1}^{\;\tau}B_x + {}^{\tau+1}_{g}B_x\right)} = \frac{{}_{g-1/g}^{\;\tau}T_x}{{}^{\tau+\frac{1}{2}}B_x} = m_x \tag{4.1.2}$$

which is defined as the quotient of the deaths in one year divided by the mean population of that year. Instead of taking the arithmetical mean of the actual populations at the end of two years, we can also use the actual population in the middle of the year. Assuming that the population ${}^{\tau}B_x$ changes uniformly in the course of τ, i.e. the dead at age x are evenly distributed over the two generations $g-1$ and g, or in other words, the subgroup ABC = ACE $= \frac{1}{2}\,{}_{g-1/g}^{\;\tau}T_x$ (which proves to be reasonably accurate except for the ages 0 and 85 and over), it follows that

$$q_x = \frac{{}_{g-1/g}^{\;\tau}T_x}{{}^{\tau+\frac{1}{2}}B_x + \frac{1}{2}\,{}_{g-1/g}^{\;\tau}T_x}\,. \tag{4.1.3}$$

* According to the old (aprioristic) view, the probability of a chance event is defined in probability calculus as a fraction in which the numerator is the number of successes and the denominator the number of equally possible cases. Thus, for example, the probability p of throwing the number 5 with an unloaded dice is $\frac{1}{6}$, for of the 6 equally possible cases there is only one success, viz. 5. Similarly, the probability q of throwing a number other than 5 is $\frac{5}{6}$ for there are five successes and 6 of equal possibility. Thus $p+q=\frac{1}{6}+\frac{5}{6}=1$. According to this definition the relative frequency of death q_x can be conceived (under certain conditions) as the probability of death, according to which the number of deaths, i.e. the "successes" are the numerator and the number of living, i.e. the cases of equal possibility, the denominator. For further details see: WIESLER, H.: Über die Grundlagen der Lebensversicherungsmathematik, l.c. Further: NIEDERMANN, H.: Untersuchungen über den Wahrscheinlichkeitscharakter der Sterblichkeit, Mitteilungen der Vereinigung schweizerischer Versicherungsmathematiker, 46th year (1946).

Division by ${}^{\tau+1/2}B_x$ yields

$$q_x = \frac{\dfrac{{}_{g-1/g}^{\tau}T_x}{{}^{\tau+\frac{1}{2}}B_x}}{1+\dfrac{\frac{1}{2}\,{}_{g-1/g}^{\tau}T_x}{{}^{\tau+\frac{1}{2}}B_x}} = \frac{m_x}{1+\frac{1}{2}m_x} = \frac{2m_x}{2+m_x}. \tag{4.1.4}$$

Offices of statistics on the continent use the *birth year method* as a rule when constructing mortality tables. Where the figures of the living and deaths published in statistical annuals are used as a basis for the construction of tables, it is usually necessary to have recourse to a curtate method as the groups of the living and deaths are published in age groups. Such a method will be discussed in detail in section 4.6.

Observation periods of several years

As was mentioned at the commencement of this section, it is generally desirable when ascertaining statistical indices to use large numbers so as to eliminate chance elements as far as possible. According to the law of large numbers, the variance to which the statistical number is subject decreases as the number of observations increases. Thus in countries with a small or medium population, it is customary to make the observation period cover several years when computing the annual probabilities of death. However, in endeavouring to include as many years of observation as possible in order to eliminate chance variations, it must be remembered that mortality varies greatly with time, that the secular trend exercises an important influence, and that where a large interval is chosen, the life table no longer reflects the present conditions of mortality.

According to the recommendation of the International Statistical Institute*, mortality tables should be *constructed for a period of observation covering 3—5 years and including a census*. Since censuses are held at the same time in many countries, international comparisons of the conditions of mortality would thus be easy to draw. It is on these lines that official population life tables have been constructed in Switzerland since the census of 1930. Moreover, it has become the practice, particularly in small countries, to base such tables on a period covering the *whole interval between two censuses*. As we shall see, this permits a better allowance to be made for migrations. In Switzerland a population life table has been computed for every intermediate period since 1881 with the exception of the decade 1911—1920, when no table was constructed because of the influenza epidemic of 1918 and its repercussions.

Another factor must be taken into account when fixing the limits of the period of observation. If it is intended to show the average mortality in the table, which must be done when, for instance, the table is to be used as a basis for life assurance or for international comparisons, a period of observation must be

* Bulletin de l'Institute international de Statistique, Congrès de Madrid, 1931, Vol. XXVI.

selected which does not contain years departing substantially from the norm by virtue of exceptionally high or low mortalities.

If we combine several years of observation τ, $\tau+1$, $\tau+2$, ... where the corresponding years of birth are g, $g+1$, $g+2$, ... for age x, (according to the equation $x=\tau-g$), then the average probability of dying of persons aged x can be determined in two ways, viz. either as an ordinary arithmetical mean from the individual probabilities of dying

$$q_x = \frac{1}{n}\left(\frac{{}_{g}^{\tau/\tau+1}T_x}{{}_{g}^{\tau}L_x} + \frac{{}_{g+1}^{\tau+1/\tau+2}T_x}{{}_{g+1}^{\tau+1}L_x} + \frac{{}_{g+2}^{\tau+2/\tau+3}T_x}{{}_{g+2}^{\tau+2}L_x} + \cdots\right) = \frac{1}{n}\left({}_{g}q_x + {}_{g+1}q_x + {}_{g+2}q_x + \cdots\right), \quad (4.1.5)$$

or as a weighted arithmetical mean

$$q_x = \frac{{}_{g}^{\tau/\tau+1}T_x + {}_{g+1}^{\tau+1/\tau+2}T_x + {}_{g+2}^{\tau+2/\tau+3}T_x + \cdots}{{}_{g}^{\tau}L_x + {}_{g+1}^{\tau+1}L_x + {}_{g+2}^{\tau+2}L_x + \cdots} = \frac{{}_{g}^{\tau}L_x\,{}_{g}q_x + {}_{g+1}^{\tau+1}L_x\,{}_{g+1}q_x + {}_{g+2}^{\tau+2}L_x\,{}_{g+2}q_x + \cdots}{{}_{g}^{\tau}L_x + {}_{g+1}^{\tau+1}L_x + {}_{g+2}^{\tau+2}L_x + \cdots}. \quad (4.1.6)$$

As will be seen from this formula, the actual living populations L_x in the years in question are employed as weights, i.e. allowance is made for the varying number of lives in age groups where these are of unequal size. For this reason the second formula is to be preferred. Of the observations made in the two marginal years approximately one half is taken into account. The populations ${}_{g}^{\tau}L$, ${}_{g}^{\tau+1}L$ ... are usually determined by intercensal estimation (see p. 42).

Example: We will illustrate the foregoing by taking the Swiss life table during the period of observation 1939/44 (abbreviated to Swiss men 1939/44) as an example. Fig. 3 shows the groups of observed deaths according to statistics for the ages 0 to 14, i.e. for the years of birth 1928 to 1943 entered in

Table III. *Groups and subgroups of the living and dead. Annual probabilities of death**
(Swiss men, 1939—1944)

Age	Second group of the living**	First sub-group of deaths	*First group of the living*	First subgroup of deaths	Second sub-group of deaths	*First group of deaths*	*Crude annual probability of death*
(1)	(2)	(3)	(4) = (2) + (3)	(5) = (3)	(6)	(7) = (5) + (6)	(8) = (7) : (4)
0	178,035	7,116	185,151	7,116	1,578	8,694	0.04696
1	166,796	508	167,304	508	527	1,035	619
2	157,860	260	158,120	260	253	513	324
3	153,861	196	154,057	196	196	392	254
4	154,916	159	155,075	159	151	310	200
5	156,070	130	156,200	130	133	263	0.00168
6	156,976	128	157,104	128	98	226	144
7	159,563	105	159,668	105	111	216	135
8	160,791	119	160,910	119	116	235	146
9	162,164	95	162,259	95	92	187	115
10	162,509	95	162,604	95	88	183	0.00113
11	163,689	98	163,787	98	118	216	132

* Swiss population life tables 1931/41 and 1939/44, Stand und Entwicklung der Sterblichkeit in der Schweiz. Eidgenössisches Statistisches Amt. Berne 1951.

** The computation of these numbers is explained on page 43.

the Lexis diagram. By adding the columns we obtain the first and second subgroups reproduced in columns (5) and (6) of the table III, and by the addition of these figures, the first group of deaths.

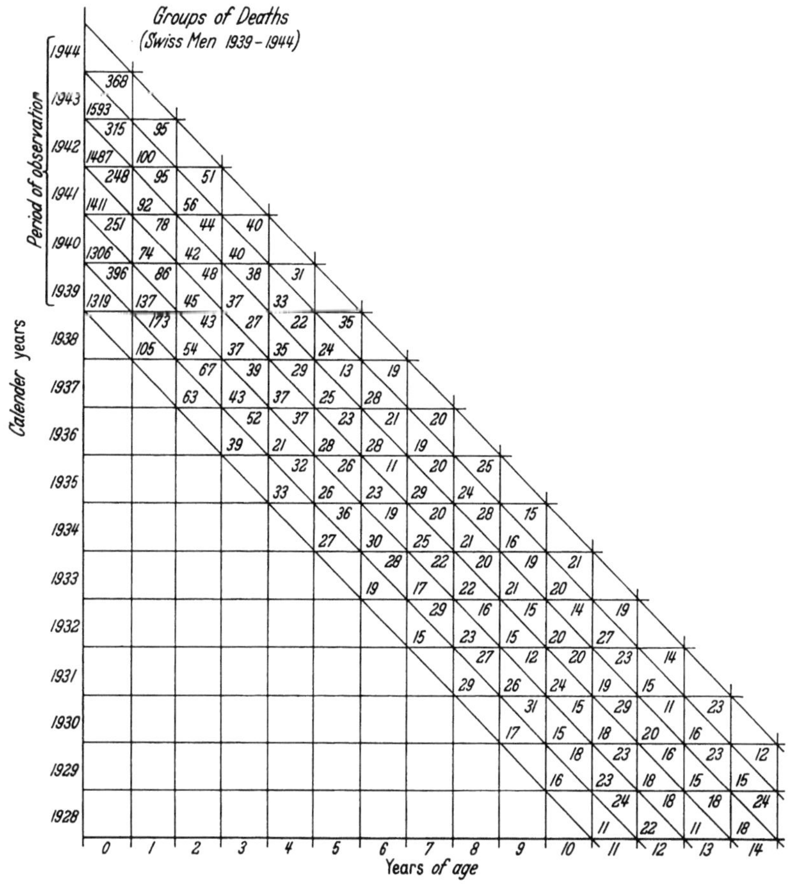

Fig. 3. Groups of deaths (Swiss Men 1939—1944)

As may be seen, in the case of the marginal years 1944 and 1939, only the second and first subgroups respectively have been counted.

The method of computing the second group of the living will be explained in the section on intercensal estimates.

Migration

In our previous computations only births and deaths have been considered as factors of change in population movement, but not migrations to and from the population. If these migrations are also to be taken into account, we must think on these lines: At the beginning of the year we have an actual population B. This increases in the course of the year by the number of entries E and decreases by the number of exits due to death T and other causes A. It may be assumed (according to Becker) that the entries and exits are evenly distributed over the whole year. Thus the lives migrating to and from the population are under observation for an average of half a year, i.e. we increase the exposed to risk L by half the migration balance $E-A$ and obtain for the annual probability of death

$$q_x = \frac{T_x}{L_x + \frac{E_x - A_x}{2}}.$$

(We shall revert to this formula when computing the probabilities of exit where several causes of exit are in operation; formally the same process of thought is involved.)

In constructing life tables it is not customary to make such corrections for migration for the following reasons:

In *life tables with a short interval of observation* symmetrically including a census, migrations before and after the census largely cancel each other out if they are fairly evenly distributed in each age group and year of observation. As a rule, the shorter the interval of observation, the smaller becomes the error due to omitting a correction for migrations.

In *life tables where censuses form the limits of the period of observation,* intercensal estimates are used to ascertain the actual population in each year of observation. In making these estimates, we apply for each year a migration component of such a kind that the final population obtained from the estimates tallies with the data of the census.

Intercensal estimates

Censuses provide information on the classification of the population according to sex, age, marital status, domicile, profession, religion etc., which is of particular importance for the investigation of mortality. Such censuses are held in most countries at regular intervals — as a rule every 5 to 10 years (every 10 years in Switzerland commencing in 1850). The registry offices and courts also ascertain the number of births, deaths, marriages and divorces. These notifications of births and deaths enable us to compute the age structure of the population, which is of particular interest to us, in years other than those when a census is taken. This is done by means of the intercensal estimate. In principle the method is as follows: From the lives enumerated in the census at the end of the year, we deduct the deaths occurring in the following year, and add the migration balance of the same year, thus obtaining the actual number of living at the end of the year following the census. This procedure is applied to every age. If the actual numbers for each year between two census years are to be obtained, we determine the migration components in advance in such a manner that, starting with the first census, the last estimated population coincides exactly with the figures of the second census.

Example: (see table IV page 43)

Starting with the census on December 1, 1941, we first ascertain the actual

Table IV. *Intercensal estimate of the Swiss population, starting with the census of December 1, 1941*

Year of birth	1940			1941			*Census* Living on Dec. 1, 1941	Deaths in Dec. 1941	1942			1943			1944	
	Age	Living[1]	Deaths[2]	Age	Living[1]	Deaths[2] Jan.—Nov.			Age	Living[1]	Deaths[2]	Age	Living[1]	Deaths[2]	Age	Living[1]
(1)	(2)	(3)	(4)	(5)	(6)	(7)	(8)	(9)	(10)	(11)	(12)	(13)	(14)	(15)	(16)	(17)
1943	—	—	—	—	—	—	—	—	—	—	—	—	*42,440*	1,593	0	40,847
1942	—	—	—	—	—	—	*3,135* Dec.	—	—	*40,364*	1,487	0	38,877	415	1	38,462
1941	—	—	—	—	*33,685*	1,283	32,402	128	0	35,409	340	1	35,069	151	2	34,918
1940	—	*32,493*	1,306	0	31,187	309	30,878	16	1	30,862	120	2	30,742	84	3	30,658
1939	0	31,715	533	1	31,182	122	31,060	9	2	31,051	85	3	30,966	71	4	30,895
1938	1	31,221	227	2	30,994	75	30,919	5	3	30,914	62	4	30,852	46	5	30,806
1937	2	30,155	110	3	30,045	70	29,975	6	4	29,969	54	5	29,915	41	6	29,874
1936	3	31,278	73	4	31,205	63	31,142	2	5	31,140	51	6	31,089	40	7	31,049
1935	4	31,995	58	5	31,937	45	31,892	4	6	31,888	40	7	31,848	44	8	31,804
1934	5	32,272	66	6	32,206	42	32,164	2	7	32,162	41	8	32,121	44	9	32,077
1933	6	31,919	45	7	31,874	41	31,833	3	8	31,830	41	9	31,789	39	10	31,750
1932	7	32,630	52	8	32,578	30	32,548	1	9	32,547	35	10	32,512	41	11	32,471
1931	8	32,458	53	9	32,405	34	32,371	2	10	32,369	39	11	32,330	33	12	32,292
1930	9	33,346	46	10	33,300	27	33,273	6	11	33,267	49	12	33,218	27	13	33,191
1929	10	32,578	41	11	32,537	36	32,501	5	12	32,496	31	13	32,465	38	14	32,427
1928	11	33,084	46	12	33,038	28	33,010	1	13	33,009	36	14	32,973	43	15	32,930

The figures in italics refer to births.

[1] Second group of the living; living at the beginning of the year in question.

[2] Second group of the dead.

population on January 1, 1942 by adding the births in December and subtracting the deaths in December, this being done for each individual age. By adding the births and subtracting the deaths for each year of observation, the number of living is obtained at the beginning of each succeeding year. The procedure is similar for retrospectice estimates, i.e. for computing the actual populations on January 1, 1940 and 1939. No account was taken in this example of any migration component.

The table IV can be read in three ways:

— vertically, the age distribution of the population at the commencement of a specified year of observation,
— horizontally, decrements in a generation due to death,
— diagonally, the coevals at the beginning of a year of observation. By adding these populations we obtain the second group of the living we need for computing the probabilities of death.

4.2. Graduation

If the annual probabilities of death obtained by formula (4.1.1) or (4.1.3) are plotted on a graph against age, we do not normally obtain a smooth curve, for the ordinates usually display certain variations. The causes of these variations are manifold. Mortality is conditioned by a diversity of factors such as habits, occupational conditions, constitution, environment, genetic inheritance etc.; moreover, the population exposed to risk is of such a heterogeneous character that influences do not necessarily impinge on all persons equally. An epidemic, for instance, may affect certain age groups more seriously than others. And to these causes of variation, which are in the nature of things or of a biological character, must be added those of a statistical kind. Every survey involves errors which are either constant or random in character. The difficulties inherent in collecting data on the exposed to risk, when the composition of this group is constantly changing, have been repeatedly stressed, and the classification of the living and dead according to place of residence must always be somewhat arbitrary.

In spite of these variations, the trend of mortality tends to be uniform. In order to disengage the basic trend as far as possible from more or less random irregularities, various graduation procedures have been evolved. These should be so contrived that, while producing as smooth a curve as possible for the values, they do not efface variations which are inherent in the subject matter.

There are three forms of graduation:

— the *graphic:* as smooth a curve as possible is plotted free-hand between the marked values.
— the *mechanical:* the value to be graduated is taken to be the mean value of its adjacent values.
— the *analytical:* the empirical curve is replaced by a mathematical one which is fitted as closely as possible to the given values. For life tables over the age

of 30 such a mathematical function is provided by the GOMPERTZ-MAKEHAM mortality formula

$$l_x = k\, s^x\, g^{c^x},$$

which is very popular especially in actuarial science.

We shall not go further into graduation methods here; they are of no particular importance to the reader who wishes primarily to study the phenomenon of mortality, and those who are interested in pursuing the matter further will find that there is an extensive literature on the subject*.

4.3. Biometric functions

By "biometric functions" we generally mean the probability of death, the probability of survival, the numbers living at successive ages and the mean expectation of life; these are all deemed to be functions of age. All these values taken together for all ages, or often just the probabilities of death or the numbers living alone, are called the life table. — In the following section we shall define these values for *one* cause of exit only, i.e. for so-called *simple decrement tables***.

To construct a life table we must, as we saw in section 4.1, first compute the *annual probability of death* q_x for all ages x from the empirical figures according to formula (4.1.1) or (4.1.2). It is the normal practice to graduate these values as described in section 4.2.

The following fundamental relations can then be derived by means of q_x:

If we start from a specified initial population

$$l_0 = \text{lives aged } 0$$

then $l_0\, q_0 = d_0 = \text{deaths at age } 0\,.$

There thus remains $l_1 = l_0 - d_0 = \text{living at age } 1\,.$

From this population $l_1\, q_1 = d_1$ are removed by death.

This procedure can be continued and we obtain the *series of deaths****

$$\begin{aligned} d_0 &= l_0 - l_1 \\ d_1 &= l_1 - l_2 \\ d_2 &= l_2 - l_3 \\ d_3 &= l_3 - l_4 \\ &\cdots\cdots\cdots \end{aligned}$$

or the *series of survivors*

$$\begin{aligned} &l_0 \\ l_1 &= l_0 - d_0 \\ l_2 &= l_1 - d_1 \\ l_3 &= l_2 - d_2 \\ &\cdots\cdots\cdots \end{aligned}$$

* E.g. in HENDERSON, R.: Mathematical Theory of Graduation, New York 1938. — JOHNSON, M. L., and TETLEY: Statistics II, 1950. — ZWINGGI, ERNST: Versicherungsmathematik, Basel 1958. — SAXER, WALTER: Versicherungsmathematik, Part 2, Springer-Verlag, 1958.

** For several causes of exit see section 4.5.

*** The series of numbers l and d is shown graphically on page 49.

Clearly, $\Sigma d_x = l_0$, i.e. the sum of deaths at all ages must be equal to the initial population. It is the international practice to take for l_0 an integral multiple of 10, usually 100,000.

Then there is the equation

$p_x = 1 - q_x = \frac{l_{x+1}}{l_x}$ = probability that a person aged x years will survive one year (*probability of surviving* one year).

Among these quantities q_x, p_x, l_x, d_x exist the fundamental relations

$$q_x = 1 - p_x = 1 - \frac{l_{x+1}}{l_x} = \frac{l_x - l_{x+1}}{l_x} = \frac{d_x}{l_x}.$$

Hence, according to the definition of probability

$_np_x = \frac{l_{x+n}}{l_x}$ Probability that a person aged x will survive at least n years,

$_nq_x = \frac{l_x - l_{x+n}}{l_x} = 1 - {}_np_x$ Probability that a person aged x will die within n years,

$_{n|}q_x = \frac{d_{x+n}}{l_x}$ Probability that a person aged x will die at age $x+n$.

The total number of years which, according to the mortality table, *all* persons aged x still have to live is given by the sum $l_{x+1} + l_{x+2} + l_{x+3} \ldots$ up to the upper limiting age of the mortality table. If this sum is divided by the initial group of lives l_x, we obtain e_x or the mean length of life at age x (also called *mean expectation of life*), i.e. the average number of years which a person aged x still has to live.

$$e_x = \frac{l_{x+1} + l_{x+2} + l_{x+3} + \cdots}{l_x}, \text{ or}$$

$$\mathring{e}_x = e_x + {}^1/_2 = \frac{l_x + l_{x+1} + l_{x+2} + \cdots}{l_x} - {}^1/_2.$$

In the formula for e_x it is assumed thet the deaths do not occur until the end of a year; in the case of $\mathring{e}_x$ they are assumed to occur in the middle of the year*.

The mean expectation of life is one of the most important indices of mortality; it is not only easy to visualize but also indicates in a single figure the complete future trend of mortality in a given group of lives. Thus the *mean length of life* of those aged 0 in a population is commonly accepted as a measure of the mortality in a country. As we saw in section 3.3, this figure is equal to the reciprocal value of the death rate of the stationary population and also identical with the *average age at death in the mortality table,* for

$$e_0 = \frac{l_1 + l_2 + l_3 + \cdots}{l_0} = \frac{0\,d_0 + 1\,d_1 + 2\,d_2 + 3\,d_3 + \ldots}{d_0 + d_1 + d_2 + d_3 + \cdots}.$$

In this formula, the numbers 0, 1, 2, 3 ... are the ages and the deaths d_0, d_1, d_2, d_3 ... are the weights.

* To distinguish it from e_x, the value $\mathring{e}_x$ is often called the complete expectation of life.

Some applications and examples

The life tables constructed from time to time are the most reliable barometer of the mortality rate in a nation. The life table clearly shows the changes in the age structure of a population due solely to a decrease in mortality and also the differences in the age structures of the two sexes in the stationary population. Moreover, the fundamental idea of the life table also forms the basis for the computation of marriage and divorce tables as well as the tables and figures of marriage, fertility, etc. The principal use of life tables, however, is to afford a mathematical basis for all life assurances. These problems cannot be discussed at length in the compass of this paper; they are dealt with in text books on actuarial mathematics. However, here are some simple applications derived from the theory of probability.

The quotient $p_x = \frac{l_{x+1}}{l_x}$ has been defined as the probability that a man aged x will live to age $x+1$. Question: How great is the probability that a newborn male child will live to the age of 65? Answer: according to the Swiss population life table 1948/53, a number of 66,625 out of 100,000 lives aged 0 will survive to 65; thus of the 100,000 cases of "equal possibility" only 66,625 are "successes". Thus the probability we are seeking is ${}_{65}p_0 = \frac{66{,}625}{100{,}000} = 0.66\,625$.

Generally speaking, the probability that a man aged x will survive at least n years is given, as we have seen, by ${}_np_x = \frac{l_{x+n}}{l_x}$. Where the numerical value of the fraction

$$\frac{l_{x+n}}{l_x} = {}^1/_2$$

there is an equal possibility that a person aged x will die before or after $x+n$. In this case the duration n is called the *median duration of a life aged* x or probable lifetime. Since $l_{x+n} = \frac{l_x}{2}$, the median duration of life is equivalent to the period in which the original total of l_x persons has been reduced by half. According to the Swiss population life table 1948/53, the median duration of life for a boy aged 0 is about 72 years, for after this time the original population of 100,000 has been reduced to half. For the $l_x = 94{,}272$ lives aged 20 according to the life table mentioned above we have $l_{x+n} = \frac{l_x}{2} = 47{,}136$, which number corresponds approximately to the age 73. Thus the median length of a life aged 20 is $73-20=53$ years.

Question: How great is the probability that a married couple will still be alive in 30 years if the husband is 30 and the wife 25 years old? Answer: upon the assumption that the probabilities of survival for both sexes are independent, the probability P we are seeking is the product of the probability that the husband will reach age 60 and the probability that the wife will live to age 55; that is to say, using the values of the Swiss population life table

$$P = {}_{30}p_{30}\ {}_{30}p_{25} = \frac{75\,355}{92\,530} \times \frac{87\,225}{95\,322} = 0.74\,521.$$

In general the formula

$$P = {}_np_x \, {}_np_y$$

gives the probability that a man aged x and a woman aged y will survive n years. If in the case of a married couple the product ${}_np_x \, {}_np_y = {}^1/_2$, n is called the *median duration of the marriage* on the assumption that only death will separate the couple and that the expectations of life for (x) and (y) are independent. Accordingly we have the following probabilities (P.):

${}_np_x \, {}_nq_y = {}_np_x(1 - {}_np_y)$	P. that (x) is still alive after n years but that (y) has died.
${}_np_y \, {}_nq_x = {}_np_y(1 - {}_np_x)$	P. that (y) is still alive after n years but that (x) has died.
${}_nq_x \, {}_nq_y$	P. that both (x) and (y) have died after n years.

4.4. Hypothetical character of the life table

The life table is derived from the actual number of lives *living at the same time*, i.e. from the mortality rates prevailing at that instant. Thus when we say that the life table shows how a population of l_0 aged 0 will decrease in the course of time, this statement is only hypothetical in character. During the 100 years or so which would elapse by the time the initial generation l_0 had died out completely, the mortality would change, and by the time those now aged 0 had reached age 10, 20 etc., the mortality rates applying to them would differ from those obtaining when the table was constructed. Even so, the type of population represented by the life table is of great importance in measuring mortality and in population statistics generally. It is known as the *stationary population.* This is a population of constant size, i.e. increments by birth exactly balance decrements by deaths. Migrations leave it unaffected.

It will be clear that the *real population* differs in its composition from this type. Actually we never have a constant but always a fluctuating number of births; moreover, the number of births is sometimes larger and sometimes smaller than the number of deaths. Again, migrations to and from the population are constantly altering its structure. In figure 4 the actual age structure of the Swiss population in the years 1939—44 is compared with the stationary population according to the life table of 1939/44.

What has just been said about the living applies with equal force to deaths. The series d_x, d_{x+1}, $d_{x+2} \ldots$ is also of a hypothetical character because it is derived from the fictitious populations l_x, l_{x+1}, $l_{x+2} \ldots$ Opposed to these we again have the actual series of deaths at the various ages D_x, D_{x+1}, $D_{x+2} \ldots$ Figure 5 compares the two populations, showing the theoretical and actual number of deaths.

It will be asked which of the two populations, the theoretical or the actual one, is of greater importance for the investigation of mortality. In general it may be said that although the actual figures afford information as to the present mortality rate, comparison with another population (in time or place) may lead to false conclusions (cf. section on crude and life table death-rates). The theoretical populations, on the other hand, provide a less graphic but more accurate picture of present mortality conditions and also permit comparisons with the figures of other periods or regions.

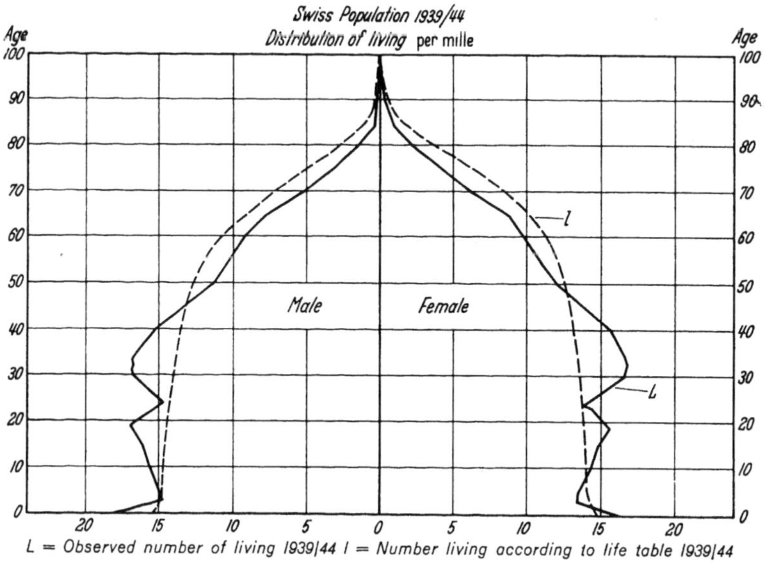

Fig. 4. Distribution of living per mille, (Swiss Population 1939/44)

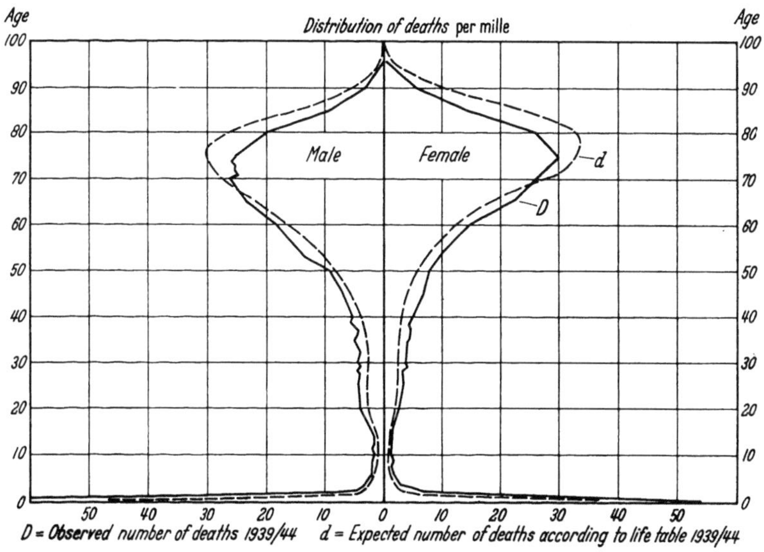

Fig. 5. Distribution of deaths per mille, (Swiss Population 1939/44)

4.5. Multiple causes of exit; multiple decrement tables

So far we have assumed that the decrements in the initial population l_0 were due solely to death, i.e. we considered only *one* cause of exit. But there are very many cases where decrements in the population occur as the result of more than one cause. This is true, for instance, if we consider decrements as being due not simply to death in general but to various causes of death. Again, if we wish to ascertain the mortality of married persons, we must remember that these groups are also reduced by divorce and the death of one of the partners as well as by the death of both, and that new marriages are added to the group in the course of the year.

Let the following symbols have the meaning indicated:

L_x = Total number of persons of the same age at the beginning of age x,

$T_x^{(i)}$ = Exits from L_x due cause (i) within year of age x,

A_x = Other exits from L_x within year of age x,

E_x = Entries into L_x within year of age x,

$$\left.\begin{aligned} \Delta_x &= T_x^{(i)} + A_x - E_x \\ \Delta_x &= L_x - L_{x+1} \end{aligned}\right\} \text{ Total change.}$$

For simplicity, we assume that the population L_x changes linearly within one year of age and that the exits due to cause (i) are evenly distributed over the year of age in question.

The annual independent, partial probability of exit due to cause (i) can then be defined as*

$$q_x^{(i)} = 1 - \left(1 - \frac{\Delta_x}{L_x}\right)^{T_x^{(i)}/\Delta_x} . \tag{4.5.1}$$

By expanding the binomial and approximating it by an infinite geometrical series we obtain

$$q_x^{(i)} \approx \frac{T_x^{(i)}}{L_x - \dfrac{\Delta_x - T_x^{(i)}}{2}} . \tag{4.5.1'}$$

The independent probabilities of exit are computed in practice by formula (4.5.1) or (4.5.1′). Formula (4.5.1) yields better values.

The *annual independent partial probability of survival* is expressed by

$$p_x^{(i)} = 1 - q_x^{(i)} .$$

The table of decrements due to cause (i) alone takes the form

$$\begin{aligned} &l_0^{(i)} \\ &l_1^{(i)} = l_0^{(i)}\, p_0^{(i)} \\ &l_2^{(i)} = l_1^{(i)}\, p_1^{(i)} \\ &l_3^{(i)} = l_2^{(i)}\, p_2^{(i)} \\ &\cdots\cdots\cdots \end{aligned} \tag{4.5.2}$$

* For the derivation of this formula cf. for instance ZWINGGI, E.: Versicherungsmathematik, l.c. — Also in: Berechnung und Darstellung der unabhängigen und abhängigen Wahrscheinlichkeiten. Mitteilungen der Vereinigung schweizerischer Versicherungsmathematiker, 49. Berne 1949.

According to the multiplication theorem of the theory of probability

$$p_x = p_x^{(1)}\, p_x^{(2)}\, p_x^{(3)} \dots p_x^{(k)}, \tag{4.5.3}$$

where k represents the number of causes of exit. The probabilities $q_x^{(i)}$ and $p_x^{(i)}$ are termed independent because exit due to cause (i) is considered to be independent of other causes.

From (4.5.2) and (4.5.3) it follows that

$$l_x = C\, l_x^{(1)}\, l_x^{(2)}\, l_x^{(3)} \dots l_x^{(k)}, \tag{4.5.4}$$

where

$$C = \frac{l_0}{l_0^{(1)}\, l_0^{(2)}\, l_0^{(3)} \dots l_0^{(k)}}.$$

Equation (4.5.3) thus signifies that the *total probability of survival is equal to the product of the independent, partial probabilities of survival,* and equation (4.5.4) *that the series of numbers surviving to successive ages in the total table is proportional to the product of the series in the partial tables.*

The partial tables show the exits from a group when only *one* of the various causes is operative. This is a very important theoretical construction in measuring mortality — theoretical because such partial exits do not occur in actual practice. They are used when it is desired, for instance, to isolate the effect of a specific cause of exit, or compare the effects of several causes operating together.

Application

a) Causes of death. Let $T_x^{(i)}$ = deaths in the population L_x due to cause (i), thus $T_x - T_x^{(i)}$ = deaths due to another cause.

Assuming that there are no entries (cf. page 50)

$$\Delta_x = T_x^{(i)} + (T_x - T_x^{(i)}) = T_x$$

and from equation (4.5.1) and (4.5.1′) it follows that

$$q_x^{(i)} = 1 - \left(1 - \frac{T_x}{L_x}\right)^{T_x^{(i)}/T_x},$$

$$q_x^{(i)} \approx \frac{T_x^{(i)}}{L_x - \dfrac{T_x - T_x^{(i)}}{2}}.$$

Annual independent partial probability that a life aged x will die from cause (i).

b) Migrations. In addition to exits due to death (T) there is also the possibility of migrations, i.e. exits (A) and entries (E). Then

$$\Delta_x = T_x + A_x - E_x$$

and, according to (4.5.1) and (4.5.1′), the annual probability of death

$$q_x = 1 - \left(1 - \frac{\Delta_x}{L_x}\right)^{T_x/\Delta_x},$$

$$q_x \approx \frac{T_x}{L_x - \dfrac{A_x - E_x}{2}}.$$

c) Changes of marital status. The groups of living L_x and dead T_x can be subdivided as follows:

L_x^s or T_x^s single persons
L_x^m or T_x^m married persons
L_x^w or T_x^w widows or widowers
L_x^d or T_x^d divorced persons.

Thus
$$L_x = L_x^s + L_x^m + L_x^w + L_x^d,$$
$$T_x = T_x^s + T_x^m + T_x^w + T_x^d.$$

Using registry offices records we can, by applying the same principle as in the case of deaths, construct first and second subgroups of the marriages of single, divorced and widowed persons and of divorces, widowhoods and widowerhoods. With these figures it is possible to make intercensal estimates of the population according to marital status and also to compute the relevant probabilities of death.

Where

M_x = Marriages, $M_x = M_x^s + M_x^w + M_x^d$,

W_x = Widowhoods or widowerhoods,

D_x = Divorces ,

the *independent probabilities of death for lives aged x* may be computed as follows:

Single persons
$$\Delta_x^s = T_x^s + M_x^s,$$
$$q_x^s = 1 - \left(1 - \frac{\Delta_x^s}{L_x^s}\right)^{T_x^s/\Delta_x^s},$$
$$q_x^s \approx \frac{T_x^s}{L_x^s - \dfrac{M_x^s}{2}}.$$

Married persons
$$\Delta_x^m = T_x^m + W_x + D_x - M_x,$$
$$q_x^m = 1 - \left(1 - \frac{\Delta_x^m}{L_x^m}\right)^{T_x^m/\Delta_x^m},$$
$$q_x^m \approx \frac{T_x^m}{L_x^m - \dfrac{W_x + D_x - M_x}{2}}.$$

Widowed persons
$$\Delta_x^w = T_x^w + M_x^w - W_x,$$
$$q_x^w = 1 - \left(1 - \frac{\Delta_x^w}{L_x^w}\right)^{T_x^w/\Delta_x^w},$$
$$q_x^w \approx \frac{T_x^w}{L_x^w - \dfrac{M_x^w - W_x}{2}}.$$

Divorced persons

$$\Delta_x^d = T_x^d + M_x^d - D_x,$$

$$q_x^d = 1 - \left(1 - \frac{\Delta_x^d}{L_x^d}\right)^{T_x^d/\Delta_x^d},$$

$$q_x^d \approx \frac{T_x^d}{L_x^d - \frac{M_x^d - D_x}{2}}.$$

Numerical examples

a) Causes of death. Of the 3,244 that died in Switzerland between 1939—1944, out of a total of 55,495 men aged 70, there were 684 deaths due to cancer. The annual, independent probability that a man aged 70 will die of cancer can thus be calculated from (4.5.1) and (4.5.1′), [since $L_x = 55{,}495$, $T_x = 3{,}244$, $T_x^{(i)} = 684$]

$$q_{70}^{(i)} = 1 - \left(1 - \frac{3{,}244}{55{,}495}\right)^{684/3{,}244} = 0{,}01\,180,$$

$$q_{70}^{(i)} \approx \frac{684}{55{,}495 - \frac{3{,}244 - 684}{2}} = 0{,}01\,292.$$

b) Changes of marital status. A total of 118,213 men aged 50 (first group of the living) observed during the period from 1939—1944 were classified according to marital status as follows:

$$L_{50}^s = 15{,}410$$
$$L_{50}^m = 97{,}201$$
$$L_{50}^w = 2{,}938$$
$$L_{50}^d = 2{,}664$$
$$L_{50} = 118{,}213$$

Between the ages 50 and 51, the following exits and entries were observed:

Marital status	Exits or entries[1] owing to				Total change[1]
	Death	Marriage	Widowerhood	Divorce	
Single persons	$T^s = 221$	$M^s = 180$	*	*	$\Delta^s = 401$
Married persons	$T^m = 846$	$M = \mathit{630}$	$W = 534$	$D = 227$	$\Delta^m = 977$
Widowers	$T^w = 39$	$M^w = 262$	$W = \mathit{534}$	*	$\Delta^w = -233$
Divorced persons	$T^d = 41$	$M^d = 188$	*	$D = \mathit{227}$	$\Delta^d = 2$
Total	$T = 1147$	—	—	—	$\Delta = 1147$

With these figures as a basis, the annual independent probabilities of death for men aged 50 of the various marital statuses can be computed according to (4.5.1)

[1] Increments are *italicized;* they constitute negative quantities for the changes.

and (4.5.1′) as follows:

$$q_{50}^{s}=1-\left(1-\frac{401}{15{,}410}\right)^{221/401}=0.01\,440,$$

$$q_{50}^{s}\approx\frac{221}{15{,}410-\frac{180}{2}}=0.01\,443.$$

$$q_{50}^{m}=1-\left(1-\frac{977}{97{,}201}\right)^{846/977}=0.00\,871,$$

$$q_{50}^{m}\approx\frac{846}{97{,}201-\frac{534+227-630}{2}}=0.00\,871.$$

$$q_{50}^{w}=1-\left(1-\frac{-233}{2{,}938}\right)^{39/-233}=0.01\,374,$$

$$q_{50}^{w}\approx\frac{39}{2{,}938-\frac{262-534}{2}}=0.01\,392.$$

$$q_{50}^{d}=1-\left(1-\frac{2}{2664}\right)^{41/2}=0.01\,524,$$

$$q_{50}^{d}\approx\frac{41}{2{,}664-\frac{188-227}{2}}=0.01\,550.$$

The total exits d_x for each year of age can be classified according to the k different causes of exit:

$$d_x=d_x^{(1)}+d_x^{(2)}+\cdots+d_x^{(k)}.$$

If these figures are divided by the population from which they are derived, we obtain the *dependent* partial probabilities of exit

$$\frac{d_x}{l_x}=\frac{d_x^{(1)}}{l_x}+\frac{d_x^{(2)}}{l_x}+\cdots+\frac{d_x^{(k)}}{l_x},$$

or

$$q_x={}^*q_x^{(1)}+{}^*q_x^{(2)}+\cdots+{}^*q_x^{(k)}.$$

This equation signifies: *The total probability of exit is equal to the sum of the dependent partial probabilities.*

As is clear from the definition equation for the dependent probability of exit

$${}^*q_x^{(i)}=\frac{d_x^{(i)}}{l_x},$$

the ratio is established between the number dying from cause (i) and the number living at the beginning of the year, and no account is taken of exits among these lives which are due to other causes. Hence these probabilities are not independent of the effects of other causes of exit and entries there may be, hence their special designation.

Independent and dependent probabilities can be converted one into the other by means of the following formulae:

$$*q^{(1)}=q_x^{(1)}\left(1-\frac{q_x^{(2)}}{2}\right)\cdots\left(1-\frac{q_x^{(k)}}{2}\right),$$

$$q^{(1)}=1-(1-q_x)^{*q_x^{(1)}/q_x}.$$

Of course, these equations hold good not only for cause 1, but also for each of the k causes if the indices are changed appropriately.

As a rule, however, the dependent probabilities can also be computed *directly from the observations,* namely by classifying the dead T_x according to the various causes of death from 1 to k

$$T_x=T_x^{(1)}+T_x^{(2)}+T_x^{(3)}+\cdots+T_x^{(k)}$$

and by dividing these groups by the number of persons under observation L_x, from which it follows that

$$\frac{T_x}{L_x}=\frac{T_x^{(1)}}{L_x}+\frac{T_x^{(2)}}{L_x}+\frac{T_x^{(3)}}{L_x}+\cdots+\frac{T_x^{(k)}}{L_x},$$

or

$$q_x={}^*q_x^{(1)}+{}^*q_x^{(2)}+{}^*q_x^{(3)}+\cdots+{}^*q_x^{(k)}.$$

If each of these quantities is multiplied by the mortality table population l_x, we obtain

$$l_x\,q_x=l_x\,{}^*q_x^{(1)}+l_x\,{}^*q_x^{(2)}+l_x\,{}^*q_x^{(3)}+\cdots+l_x\,{}^*q_x^{(k)},$$

or

$$d_x=d_x^{(1)}+d_x^{(2)}+d_x^{(3)}+\cdots+d_x^{(k)},$$

i.e. the deaths expected according to the life table are allotted to the various causes. In this way we can also *analyze the life table death-rate into the components assignable to the various causes of death,* namely

$$r=\frac{1}{e_0}=\frac{\Sigma d_x}{\Sigma l_x}=\frac{\Sigma d_x^{(1)}}{\Sigma l_x}+\frac{\Sigma d_x^{(2)}}{\Sigma l_x}+\frac{\Sigma d_x^{(3)}}{\Sigma l_x}+\cdots+\frac{\Sigma d_x^{(k)}}{\Sigma l_x}.$$

4.6. Method of constructing an "abridged" life table

For the construction of a complete life table by the classical method, we need the actual numbers of living and deaths for *all* ages. The exact number of the living according to age is known only for the actual dates of censuses, the results of which are normally published. In most civilized countries intercensal estimates of the population are made according to age, but the results are usually published only in *age groups,* particularly in statistical year books. Similarly annual deaths are usually given simply in age groups in mortality statistics. This fact — and aversion to the long calculations necessary for the construction of a complete mortality table — probably explains why the life table method is still so little used in population statistics. Below we shall explain a simple method of obtaining a sufficiently accurate life table even where the numbers of living and dead are known only in age groups.

Explanation of the method *

If we restrict ourselves to the ages 0, 1, 5, 10, 15 etc., the number of lives surviving to successive ages in such an abridged life table would be expressed by the formulae:

$$\begin{aligned}
&l_0\\
&l_1 = l_0 p_0\\
&l_5 = l_1 p_1 p_2 p_3 p_4\\
&l_{10} = l_5 p_5 p_6 p_7 p_8 p_9\\
&l_{15} = l_{10} p_{10} p_{11} p_{12} p_{13} p_{14}\\
&\ldots\ldots\ldots\ldots\ldots\ldots
\end{aligned} \tag{4.6.1}$$

Where the population statistics do not supply the numbers of living and dead for each year of age but only for age groups, we cannot determine the individual probabilities of survival $p_1, p_2, p_3 \ldots$; it becomes a question therefore of finding another expression for the products $p_x p_{x+1} p_{x+2} \ldots p_{x+n-1}$. Thus in the system of equations (4.6.1) we set

$$\begin{aligned}
&l_0\\
&l_1 = l_0 p_0\\
&l_5 = l_1 p_1 p_2 p_3 p_4 = l_1 (p_{1-4})^{t_{1-4}}\\
&l_{10} = l_5 p_5 p_6 p_7 p_8 p_9 = l_5 (p_{5-9})^{t_{5-9}}\\
&l_{15} = l_{10} p_{10} p_{11} p_{12} p_{13} p_{14} = l_{10} (p_{10-14})^{t_{10-14}}\\
&\ldots\ldots\ldots\ldots\ldots\ldots\ldots\ldots
\end{aligned} \tag{4.6.1'}$$

where in general

$$p_{x \to x+n-1} = 1 - q_{x \to x+n-1} = \frac{l_{x+1} + l_{x+2} + \cdots + l_{x+n}}{l_x + l_{x+1} + \cdots + l_{x+n-1}} \tag{4.6.2}$$

is the annual probability of survival of the age group x to $x+n-1$.

---

* The first exposition of this method was in:

WIESLER, H.: The construction of mortality tables on the basis of incomplete data. J. Ind. Med. Prof. 7, 3427—3435 (1960).

WIESLER, H.: Einfache Methode für die Erstellung einer abgekürzten Sterbetafel. Schweiz. Z. f. Volkswirtschaft u. Statistik. 87, 310—328 (1951).

For its application to causes of death see especially:

WIESLER, H.: Methodisches zur Sterblichkeitsmessung. Schweiz. Z. f. Volkswirtschaft u. Statistik. 88, 241—249 (1952).

— Une méthode simple pour la construction de tables de mortalité abrégées. World Population Conference, Rome 1954, Vol. IV, p. 1063—1073. United Nations, New York.

The method is also explained and applied in:

ROS, JIMENO: Mortalidad y esperanza de vida. Revista Internacional de Sociología, núm. 43, julio-septiembre 1953.

Also in: Tablas abreviadas de mortalidad de la Población española, Año 1950. Seria A, Demografía — 2. Instituto de estadística. Madrid 1958.

MICHALUP, E.: Procedimientos para confeccionar tablas de mortalidad. Revista de economía. Número 2, oct., nov., dic. 1957.

HANSLUWKA, H.: Entwicklung der Sterblichkeit in der Republik Österreich. Beiträge zur Österreichischen Statistik. Published by the Austrian Central Office of Statistics. Fasc. 47, Vienna 1960.

The indices t in (4.6.1′) may be expanded as follows:

$$\begin{aligned} t_{1-4} &= \frac{\log l_5 - \log l_1}{\log p_{1-4}}, \\ t_{5-9} &= \frac{\log l_{10} - \log l_5}{\log p_{5-9}}, \\ t_{10-14} &= \frac{\log l_{15} - \log l_{10}}{\log p_{10-14}}, \\ &\dots\dots\dots\dots \end{aligned} \tag{4.6.3}$$

If we now determine according to the formula (4.6.3) the values t from various life tables, it will be found — and this is the essence of the method — *that these values are almost the same however different the table.* We have calculated the indices t for five-year age groups from various tables and compiled them in Table V. Any number of examples may be cited. As will be seen, values which are identical or only slightly different are obtained from tables with similar mortality (e.g. Switzerland—England) as well as from those where the mortality differs widely (e.g. England—Portugal). Except for the highest age groups, the probability of survival p_u for a five-year group is generally equivalent in all life tables to the *geometric mean* of the separate values p_x of this group, i.e. the rise or fall of the curve is simply exponential within these intervals. In the last column of Table V we have compiled mean values t_u from the various values of the separate life tables and we recommend these for constructing an abridged life table.

The method rests therefore upon the *hypothesis* that the values t_u are the same for all life tables, i.e. the average values given in the last column of Table V are generally valid for our computations. Apart from its empirical foundation in the statistics of Table V, the hypothesis can also be substantiated a priori: the mortality of mankind displays by and large the same trend everywhere, for, although it is not a natural law, it does proceed in accordance with biological principles.

Let it be supposed that the groups of the living (L_u) and dead (T_u) are available for the age groups u classified as 0, 1—4, 5—9, 10—14, 15—19 etc.*; then, from these, the (crude) annual probabilities of dead may be computed

$$\frac{T_0}{L_0} = \bar{q}_0, \quad \frac{T_{1-4}}{L_{1-4}} = \bar{q}_{1-4}, \quad \frac{T_{5-9}}{L_{5-9}} = \bar{q}_{5-9}, \quad \frac{T_{10-14}}{L_{10-14}} = \bar{q}_{10-14}, \text{ etc.} \tag{4.6.4}$$

the dash over the q denoting that these are unadjusted values.

Now

$$\bar{q}_u = \frac{T_u}{L_u} \approx \frac{\Sigma d_x}{\Sigma l_x} = \frac{d_u}{l_u} = q_u, \tag{4.6.5}$$

the sums covering the years of age x to $x+n-1$ occurring in group u. We now propose a *second hypothesis* and equate both sides of this approximation. This

* The Demographic Year Book of the UNO, for example, publishes the population figures and deaths in these age groups for most countries.

Table V. *Values of t_u from various mortality tables*

Age group u	Switzerland 1939–1944	Belgium 1928–1932	Germany 1932–1934	France 1933–1938	England and Wales 1930–1932	Japan 1952	Portugal 1939–1942	*Mean values*
				Males				
1—4	3,990	3,977	3,990	3,982	3,981	3,993	3,925	*3,99*
5—9	5,01	4,99	5,00	5,00	5,00	4,99	4,99	*5*
10—14	5,02	5,00	5,00	5,00	5,00	4,98	5,00	*5*
15—19	5,01	5,00	5,00	5,00	5,00	5,00	5,00	*5*
20—24	5,00	4,99	5,00	5,00	5,00	5,00	5,00	*5*
25—29	5,00	5,00	5,00	5,00	5,00	5,00	5,00	*5*
30—34	5,00	5,00	5,00	5,00	5,00	5,00	5,00	*5*
35—39	5,00	5,00	5,00	5,00	5,00	5,00	5,00	*5*
40—44	5,00	5,00	5,00	5,00	5,00	5,00	5,00	*5*
45—49	5,004	5,008	5,005	5,008	5,007	5,007	5,005	*5,005*
50—54	5,012	5,008	5,010	5,010	5,010	5,009	5,010	*5,010*
55—59	5,016	5,016	5,015	5,017	5,016	5,019	5,016	*5,016*
60—64	5,024	5,026	5,024	5,025	5,027	5,028	5,027	*5,026*
65—69	5,041	5,042	5,040	5,034	5,045	5,045	5,050	*5,045*
70—74	5,067	5,067	5,067	5,069	5,072	5,063	5,081	*5,068*
75—79	5,113	5,110	5,106	5,112	5,109	5,094	5,110	*5,110*
80—84	5,162	5,177	5,179	5,165	5,154	5,140	5,150	*5,165*
				Females				
1—4	3,995	3,982	3,991	3,984	3,979	3,994	3,927	*3,99*
5—9	5,00	5,00	5,00	5,00	5,00	4,98	5,00	*5*
10—14	5,00	5,00	5,00	5,00	5,00	5,01	5,00	*5*
15—19	5,00	5,00	5,00	5,00	5,00	4,99	5,00	*5*
20—24	5,00	5,00	5,00	5,00	5,00	5,00	5,00	*5*
25—29	5,00	5,00	5,00	5,00	5,00	5,00	5,00	*5*
30—34	5,00	5,00	5,00	5,00	5,00	5,00	5,00	*5*
35—39	5,00	5,00	5,00	5,00	5,00	5,00	5,00	*5*
40—44	5,00	5,00	5,00	5,00	5,00	5,00	5,00	*5*
45—49	5,004	5,004	5,005	5,005	5,005	5,006	5,003	*5*
50—54	5,007	5,007	5,007	5,006	5,007	5,007	5,006	*5,007*
55—59	5,011	5,012	5,012	5,011	5,012	5,012	5,011	*5,012*
60—64	5,020	5,021	5,021	5,018	5,019	5,019	5,019	*5,020*
65—69	5,035	5,036	5,037	5,033	5,033	5,031	5,038	*5,036*
70—74	5,061	5,062	5,065	5,057	5,059	5,052	5,067	*5,062*
75—79	5,092	5,107	5,096	5,093	5,095	5,087	5,105	*5,100*
80—84	5,160	5,184	5,153	5,145	5,138	5,145	5,127	*5,151*

Where the actual numbers of living and deaths are given in *10-year* age groups, the following values may be used for t:

Age groups	1—9	10—19	20—29	30—39	40—49	50—59	60—69	70—79	80—89
t for males	8.97	10	10	10	10.04	10.108	10.269	10.747	11.564
t for females	8.97	10	10	10	10	10.067	10.222	10.617	11.535

equality is, of course, precisely attained only in rare instances, for in the first place we are using unadjusted probabilities on one side and adjusted probabilities on the other; secondly $\bar{q}_u$ is a mean weighted with the actual population whereas

q_u is weighted with the stationary population; this is clearly apparent when (4.6.5) is written in the form

$$\bar{q}_u = \frac{\Sigma L_x \bar{q}_x}{\Sigma L_x} \approx \frac{\Sigma l_x q_x}{\Sigma l_x} = q_u. \tag{4.6.5'}$$

The examples will show us the magnitude of the "errors" we make through these two assumptions.

Computation of the numbers dying at successive ages

The actual numbers of deaths T_u and living L_u are taken from the statistics. This can be done in two ways:

a) The number of deaths is given according to years of birth and ages. The probabilities of death q_u can then be calculated directly by BECKER and ZEUNER's method [see formula (4.1.1)].

b) The actual numbers of deaths are published only according to age. In this case we first compute the central death rate $m_u = \frac{T_u}{L'_u}$ (the number L'_u referring to the middle of the year) and then the probabilities of death q_u according to the formula $q_u = \frac{2\,m_u}{2+m_u}$ [see formula (4.1.2)]. The latter method is the more customary; it is used in Anglo-Saxon countries for the construction of official mortality tables. The differences in the results yielded by the two methods are negligible. Needless to say, in computing age 0 reference must be made directly to the number of births (cf. discussion on page 32).

From the probabilities of survival determined by formulae (4.6.4) $p_u = 1 - q_u$, and the values given in the last column of Table V, we can obtain the numbers surviving to successive ages as follows

$$\begin{array}{lcl} l_0 & \text{or} & \log l_0 \\ l_1 = l_0 p_0 & & \log l_1 = \log l_0 + \log p_0 \\ l_5 = l_1 (p_{1-4})^{t_{1-4}} & & \log l_5 = \log l_1 + t_{1-4} \log p_{1-4} \\ l_{10} = l_5 (p_{5-9})^{t_{5-9}} & & \log l_{10} = \log l_5 + t_{5-9} \log p_{5-9} \\ l_{15} = l_{10} (p_{10-14})^{t_{10-14}} & & \log l_{15} = \log l_{10} + t_{10-14} \log p_{10-14} \\ \dots\dots & & \dots\dots \end{array} \tag{4.6.6}$$

The logarithms of the numbers surviving to successive ages are thus simply obtained by multiplying the logarithms of the probabilities of survival p_u by the various values t_u and adding the preceding value.

Computation of the average expectation of life

According to (4.6.5)

$$\bar{q}_u = \frac{T_u}{L_u} \approx \frac{d_u}{l_u},$$

so that

$$l_u \approx \frac{d_u L_u}{T_u} = \frac{(l_x - l_{x+n}) L_u}{T_u} \tag{4.6.7}$$

since d_u denotes the number of dead in the age interval x to $x+n-1$. If we have used this formula to obtain the sum of the living per age group u, the total number surviving to age x will be $\Sigma l_u = \Sigma l_x$, and the average expectation of life

$$\mathring{e}_x = \frac{\Sigma l_u}{l_x} - 0.5. \tag{4.6.8}$$

If the central death rates

$$m_u = \frac{T_u}{L'_u} \approx \frac{\Sigma d_x}{\sum \frac{l_x + l_{x+1}}{2}} = \frac{d_u}{l'_u}$$

are available, then

$$l'_u \approx \frac{d_u L'_u}{T_u} = \frac{(l_x - l_{x+n}) L'_u}{T_u}, \tag{4.6.7'}$$

and

$$\mathring{e}_x = \frac{\Sigma l'_u}{l_x}. \tag{4.6.8'}$$

This method can also be used to investigate *mortality according to causes of death* for the purpose, for example, of constructing life tables in which certain causes of death are eliminated or tables showing the numbers of deaths at successive ages due solely to specified causes. From such (fictitious) constructions it is possible to determine with accuracy what effect each separate cause has within the total number of deaths.

If $T_u^{(i)}$ is the number of lives aged u who died of cause (i), then (see formula page 51)

$$q_u^{(i)} = \frac{T_u^{(i)}}{L_u - \frac{T_u - T_u^{(i)}}{2}}$$

is the independent probability that a life aged u will die of cause (i).

The life table of a group in which decrements are due solely to a specified cause (i) is expressed for ages 0, 1, 5, 10, 15 ... by

$$\begin{aligned}
&l_0^{(i)} \\
&l_1^{(i)} = l_0^{(i)} p_0^{(i)} \\
&l_5^{(i)} = l_1^{(i)} p_1^{(i)} p_2^{(i)} p_3^{(i)} p_4^{(i)} \\
&l_{10}^{(i)} = l_5^{(i)} p_5^{(i)} p_6^{(i)} p_7^{(i)} p_8^{(i)} p_9^{(i)} \\
&l_{15}^{(i)} = l_{10}^{(i)} p_{10}^{(i)} p_{11}^{(i)} p_{12}^{(i)} p_{13}^{(i)} p_{14}^{(i)} \\
&\cdots\cdots\cdots\cdots
\end{aligned} \tag{4.6.9}$$

In order to obtain this life table we employ the same method as for the total mortality and then find the relations by analogy with (4.6.6)

$$\begin{aligned}
&\log l_0^{(i)} \\
&\log l_1^{(i)} = \log l_0^{(i)} + \log p_0^{(i)} \\
&\log l_5^{(i)} = \log l_1^{(i)} + t_{1-4} \log p_{1-4}^{(i)} \\
&\log l_{10}^{(i)} = \log l_5^{(i)} + t_{5-9} \log p_{5-9}^{(i)} \\
&\log l_{15}^{(i)} = \log l_{10}^{(i)} + t_{10-14} \log p_{10-14}^{(i)} \\
&\cdots\cdots\cdots\cdots
\end{aligned} \tag{4.6.9'}$$

As experience has shown, the coefficients t_u can also be used to compute life tables for specified causes or the total mortality excluding certain causes. The reason is as follows: either the partial probabilities of death are so small that the last digits of the t_u coefficients in the upper age groups are negligible, or the partial probabilities of death are so great that their trend approximates to that of the total mortality.

Examples

Example 1: Computation of an abridged Swedish national life table 1931—1940, females. The process of calculation can be clearly seen from Table VI. The groups of living and deaths are of the first type* (year of birth method), so that the values of q_u are immediately obtainable as their quotient according to formula (4.1.1) on page 38. The multipliers t_u may be taken from the last column of table V. We calculate log l_x according to the recurrence formulae (4.6.6), the values l_u are obtainable from (4.6.7) and the average expectation of life e_x from (4.6.8).

Example 2: Computation of a mortality table excluding tuberculosis as a cause of death, Swiss males, 1939/44. The process of calculation can be seen from Table VII. The numbers living at successive ages and the average expectation of life are computed when tuberculosis (i) is excluded as a primary cause of death; the symbol $(-i)$ denotes all causes of death exclusive of tuberculosis.

Accuracy

In the Table VIII we shall compare the values computed for the numbers living at exact age x and the average expectation of life in example 1 (Table VI) and the exact values of the complete Swedish population life table constructed by the classical method. With a standard population of $l_0 = 100{,}000$, it will be seen the deviations in the numbers living at exact age x amount to only a few lives; the maximum absolute deviation is 55 lives at age 65, which is equivalent to a relative error of not quite one per mille. If we follow the usual practice and base the comparison on $l_0 = 10{,}000$ persons, we find that the values virtually tally. Again, the deviations for the average expectation of life are negligible; the greatest difference is 3/100 of a year, i.e. a little more than one week. Moreover, the exact values of the Swedish table are unadjusted figures. As a rule, the deviations between an unadjusted and an adjusted table are greater than the differences shown here between the exact and the approximate processes.

As the following review of the figures shows, the process is also very suitable for computing life tables in which specific causes of death are excluded. Tables of this kind were constructed for Switzerland for the period 1939/44 and cancer, tuberculosis and violence excluded successively as causes of death.

* These figures are taken from "Dödlighets- och Livslängdstabeller för Årtiondet 1931—1940 av Statistiska Centralbyrån", Stockholm, 1944.

Table VI. *Example for the computation of a abridged life table, Swedish female population, 1931—1940*

Age group u x to $x+n-1$	First group: Living L_u	First group: Dead T_u	Death rate q_u	$\log p_u = \log(1-q_u)$	$t_u \cdot \log p_u$	$\log l_x$ formula (4.6.6)	Number living at exact age x l_x	l_u formula (4.6.7)	Σl_u	Expectation of life $\overset{\circ}{e}_x$
(1)	(2)	(3)	(4) = (3):(2)	(5)	(6)	(7)	(8)	(9)	(10)	(11)
0	*	*	0.03,878	—0.017,1772	—0.017,1772	5	100,000	100,000	6,662,061	66.12
1— 4	1,669,861	5,013	0.00300	—0.001,3048	—0.005,2062	4.982,8228	96,122	381,407	6,562,061	67.77
5— 9	2,234,024	2,754	123	—0.000,5345	—0.002,6725	4.977,6166	94,977	472,925	6,180,654	64.58
10—14	2,526,008	3,067	121	—0.000,5258	—0.002,6290	4.974,9441	94,394	469,457	5,707,729	59.97
15—19	2,670,459	5,991	224	—0.000,9739	—0.004,8695	4.972,3151	93,824	466,249	5,238,272	55.33
20—24	2,693,670	8,034	298	—0.001,2961	—0.006,4805	4.967,4456	92,778	460,680	4,772,023	50.93
25—29	2,685,936	8,185	305	—0.001,3266	—0.006,6330	4.960,9651	91,404	454,493	4,311,343	46.67
30—34	2,537,387	8,090	319	—0.001,3876	—0.006,9380	4.954,3321	90,019	447,571	3,856,850	42,34
35—39	2,339,006	8,445	361	—0.001,5706	—0.007,8530	4.947,3941	88,592	439,827	3,409,279	37.98
40—44	2,140,671	9,517	445	—0.001,9369	—0.009,6845	4.939,5411	87,004	431,418	2,969,452	33.63
45—49	1,961,455	11,836	603	—0.002,6267	—0.013,1335	4.929,8566	85,086	420,099	2,538,034	29.33
50—54	1,763,078	14,669	832	—0.003,6284	—0.018,1674	4.916,7231	82,551	406,485	2,117,935	25.16
55—59	1,547,777	18,389	1,188	—0.005,1903	—0.026,0138	4.898,5557	79,169	387,428	1,711,450	21.12
60—64	1,311,257	23,738	1,810	—0.007,9327	—0.039,8222	4.872,5419	74,566	360,875	1,324,022	17.26
65—69	1,113,048	32,943	2,960	—0.013,0492	—0.065,7158	4.832,7197	68,033	322,768	963,147	13.66
70—74	936,643	46,194	4,932	—0.021,9656	—0.111,1899	4.767,0039	58,480	267,850	640,379	10.45
75—79	663,670	54,470	8,207	—0.037,1904	—0.189,6710	4.655,8140	45,270	195,178	372,529	7.73
80—84	367,951	48,632	13,217	—0.061,5653	—0.317,1229	4.466,1430	29,251	114,678	177,351	5.56
85 and more	195,117	43,878	22,488			4.149,0201	14,094	62,673	62,673	3.95

* For the first year of life the death-rate was determined as the quotient of the number dying divided by the number of live births.

Table VII. *Example for the computation of a life table excluding tuberculosis as a cause of death, Switzerland, males, 1939/44*

Age group u x to $x+n-1$	First group			$q_u^{(-i)} = \frac{T_u - T_u^{(i)}}{L_u - \frac{T_u^{(i)}}{2}}$	$\log(1 - q_u^{(-i)}) = \log p_u^{(-i)}$	$t_u \log p_u^{(-i)}$	$\log l_x^{(-i)}$ according to formula (4.6.9′)	Number living at exact age x $l_x^{(-i)}$	$l_u^{(-i)} = \frac{l_x^{(-i)} - l_{x+n}^{(-i)}}{q_u^{(-i)}}$	$\sum l_u^{(-i)}$	Expectation of life $\mathring{e}_x^{(-i)} = \frac{\sum l_u^{(-i)}}{l_x^{(-i)}} - {}^1/_2$
	Living L_u	Dead									
		total T_u	of Tb $T_u^{(i)}$								
(1)	(2)	(3)	(4)	(5)	(6)	(7)	(8)	(9)	(10)	(11)	(12)
0	185,151	8,694	83	0.04,652	—0.020,6884	—0.020,6884	5	100,000	100,000	6,471,115	64.21
1—4	634,556	2,250	184	326	—0.001,4181	—0.005,6582	4.979,3116	95,348	378,528	6,371,115	66.32
5—9	796,141	1,127	119	127	—0.000,5519	—0.002,7595	4.973,6534	94,114	469,291	5,992,587	63.17
10—14	823,393	979	121	104	—0.000,4519	—0.002,2595	4.970,8939	93,518	467,308	5,523,296	58.56
15—19	860,027	1,764	360	163	—0.000,7085	—0.003,5425	4.968,6344	93,032	463,190	5,055,988	53.85
20—24	815,520	2,479	660	223	—0.000,9696	—0.004,8480	4.965,0919	92,277	459,641	4,592,798	49.27
25—29	826,506	2,612	812	218	—0.000,9478	—0.004,7390	4.960,2439	91,252	454,128	4,133,157	44.79
30—34	873,186	2,701	784	220	—0.000,9565	—0.004,7825	4.955,5049	90,262	449,545	3,679,029	40.26
35—39	830,498	3,040	722	279	—0.001,2134	—0.006,0670	4.950,7224	89,273	443,728	3,229,484	35,68
40—44	750,812	3,841	776	408	—0.001,7755	—0.008,8775	4.944,6554	88,035	436,520	2,785,756	31.14
45—49	646,865	4,961	704	658	—0.002,8671	—0.014,3498	4.935,7779	86,254	426,140	2,349,236	26.74
50—54	566,166	6,629	664	1,054	—0.004,6018	—0.023,0550	4.921,4281	83,450	409,298	1,923,096	22.54
55—59	517,610	9,295	728	1,656	—0.007,2521	—0.036,3765	4.898,3731	79,136	383,998	1,513,798	18.63
60—64	453,654	12,787	691	2,668	—0.011,7444	—0.059,0274	4.861,9966	72,777	346,627	1,129,800	15.02
65—69	355,785	15,126	621	4,080	—0.018,0908	—0.091,2681	4.802,9692	63,529	295,147	783,173	11.83
70—74	233,279	15,869	396	6,638	—0.029,8299	—0.151,1779	4.711,7011	51,487	228,005	488,026	8.98
75—79	139,195	14,735	262	10,407	—0.047,7259	—0.243,8793	4.560,5232	36,352	150,091	260,021	6.65
80—84	59,943	9,777	90	16,172	—0.076,6109	—0.395,6953	4.316,6439	20,732	76,651	109,930	4.80
85 and more	20,218	5,074	11	25,049	—	—	3.920,9486	8,336	33,279	33,279	3.49

Table VIII. *Swedish life table, females, 1931—1940*

Age x	Number living at exact age x		Expectation of life $\overset{\circ}{e}_x$	
	Exact values	Approximation method	Exact values	Approximation method
0	100,000	100,000	66.13	66.12
1	96,122	96,122	67.78	67.77
5	94,973	94,977	64.59	64.58
10	94,387	94,394	59.97	59.97
15	93,818	93,824	55.32	55.33
20	92,722	92,778	50.91	50.93
25	91,397	91,404	46.64	46.67
30	90,013	90,019	42.32	42.34
35	88,586	88,592	37.96	37.98
40	86,995	87,004	33.61	33.63
45	88,075	85,086	29.31	29.33
50	82,532	82,551	25.13	25.16
55	79,144	79,169	21.10	21.12
60	74,532	74,556	17.24	17.26
65	67,978	68,033	13.64	13.66
70	58,441	58,480	10.44	10.45
75	45,269	45,270	7.71	7.73
80	29,237	29,251	5.55	5.56
85	14,071	14,094	3.94	3.95

Comparison of the exact values and those obtained by our method of approximation reveals only negligible differences in the average expectation of life. This is particularly remarkable in view of the fact that the causes of death operative here vary considerably in their trend. Cancer, for example, is predominantly a disease of old age whereas tuberculosis and violent deaths are of variable pattern and show little tendency to increase in the upper age groups.

Average expectation of life in years. Switzerland, males, 1939/44

Age	All causes of death excluding cancer		All causes of death excluding tuberculosis		All causes of death excluding violence	
	Exact values	Approximation method	Exact values	Approximation method	Exact values	Approximation method
0	64.42	64.47	64.19	64.21	64.90	64.92
20	49.82	49.87	49.25	49.27	49.65	49.68
65	12.84	12.91	11.76	11.83	11.87	11.93

Instead of calculating the decrements in a standard group for the total mortality excluding cause (i), it is also possible, by using (4.6.9′), to determine the decrements for cause (i) alone. The two tables are interrelated according to (4.5.4) on page 51, so that the one may derived from the other. In the case of one cause (i) and with a standard population of 100,000

$$\frac{l_x^{(i)}\, l_x^{(-i)}}{100{,}000} = l_x; \quad l_x^{(i)} = 100{,}000\, \frac{l_x}{l_x^{(-i)}} .$$

We have calculated the decrements in the Swiss population due to tuberculosis as a cause of death first by applying this formula [l_x divided by column (9) of Table VII and secondly direct by formula (4.6.9′)] and then compared them in the Table IX with the exact values, i.e. those obtained from the complete and adjusted life table constructed by the classical method. The agreement between the three sets of figures is good. An equally good approximation can be obtained for cancer, which has an entirely different trend as a cause of death.

Table IX. *Life table for tuberculosis as a cause of death. Switzerland, males, 1939/1944*

Age x	Exact values	Method of approximation	
		$l_x^{(i)}$ according to formula (4.6.9′)	$l_x^{(i)} = \frac{l_x}{l_x^{(-i)}} 100{,}000$
0	100,000	100,000	100,000
1	99,954	99,954	99,954
5	99,844	99,838	99,837
10	99,763	99,764	99,763
15	99,684	99,689	99,688
20	99,471	99,480	99,479
25	99,055	99,077	99,076
30	99,590	98,593	98,590
35	98,163	98,150	98,152
40	97,731	97,724	97,724
45	97,224	97,217	97,213
50	96,680	96,688	96,678
55	96,108	96,117	96,107
60	95,433	95,435	95,423
65	94,675	94,699	94,681
70	93,876	93,851	93,833
75	93,008	93,017	92,994
80	92,100	92,075	92,051
85	91,412	91,302	91,267

Possible applications

In conclusion we may mention a few possible applications of the method. Since it is based on group numbers it ensures a certain graduation in the trend of mortality. Hence it is particularly valuable where the actual numbers of living and deaths are available in figures that are *too small* to permit the calculation of the probabilities of death for each age x without large discontinuities having to be tolerated. This arises, for example, when life tables have to be constructed not only for large countries or very numerous insurance populations but also for smaller areas, towns, occupational groups, marital status groups or special groups of lives such as under-average risks. Moreover, it is also possible to use reliable old statistics for the construction of life tables at a later date. This possibility is of particular value when it is desired to compare the mortality in various places *at the same time;* it is notorious that official life tables seldom coincide in time.

Where intercensal estimates are available, it is also feasible to construct life tables between the dates fixed for national censuses, and in this way we obtain suitable index figures for changes in mortality. Also, because the populations observed need not be so large as for a complete life table, we can select a shorter interval of observation and thus permit the disturbing influence of the secular mortality trend to be eliminated with greater success.

The *net reproduction rate* is computed by multiplying the relative number of live girl births per woman by the probability that these girls will attain the age of their mother. In most civilized countries reproduction rates are determined for each year; that is to say, the ratio is established between the number of girl births observed annually and the actual population of women as obtained by intercensal estimate and then multiplied by the last available life table. However, it sometimes happens that this table is very much out of date as compared with the observed numbers and hence the net reproduction rate may be illusory. The same applies to the life potential. The construction of a life table referring to the period under consideration, however, would permit comparable figures with a common origin in time to be correlated.

The method is based on the assumption that the values t_u are valid for all tables. Strict adherence to these values, however, is not essential; in the age group 1—4 in particular the values vary in the second place of decimals according to whether it is a country with a high or low infant mortality rate. Hence, depending on the type of table to be constructed, we can compute with a higher or a lower value for t_{1-4}. Generally speaking, however, we need have no hesitation in taking the mean values of t_u.

The considerations upon which this method is based hold good, of course, for any other classification of the age groups; if the method is used for another classification the values t_u applicable to it will have to be determined. The smaller the age group, however, the better the approximation, for under these circumstances, as may be seen from the equivalence (4.6.5′), the differences in the age structure of the population observed are not of great consequence. As UNO has published the population figures for most countries in 5-year groups in its Demographic Year Book, we shall refrain here from discussing any other age division in detail.

4.7. *Kinds of life tables*

A first distinction must be made between *life tables for the population* in general and those for *assured lives,* for the assured lives constitute a selection from the general population in various respects. The first important difference is that the assured must either submit to a medical examination or complete a detailed medical questionnaire before taking out his policy. In this way the assurer wants to protect himself from the admission of sick persons in the interests of the healthy lives assured. Aggravated risks, i.e. persons with abnormal mortality, are either excluded by the companies or accepted only on different conditions since the premium rates are based on a group of healthy lives exhibiting the greatest possible homogeneity. For this reason the life tables of assured lives show a slightly lower mortality than the population life tables.

This selection on grounds of health that distinguishes assured lives from the rest of the population when insurance is first purchased disappears with time and after a certain period the mortality of insured and non-insured lives is nearly the same. This period is known as the selection period and life tables which show mortality experienced relative to this period are called *select tables*. Tables taking no account of selection are called *aggregate tables*. Thus, whereas the aggregate tables are related solely to age, select tables have a double relationship, viz. to age and to the period elapsed since the date of assurance. A life table showing the mortality of lives assured after the selection period is called an *ultimate table* (cf. Fig. 6).

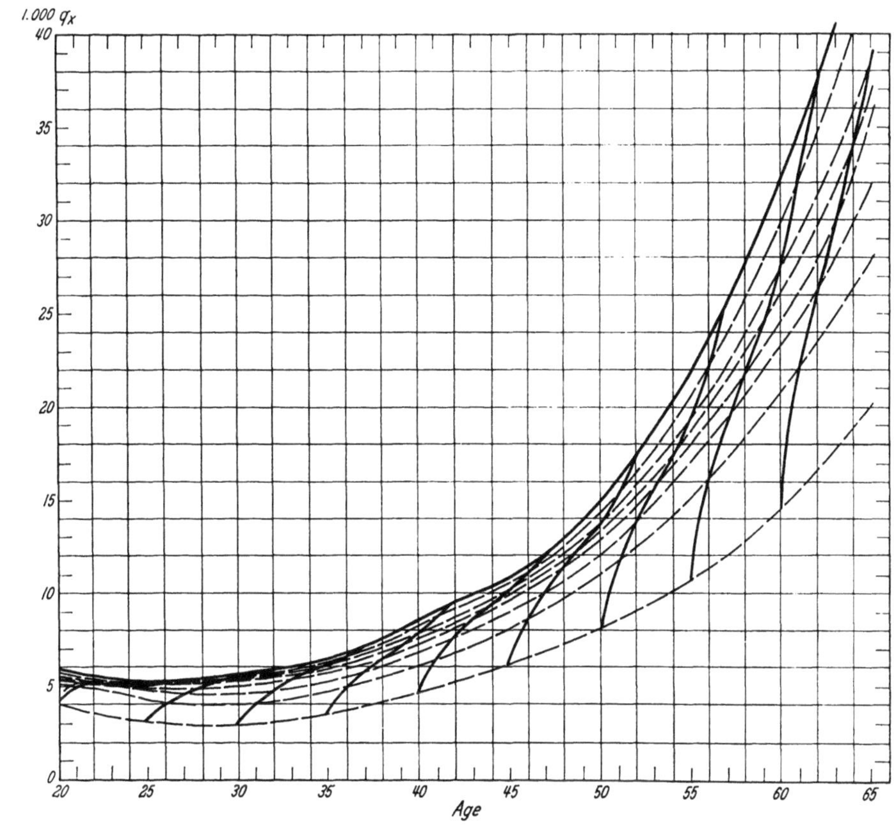

Fig. 6. Select tables (New Gotha-Table)
— — — Select tables (Probabilities of death for assured lives in the 1st, 2nd, 3rd . . . year of assurance. The Mortality thus always refers to different lives.)
—— { Ultimate table (Mortality on conclusion of the selection period)
Transversals (They denote the true mortality of an initial population and merge into the ultimate curve on conclusion of the selection period)

The graph is taken from: N. R. Jörgensen: Grundzüge einer Theorie der Lebensversicherung, Jena 1913, p. 12.

Distinctions according to the type of insurance. Life assurances can be divided into two principal classes, assurances for a capital sum and annuity assurances. The predominant forms of assurances for a capital sum are assurances payable at death and, more particularly, so-called endowment assurances in which the sum assured is payable either on the death of the assured life or on survival up to a certain age. By and large, persons taking out assurances payable on death have a higher mortality than those who buy an annuity, for in both groups selection against the insurer is operative. Proposers for annuities in particular include a certain number who enjoy exceptional health and hope therefore to draw their annuity for as long as possible. For this reason different tables are used for *annuitants* and for *assured lives.*

The assurer must often make a further distinction between *individual and group insurance.* Whereas population life tables are used for the assurance of individual lives, these rates cannot as a rule be simply applied to group assured lives. The latter normally constitute a selection in as much as they usually include only healthy lives or at least persons capable of work.

Distinction between normal and abnormal risks. By normal risks we mean lives that exhibit no abnormalities which might be considered to aggravate the risk at the time the assurance is taken out. Life tables based on such individuals are largely a reflection of the policy adopted by the company or companies in accepting new lives. Lives displaying abnormalities are grouped together in classes and *tables are constructed for abnormalities of the same type* (life tables for cardiac, diabetic cases etc.) or *tables for the same degree of excess* mortality (e.g. tables for 25%, 50% etc. greater mortality than the normal table indicates). For further discussion on this point see chapter 5.2.

The population life tables of the various countries are normally published in their statistical year books or appear in special publications brought out by the statistical offices. The Demographic Year Book of the United Nations as a rule contains the average expectation of life for several ages from most of the known life tables of recent date. The volume for 1957 also includes for these ages the values of the number living at exact age x (l_x) and the probabilities of death (q_x).

5. The investigation of mortality in life assurance — special features

5.0. *General observations*

The problem of investigating the mortality of assured lives involves material and formal peculiarities as compared with the mortality of a general population, and for this reason a special section must be devoted to it.

In the first place the exposed to risk differ fundamentally in their age structure from the general population. Assured lives are drawn as a rule only from persons earning their own living or having independent means. Also these people represent a *selection* from the general population in various respects: first, an assurance can be taken out and maintained only by a social class enjoying a certain income and thus standing on a certain social level (class selection). Then, insurance is very frequently sought by persons who hope to find the transaction especially profitable. Thus annuities are bought particularly by persons with exceptionally robust health whereas assurances payable on death are often considered desirable by those whose expectation of life is diminished. However, this latter selection is modified by the *medical examination on entry*, which is designed to prevent persons with aggravated life risks from being assured at rates which were established for exposed to risk with a normal mortality. This selection, which is of course based on health findings at a particular moment, disappears in time, with the result that mortality is also a *function of the number of years of assurance that have elapsed*. Finally it may be mentioned that *males* figure more prominently among assured lives and this must be borne in mind when comparing tables for both sexes.

As to methodology, it should be said at the outset that an assurance life table must usually cover a longer period of observation than a population life table so that the numbers involved may be sufficiently large. One advantage of the life table for assured lives is that account may be taken of all the entries and exits affecting the exposed to risk in contradistinction to the population life tables where no allowance is usually made for migrations, or at most only indirectly (cf. section 4.1).

In constructing population life tables there is no doubt that the individual, i.e. the person, must be taken as the *unit of enumeration*. This choice is more difficult when investigating the mortality of assured lives in view of the special character of the insurance business and the practical object it pursues. The policy, the person or the sum assured can all be used as units. In order to obtain exact values for the probabilities of death among the lives assured, it would, of course, be necessary to use the "*person*" as a unit. But it may be that one and the same person takes out several assurances. Such multiple assurances make themselves felt even in the material of a single company and much more so in a group of companies. Where there are a large number of policies, however, it is simply not possible to sort through them to eliminate the possibility of counting the same life more than once. In view of this we are usually satisfied with a substitute, namely the *policy*, as a unit. As a rule the deviations from the true mortality trend of the group of persons concerned is not large. They vary, however, with the country and its economic position. The number of multiple policies also grows with increasing age*. Where the *sum assured* is the unit, the basic principle adopted is to take each life into account and weight it in proportion to the assured sum.

---

* The copious material used in the "Impairment Study 1951" (Society of Actuaries; see also p. 77) gave the following comparative figures for all ages

$$\frac{\text{Deaths, Number of policies}}{\text{Deaths, Number of persons}} = \frac{119}{100} \text{ for normal risks and } \frac{109}{100} \text{ for abnormal risks.}$$

5.1. *The construction of an assured lives' table*

It is, of course, possible to consider the mortality of assured lives not merely as a function of country, time, age and sex but also, for example, as a variable dependent on the form of assurance (tariff), the duration of the assurance, the class of risk in general, and of occupation in particular. In the method of constructing an assurance life table described below, we need only consider time and age as variable (as in the population life table); the other variable factors mentioned are taken care of by first classifying the groups in question according to country (currency), sex, type of assurance, duration of assurance etc.

Here again (as with the general population cf. section 4.1) we are faced with the problem first of deriving the probabilities of death from the observed figures. The other biometric functions can then be determined by simple transformations. Once again we shall use only *whole number values:*

$$x = \text{age}$$
$$g = \text{year of birth}$$
$$\tau = \text{year of observation,}$$

the (approximate) age being obtainable from the equation

$$x = \tau - g .$$

Again we shall use Lexis's graph and extend it to our problem in order to render the various factors concerned easier to grasp. As a rule, it is only when people have reached a certain age that they come under observation; that is to say, they take out an assurance (this point was mentioned at the outset). In the following exposition (cf. Figure 7), the *entry* of such a person will be denoted by ○. His *life line* will continue from this point until his *exit on account of death* + or some *other cause* ● or else the person is still alive when the enumeration is made→. In the graph the life lines of four persons have been plotted: Two of the persons entered at age $x-1$; one was born in year g and the other in $g+1$. The first one died the next year (i.e. at age x) whereas the second was still alive at the end of the year of observation $\tau+2$. A person born in year g came under observation at age $x-3$ but died at age x. Then a person born in year $g+2$ took out an assurance in year τ but discontinued it in year $\tau+2$, i.e. at age x.

In order to determine the probabilities of death we shall now use the best method from the theoretical point of view, namely the year of birth method (see section 4.1). For this purpose we must establish the ratio between the first group of deaths and the first group of the living. Clearly, the first *group of deaths* is equal to the number of death points + we count in the relative squares. Thus, for example

$$^{\tau/\tau+1}_{\;g}T_x = \text{ACDE}$$

comprises all the death points in the square bounded by the two perpendiculars enclosing age x and the two horizontals marking the beginning and end of year g.

As may be seen, these deaths are distributed over the two years of observation τ and $\tau+1$; only half of the marginal years, however, is taken into account.

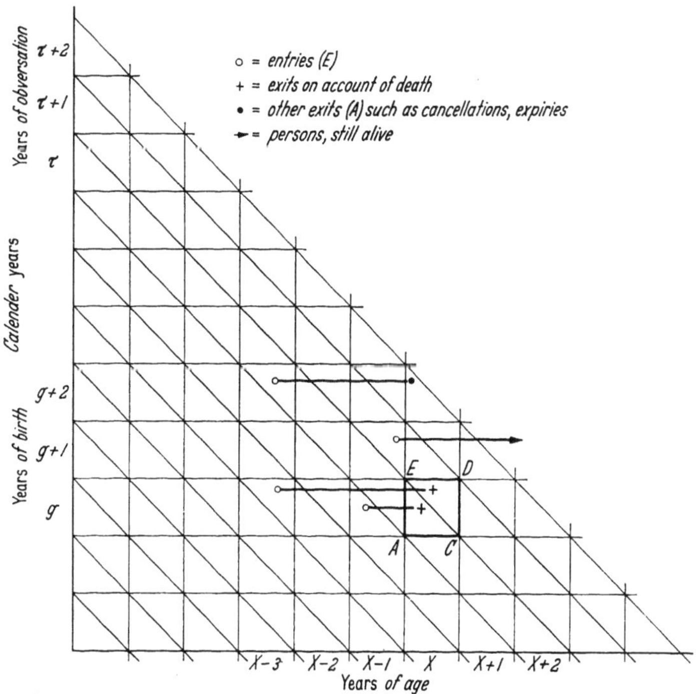

Fig. 7. *Lexis'* diagram showing entries into and exits from period of observation

At the beginning of age x there will clearly be as many lives (policies) under observation (first *group of the living* = exposed to risk = L_x) as there are life lines intersecting the vertical line $\overline{\text{AE}}$. But, as we saw when dealing with the general population, this group cannot be directly ascertained. We must determine it with the aid of the first subgroup (triangle subgroup) of deaths ACE = ${}^{\tau}_{g}T_x$ and the second group of the living ${}_{g}B_x$, which is, of course, identical with the number of lives (policies) enumerated at the end (or beginning) of the years of observation to be considered, i.e. the number of life lines cutting the diagonal $\overline{\text{CE}}$. The first group of the living is therefore

$$ {}^{\tau}_{g}L_x = \overline{\text{CE}} + \text{ACE} = {}^{\tau+1}_{\ g}B_x + {}^{\tau}_{g}T_x $$

and the probability that a life aged x will die within one year

$$ q_x = \frac{\text{ACDE}}{\overline{\text{AE}}} = \frac{\text{ACDE}}{\overline{\text{CE}}+\text{ACE}} = \frac{{}^{\tau/\tau+1}_{\ \ g}T_x}{{}^{\tau}_{g}L_x} = \frac{{}^{\tau/\tau+1}_{\ \ g}T_x}{{}^{\tau+1}_{\ g}B_x + {}^{\tau}_{g}T_x}. $$

Now we must take into account the *entries (E) and exits (A)* occurring during the years under observation. This is done with the formulae already given on page 42 and 51

$$ q_x = \frac{T_x}{L_x + \dfrac{E_x - A_x}{2}} $$

which is based upon the assumption that the entries and exits occur on average in the middle of the year; that is to say that such lives (policies) are still at risk during one half of the calendar year in question. The probability that a person aged x will die within one year during the period τ, $\tau+1$ can therefore be calculated from the formula

$$q_x = \frac{{}^{\tau/\tau+1}_{g}T_x}{{}^{\tau}_{g}L_x + \dfrac{{}^{\tau/\tau+1}_{g}E_x - {}^{\tau/\tau+1}_{g}A_x}{2}} \tag{5.1.1}$$

where as a rule ${}^{\tau}_{g}L_x = {}^{\tau+1}_{g}B_x + {}^{\tau}_{g}T_x$.

We can make another approximation by assuming that the deaths are also uniformly distributed over the whole year, i.e. the triangle subgroup ACE $= {}^{\tau}_{g}T_x$ is half the square ACDE $= {}^{\tau/\tau+1}_{g}T_x$. It follows from the above formula then that

$$q_x = \frac{{}^{\tau/\tau+1}_{g}T_x}{{}^{\tau+1}_{g}B_x + \dfrac{{}^{\tau/\tau+1}_{g}T_x + {}^{\tau/\tau+1}_{g}E_x - {}^{\tau/\tau+1}_{g}A_x}{2}}\,. \tag{5.1.2}$$

If *several years of observation* are combined, then the numbers of deaths, living, entries and exits must be totaled in accordance with formulae given on page 40. If we use

$${}^{\tau}_{g}R_x = {}^{\tau+1}_{g}B_x + \frac{{}^{\tau/\tau+1}_{g}T_x + {}^{\tau/\tau+1}_{g}E_x - {}^{\tau/\tau+1}_{g}A_x}{2} = \text{exposed to risk}$$

as the denominator in formula (5.1.2) then the probability of death in several years of observation will be

$$q_x = \frac{{}^{\tau/\tau+1}_{g}T_x + {}^{\tau+1/\tau+2}_{g+1}T_x + {}^{\tau+2/\tau+3}_{g+2}T_x + \cdots}{{}^{\tau}_{g}R_x + {}^{\tau+1}_{g+1}R_x + {}^{\tau+2}_{g+2}R_x + \cdots}\,. \tag{5.1.3}$$

Similarly, formula (5.1.1) can also be extended to the observations of several years if the actual numbers of deaths are available according to completed and non-completed years of age.

It may happen exceptionally that, instead of the years of birth, we know only the age of the assured on entry into the assurance and the year in which the deaths occurred; in this case the year of death method explained on page 38 must be applied mutatis mutandis.

5.2. *The investigation of mortality among substandard risks*

General observations

By "substandard" or "under-average" risks* we mean persons whose mortality is above normal, mortality being considered normal when all findings in the

* It is normal usage among life assurers to denote by "risk" a person exposed to a risk, i.e. an assured person. Instead of "under-average risks" the terms abnormal risks, aggravated risks, substandard risks, risks with higher mortality, impaired lives etc. are also current. Instead of "normal risks" and "abnormal (aggravated) risks" we shall simply use the expressions "normals" and "abnormals", or "standards" and "substandards".

status praesens, medical history and heredity* deemed important for the future expectation of life are normal. It is for the physician to determine the limits within which a particular finding may still be considered normal**. The actuary must decide to what extent the mortality of persons afflicted with abnormalities*** is greater than that of normal individuals.

Since the causes of increased mortality are very numerous and yet the degree of excess mortality should, in principle, be explicitly stated for each of these causes (abnormalities) and their combinations and classified according to sex, age and possibly the duration of the assurance, it will be appreciated that this problem can be solved only with the aid of a large number of observations. These must be collected with very special care and painstakingly sifted. The incidence of many of these abnormalities has changed substantially in recent years — witness the large drop in the figures for tuberculosis and the rise in those for lung cancer — and for this reason the interval of observation should not cover too many years, which in turn results in a substantial reduction in the amount of statistical material.

However, the actual number of abnormals is not great even in large assurance companies, and classification according to the various abnormalities immediately reduces these cases to a smaller number still. For this reason statistical evaluations are made according to age groups instead of single years and lives with the same kind of abnormalities are grouped together wherever possible. This can be done in the following manner:

a) All the groups of abnormalities are combined which refer to a specific organ system (e.g. heart diseases) or to a specific etiology (e.g. infectious diseases) or to specific external causes (e.g. accidents) and life tables are constructed for each of these totals. This method has been adopted more especially by Scandinavian assurance companies****. Considering that the construction of specific life tables calls for large groups in view of the considerable number of abnormalities and that the multiplicity of life tables would result in a loss of clarity and unity in technical treatment, it will be readily understood that the mortality

* A person may also have an increased mortality if he lives in an insalubrious climate, engages in particularly dangerous work, etc. In this case we speak of extra or special risks.

** For this purpose medicine makes extensive use of statistics in examining the distribution of the values and determining a purely statistical range of normality within the probable error or the single or double standard deviation round the mean value. Needless to say, such factors as age, sex, weight, domicile etc. must be considered in determining most of these values. Fixing these statistical limits is more or less a matter of judgment; moreover, considerable scope is often left to the subjective judgment or experience of the clinician. It will be clear from the foregoing that it is possible to distinguish the normal from the abnormal objectively and accurately in only a minority of cases and that a certain arbitrariness is inevitable in fixing these limits.

*** Abnormality (cause of aggravation) or impairment is thus taken to mean any departure from the norm exhibited by the assured in regard to his present condition (status praesens), his previous illnesses, (medical history) or his family history (heredity) in so far as these are deemed to produce a higher mortality.

**** Cf. especially Moltke, J.: Statistische Untersuchungen minderwertiger Leben in Dänemark. Vol. III, p. 265, 11. Congrès international d'Actuaires. Paris 1937.

of an abnormal can be ascertained only very imperfectly by this method since it requires groups of far too heterogeneous a character to be united. There is for instance a fundamental difference between the expectation of life of a person with an accidental cardiac murmur and that of one with a mitral defect and myocardial damage. Judgment is also called for when more than one abnormality is found in the same risk. The more usual way of measuring the abnormalities statistically is as follows.

b) We determine the mortality for each single type of impairment or combine these in groups only to the extent that the resultant values remain significant from the standpoint of medical prognosis and can still be applied to the individual life assured. Thus, to take an example, we do not simply group together persons who have had pulmonary tuberculosis but classify them according to the unilateral or bilateral forms of the disease, the type of residue and more especially the time elapsed since the lesions were healed, for all these distinctions are of importance for the prognosis. In the case of hepatic disease, it must be decided whether there is recurrent jaundice or only increased urobilinogen, or damage to the liver parenchyma, liver cirrhosis, liver insufficiency, a liver abscess, an enlarged liver without cardiac involvement, or bilharziosis. It will be seen that an investigation into the mortality of assured lives with "liver diseases" will yield results which are virtually worthless for assessing the medical prognosis of such proposers.

All the same, this method often leads to a dilemma, for subdivision of the material into a large number of classes often reduces the number so drastically that no useful statistical conclusion can be drawn from it.

Direct method of statistical measurement

The statistical survey is based on the report prepared by the physician (essentially prognostic in character) which also contains important findings from the family and medical history and status praesens. The physician and the underwriter decide, on the basis of the statistics, whether these findings should be deemed normal or inherently pathological (e.g. blood pressure in excess of certain values). The abnormalities thus found are now put into statistical form. As there are usually several abnormalities, the basic trouble is put first, as in causes of death. Examples of such sequences are: alcoholism, cirrhosis of the liver, esophageal varices; hyperthyreoidism, tachycardia, tremor. Moreover, it is essential that the time should be stated when each abnormality appeared and when it was cured, or if it was to be regarded as chronic, intermittent, or a relapse. It should also be noted whether an operation has been performed or not (e.g. in appendicitis) or whether a disease has been treated or not (e.g. diabetes). In regard to blood pressure, not only the (quantitative) systolic and diastolic value should be given but also the (qualitative) indication as to whether the values are labile or fixed and whether or not there is hypertension involving the kidneys.

In view of the large quantity of material, statistical processing is usually done by means of punched cards. The card should, of course, record not only the actual abnormalities discovered by medical examination but also height, weight, chest and waist measurements, the values measured for the systolic and diastolic blood pressure, and also data on race, sex, age, domicile and occupation, for there is also a connection between these features and mortality.

The investigation of the mortality of under-average risks is effected in principle in the same way as that of normal lives. The body of the assured is divided according to the various abnormalities (or abnormalities arranged in medically justifiable groups) and the number of deaths occurring in this group during a specific number of years is ascertained. The ratio of these deaths to the number of exposed to risk expresses the probability of death of those persons afflicted with the abnormality. For easier understanding and especially to facilitate the technical treatment of such risks in life assurance, it is customary to relate this probability of death to that of the normal lives concerned, thus obtaining a percentage excess mortality.

We obtain the following equations using the symbols given below:

L_x = number of normals aged x observed during one year,

T_x = observed (= actual) deaths in this observed group,

L'_x = number of abnormals aged x under observation during one year,

T'_x = observed (= actual) deaths in this observed group,

$q_x = \frac{T_x}{L_x}$ = annual probability of death for normals,

$q'_x = \frac{T'_x}{L'_x}$ = annual probability of death for abnormals.

$\Theta_x = L'_x\, q_x$ = Expected (= theoretical) number of dead from the abnormal group L'_x, if this group were subjected to normal mortality.

The excess mortality of the abnormals as compared with the normals is given by the ratio

$$\frac{q'_x}{q_x} = \frac{T'_x}{L'_x} : \frac{T_x}{L_x} = \frac{T'_x\, L_x}{T_x\, L'_x} = 1+\alpha, \tag{5.2.1}$$

or since

$$\frac{L'_x\, T_x}{L_x} = L'_x\, q_x = \Theta_x\,,$$

then

$$\frac{q'_x}{q_x} = \frac{T'_x}{\Theta_x} = 1+\alpha \tag{5.2.1'}$$

that is to say, with reference to a particular group of lives *the excess mortality α of the abnormals compared with the normals is given by the ratio of the actual to the expected deaths.*

Furthermore

$$q'_x = (1+\alpha) q_x \tag{5.2.2}$$

and

$$T'_x = (1+\alpha)\Theta_x .$$

The standard deviation can be given for Θ_x, namely

$$\sigma_\Theta = \sqrt{L'_x q_x (1-q_x)} \tag{5.2.3}$$

or if

$$1-q_x \approx 1, \quad \sigma_\Theta \approx \sqrt{\Theta}.$$

The difference between the observed and expected deaths can be regarded as significant in a first approximation if it amounts to, say, at least double the standard deviation; that is to say

$$|T'_x - \Theta_x| \geqq 2\sqrt{L'_x q_x (1-q_x)}. \tag{5.2.4}$$

The difference between the probabilities q_x and q'_x can also be checked by the χ^2 test. (This test, of course, is of general application, and the differences between various abnormalities, for example, can also be tested for significance.)

If the difference between the probabilities of death $q_x - q'_x$ is normalized by their variance, then this value is normally distributed when the exposed to risk L_x and L'_x are sufficiently large. The square

$$\chi_x^2 = \left\{ \frac{q_x - q'_x}{\sigma_{q_x - q'_x}} \right\}^2 \tag{5.2.5}$$

follows the χ^2-distribution with *one* degree of freedom. Upon the assumption that q_x and q'_x are independent the variance is given by

$$\sigma^2_{q_x - q'_x} = \frac{(T_x + T'_x)\,(L_x + L'_x - T_x - T'_x)}{L_x L'_x (L_x + L'_x)}. \tag{5.2.6}$$

To decide whether or not a χ^2 value obtained in this manner implies a significant difference, we refer to a table of probabilities corresponding to the χ^2 values, only *one* degree of freedom being supposed. Such tables may be found in any modern textbook on statistics. Assuming that the mortalities from one age group to another are independent, then the sum $\chi^2 = \sum_x \chi_x^2$ is distributed like χ^2 with the number of degrees of freedom corresponding to the number of age classes.

The direct method of investigating the excess mortality of under-average risks described here was first used on a large scale by some American life offices working in conjunction with one another. The result was the "Medico-Actuarial Mortality Investigation", a five-volume work that appeared between 1909 and 1914. The period of observation covered the years 1885 to 1908 and for this reason there is little to be found in the work on under-average risks as we understand the word today. The first major American work on under-average risks in the present sense is the "Medical Impairment Study 1929" published in 1931. It covers the period of observation from 1909 to 1927. There followed a number of other publications, a "Supplement to Medical Impairment Study", published in 1932, a "Medical Impairment Study 1936", and a further "Medical Impairment Study 1938", which treated some of the causes of impairment already dealt with and also some additional causes. Blood pressure was the subject of a special study entitled "1939 Blood Pressure Study", which appeared in 1940 and was based on about 1,300,000 policies. A year later there appeared the "Supplement to the Blood Pressure Study 1941". The last joint American investigation appeared in 1954 and was entitled "Impairment Study 1951", published by the Society of Actuaries. Twenty-seven life offices provided their material comprising 70 per cent of the total policies in the United States and Canada for this enormous undertaking. The period of observation covered the years 1935 to 1949. In 1960 a further "Build and Blood Pressure Study 1959" was published by the Society of Actuaries: it is based on investigations of several million assured lives in the USA and Canada during 1935—1953.

Example from Impairment Study 1951 (Society of Actuaries). A 16: Under-average risks with systolic apex murmur, constant, and/or mitral regurgitation without hypertrophy, found on examination, with history of tonsilitis or other streptococcic infection (not known to have been rheumatism or chorea), Males 79%, Females 21%.

Experience by age at issue

Age at issue	Exposed to risk	Actual deaths		Expected deaths (policies)	Mortality ratio %
		Policies	Lives		
15—29	17,400	63	54	19.00	332
30—39	11,577	69	53	23.86	289
40—49	5,355	64	55	25.64	250
50—64	1,196	17	16	12.44	137
15—64	35,528	213	177	80.94	263

Experience by duration

Policy year durations	Exposed to risk	Actual deaths		Expected deaths (policies)	Mortality ratio %
		Policies	Lives		
1— 2	10,785	31	30	14.22	218
3— 5	11,461	80	59	23.90	335
6—10	10,357	81	73	30.07	269
11—15	2,925	21	20	12.75	165
1—15	35,528	213	177	80.94	263

Deaths according to cause of death (only for 5 and more policies)

Cause of death	Actual deaths		Mortality ratio %
	Policies	Lives	
Malignant neoplasms	15	10	124
Vascular lesions of the central nervous system	14	7	465
Heart and circulatory diseases	129	115	493
Diseases of digestive system	7	6	136
Accidents and homicides	14	11	96
Suicides	8	4	201

Older methods of statistical investigation

a) Observation of declined lives. When the assurance of under-average lives was tentatively commenced at the turn of the century, assessment of risk was a very uncertain business, for, of course, there were still no statistics available. Thus, instead of the direct observation of deaths in groups of assured lives which we have just described, recourse was had to the method of keeping under observation proposers who were refused and analysing the causes of death.

Among the investigations of the first kind, special mention should be made of those carried out by the Consorzio Italiano from 1935 to 1942. Information was collected regarding the fate of 2,914 persons whose proposals had been refused. The investigations made by DANA between 1930 and 1941 regarding 1162 refused proposals should also be mentioned. In 1953 KAI CHRISTENSEN constructed a special mortality table MS 53 (MS – meget syge = very sick persons) on the basis of this and later analyses. Cardiac disease accounted for 42% of the deaths occurring in the material on which this table was based.

This method of investigating mortality through observation of the refused proposals, which was originated by PALME *, is very laborious since it is extremely difficult to collect information on the persons concerned. Thus in the investigation made by the Consorzio referred to above only 56% of all refused proposals could be included. Hence there is no guarantee that these are representative of the whole body.

b) Statistics of the causes of death. It was in Austria that the first attempt was made to extract the basic knowledge required for the assurance of under-average risks from the statistics of the causes of death among normal lives. ERNST BLASCHKE was the first to compile life tables for single causes of death from the material of the Gothaer Insurance Company; he published the results in his „Denkschrift zur Lösung des Problems der Versicherung minderwertiger Leben“, which appeared in 1895. He arranged the causes of death in three groups and thus obtained life tables for three classes of risk. The basis on which BLASCHKE constructed his

* PALME, S.: Beitrag zum Studium der Sterblichkeit minderwertiger Leben. Zeitschrift für das gesamte Versicherungswesen. Vol. 22, Page 58.

tables was the hypothesis that a life which is impaired in any way will die of this impairment, or of another in the same class of risk.

We encounter a new idea in an investigation carried out in 1921 by R. PALMQUIST for the Scandinavian committee for under-average risks. In this investigation F. LUNDBERG defined the abnormal life as a life whose probability of dying of certain diseases associated with the impairment is greater than the probability of normal lives dying of the same diseases. Thus, whereas BLASCHKE assumed that an under-average life will die from a cause corresponding to the impairment, LUNDBERG merely assumes that there is a certain probability of this occurring. He also adds the following important rider: the probability that an abnormal life will die of any cause unconnected with the cause of impairment is equal to the probability that normal lives will die of these diseases *.

If these ideas are expressed in mathematical terms, it will be found that, even where the number living belonging to the group in question is not known, *it is possible to compute the ratio between the probability of death for abnormal lives and that for normal lives from the number of dead alone;* that is to say, to calculate the percentage of excess mortality. If we use $(-i)$ to denote all causes of death independent of the impairment (i), then by the above hypothesis

$$q_x^{(-i)} = q_x'^{(-i)} \qquad (5.2.7)$$

or

$$\frac{T_x^{(-i)}}{L_x} = \frac{T_x'^{(-i)}}{L_x'} \, .$$

From which it follows

$$\frac{L_x'}{L_x} = \frac{T_x'^{(-i)}}{T_x^{(-i)}} \, . \qquad (5.2.8)$$

Thus in equation (5.2.1) we can replace the quotient of the living $\frac{L_x'}{L_x}$ by that of deaths and obtain

$$1+\alpha = \frac{T_x' \, T_x^{(-i)}}{T_x \, T_x'^{(-i)}} \, . \qquad (5.2.9)$$

If the age structure of the normals and abnormals is virtually the same, i.e. $L_x' = c\, L_x$ $(c = \text{const.})$, then we may write

$$1+\alpha = \frac{\Sigma T_x' \, \Sigma T_x^{(-i)}}{\Sigma T_x \, \Sigma T_x'^{(-i)}} \, . \qquad (5.2.9')$$

* This proposition was formulated by PEDERSEN as early as 1906 in the following terms: 'The difference between good and under-average lives is that there is an equal probability that both will die from n—1 causes whereas the probability that an under-average life will die from the nth cause is greater than the probability that a good life will die from it.' Similarly formulated propositions became known in the literature as "Pedersen's theorem".

As will be seen, we need only the deaths in formulas (5.2.9) and (5.2.9′) to be able to determine the excess mortality, which represents a considerable saving of work as compared with the direct method. The method is severely restricted in use, however, because of the intricate way in which the causes of death are intermixed. Thus it is not always a correct hypothesis that the probability of abnormals dying from causes apparently unconnected with their impairment is equal to that of normal lives dying from the same causes *.

Finally, there follows an example of the method (see Table X a, b and c) which ZWINGLI ** compiled from the material of Norwegian life offices. It concerns male risks subjected to medical examination. The period of investigation covered the years from 1910 to 1925. No account was taken of the expired duration of insurance. As a comparison of columns (2) and (3) in Table X c will show, the indirect method applied in this example yields for most age groups results which are at least as good as those obtained by the direct method of measuring excess mortality. If PEDERSEN's hypothesis is tenable, then the quotient must produce $\frac{q_x'^{(-i)}}{q_x^{(-i)}} \approx 1$ (cf. column (4) in Table c).

Table X a. *Normal risks*

Age group	Risks under observation	Number of deaths			Mortality rate in ‰		
		total	of tuberculosis	of other causes	total	of tuberculosis	of other causes
x	L_x	T_x	$T_x^{(i)}$	$T_x^{(-i)}$	$q_x = \frac{T_x}{L_x}$	$q_x^{(i)} = \frac{T_x^{(i)}}{L_x}$	$q_x^{(-i)} = \frac{T_x^{(-i)}}{L_x}$
14—19	112,485	670	270	400	5.96	2.40	3.56
20—29	548,332	3,402	1,470	1,932	6.20	2.68	3.52
30—39	501,573	2,375	660	1,715	4.74	1.32	3.42
40—49	310,553	1,918	238	1,680	6.18	0.77	5.41
50—59	132,180	1,555	112	1,443	11.76	0.85	10.91
60—69	31,670	922	15	907	29.11	0.47	28.64
70—79	7,010	430	2	428	61.34	0.29	61.05
80—89	1,079	138	0	138	129.9	—	129.9
all ages	1,644,882	11,410	2,767	8,643	6.93	1.68	5.25

* Cf. J. NEUHAUS and E. A. HAFNER: Über die Todesursachen anormaler Leben. Ein Beitrag zum Problem des Zusammenhanges zwischen hauptsächlicher Restriktionsursache und primärer Todesursache. Zeitschrift für die gesamte Versicherungs-Wissenschaft. 41, No. 3 (1941). This work demonstrates inter alia that impairments such as tuberculosis, diseases of the respiratory organs, and stomach and intestinal diseases in particular also influence mortality from other causes.

Cf. also H. BRAUN: Über das Abhängigkeitsverhältnis zwischen Krankheitsanlagen und Todesursachen. Vers.-Wiss. Mitt. des deutschen Vereins für Vers.-Wesen in der Čechosl. Republik. 2 fascicle, Prague 1922.

** Sterblichkeitsstatistik bei minderwertigen Leben. Skandinavisk Aktuarietidskrift, 1934 — Häft. 1.

Table X b. *Abnormal risks with tuberculosis heredity*

Age group	Risks under observation	Number of deaths			Mortality rate in ‰		
		total	of tuberculosis	of other causes	total	of tuberculosis	of other causes
x	L'_x	T'_x	$T'^{(i)}_x$	$T'^{(-i)}_x$	$q'_x = \frac{T'_x}{L'_x}$	$q'^{(i)}_x = \frac{T'^{(i)}_x}{L'_x}$	$q'^{(-i)}_x = \frac{T'^{(-i)}_x}{L'_x}$
14—19	2,700	16	9	7	5.93	3.33	2.60
20—29	15,600	117	67	50	7.50	4.29	3.21
30—39	15,141	97	45	52	6.41	2.97	3.44
40—49	9,024	54	10	44	5.98	1.11	4.87
50—59	3,056	54	4	50	17.67	1.31	16.36
60—69	587	24	3	21	40.89	5.11	35.78
70—79	113	4	0	4	35,40	0.00	35.40
80—89	19	3	0	3	157.89	0.00	157.89
all ages	46,240	369	138	231	7.97	2.98	4.99

Table X c.

Age group	$1+\alpha$ according to formula (5.2.9)	$1+\alpha$ according to formula (5.2.1)	$\frac{q'^{(-i)}_x}{q^{(-i)}_x}$	Dispersions 1.97 σ		
				for α according to formula (5.2.1)	for α according to formula (5.2.9)	for $\frac{q'^{(-i)}_x}{q^{(-i)}_x}$
(1)	(2)	(3)	(4)	(5)	(6)	(7)
14—19	1.36	0.99	0.73	0.604	0.693	0.70
20—29	1.33	1.21	0.91	0.248	0.308	0.28
30—39	1.34	1.35	1.01	0.240	0.222	0.26
40—49	1.07	0.97	0.90	0.256	0.159	0.25
50—59	1.00	1.50	1.50	0.296	0.115	0.28
60—69	1.12	1.40	1.25	0.454	0.120	0.46
70—79	1.00	0.58	0.58	0.762	0.132	0.76
80—89	1.00	1.23	1.23	1.26	0.180	1.26
all ages	1.21	1.15	0.95	0.125	0.096	0.13

The numerical method of investigating a risk where there are several abnormalities

It is commonly found that more than one abnormality is implicated in an aggravated risk. However, it is scarcely possible to determine from statistical data the rate of mortality for each abnormality and also for all the different combinations possible amongst them, so that in practice we proceed according to the following method. This method was evolved by HUNTER and ROGERS* and originally applied by the "New-York Life" office. In this method the individual excess

* HUNTER, A.: Selection of risks from the actuarial standpoint. Transactions of the Actuarial Society of America, **12**, No. 45 (1911).

mortality ratios applying to the various abnormalities affecting the assured life are simply added together (hence the name numerical method). Allowance can be made by deductions for any particularly favourable factors. Example:

	Assured life	Excess mortality %
Occupation:	Hotel-keeper, publican	25
Heredity:	Father died of pulmonary tuberculosis at 30 years Mother died at 65 years 1 brother pulmonary tuberculosis at 32 years	25
History:	Pulmonary tuberculosis 10 years ago, 6 months' treatment, cured	30
Status praesens:	Lungs: normal, x-ray good	
	Heart: mitral insufficiency, normal heart outline	75
	Pulse: 80 per minute	
	Blood pressure: systolic 130 mm diastolic 80 mm	
	Build: Height 170 cm Weight 65 kg Chest 90/80 Abdomen 78 cm	
Total excess mortality		155

An excess mortality rate of $\alpha = 155\%$ was assigned to this risk; that is to say, the excess mortality factor $1 + \alpha$ would be 2.55.

The debatable part of this method is the additive treatment of the various degrees of excess mortality. Strictly speaking, this is only permissible, of course, when the various aggravating factors may be considered independent of one another. Whether this holds good or not can be ascertained statistically with the aid of the theory of attributes which was developed in its essentials by YULE* or by means of the χ^2-tests. In the following example we shall consider simply the two abnormalities I and II and arrange the existing groups, denoted by a, b, c, d in a four-field table.

Abnormality I	Abnormality II: present	Abnormality II: not present	Sum
present	a	b	$a+b$
not present	c	d	$c+d$
Sum	$a+c$	$b+d$	$a+b+c+d=N$

* YULE, G. U., and M. G. KENDALL: An introduction to the theory of statistics. 13th edition, London 1944.

If the two attributes are not associated, then

$$\frac{a}{c} = \frac{b}{d},$$

which is equivalent to

$$\frac{a}{b} = \frac{c}{d}. \tag{5.2.10}$$

If these equations are not valid, the degree of association can be determined by reference to the χ^2-test, by making

$$\chi^2 = \frac{(ad-bc)^2 N}{(a+b)(a+c)(b+d)(c+d)}. \tag{5.2.11}$$

The more pronounced the association, the greater this value is. If a more careful check is required, a table of probabilities should be consulted, only *one* degree of freedom being considered. The method can also be extended to test the association of more than two attributes (abnormalities). However, it is the usual practice when assessing the association of various abnormalities in a specific risk and their consequences not to base conclusions simply on computational results but also on the medical experience of a physician.

It may be mentioned that, contrary to lay opinion, this numerical method does not simply involve adding the excess mortality rates of individual abnormalities together as desired; the statistics available today allow us to set down explicitly the functional dependence between the abnormalities. The connectedness of blood pressure and weight provides a simple example of this. If we were to add the excess mortality rate for any instances of overweight to the systolic and diastolic blood pressures as functions of age, sex and race, the estimate of mortality would be incorrect, because this increase is not linear.

In conclusion we have an example of how the association of two aggravating factors can be determined by means of the χ^2-criterion. The purpose of the investigation is to ascertain whether the risk of contracting lung cancer is significantly affected by residence in urban or rural areas.

Canton of Zurich, men: sum of years 1951—1957

	Died of		Total dead
	lung cancer	other diseases	
Town	590	12,329	12,919
Country	468	14,348	14,816
Total	1,058	26,677	27,735

These figures refer to men of the Canton of Zurich, domiciled either in the town of Zurich itself or in the surrounding rural district, who died in the years from 1951 to 1957. The results are directly comparable since the urban and rural areas have almost the same population and their age structures — especially for the age groups principally concerned here — are virtually the same.

If we compute the value χ^2 from these figures by formula (5.2.11), we find that $\chi^2 = 37$. But the probability is as small as 1 to 1,000 that a χ^2 as big as 11 would be attained or exceeded in such random tests. The value $\chi^2 = 37$ falls well outside these limits and thus it may be taken as proved that the influence of the town aggravates the risk of a lung cancer being formed. Needless to say, such an assertion is not a positive statement as to the cause of this increased risk. Assuming, however, that smoking habits are similar in town and country, the cause will have to be sought in the exhaust gases with which the town air is saturated, particularly in view of the fact that direct chemical analyses recently performed have repeatedly found carcinogenic materials in exhaust gases. In the case of proposed lives who are already predisposed to lung cancer as a result of serious abuse of nicotine, it cannot be a matter of indifference from the mortality point of view whether they live in an urban or rural area.

The actuarial treatment of under-average risks in life assurance

After an under-average risk has been assessed by the underwriter on the basis of the medical report and statistical results in comparable groups, it must be considered from the actuarial point of view. This consists in computing the necessary premium according to the assurance contract for the excess mortality expressed in numerical terms and then making allowances for the increased risk in the usual technical calculations.

We cannot go further into these problems in the compass of this work and refer the reader to the book mentioned below *. On the other hand, the basic ideas underlying the methods of allowing for excess mortality may be stated. This is done either by

— using special life tables for groups of medically similar impairements, e.g. life tables for cardiac patients, diabetics etc.,
— using life tables which are based on a certain excess mortality in relation to the basic table. The following methods are used:
  a) *Method of increase in age.* This method is based on the assumption that the mortality of a substandard risk is comparable to the mortality of a standard risk of higher age. The life tables for the different classes of risks are thus obtained simply by using the basic mortality table at a suitably increased age.
  b) *Method of proportionate increase in mortality.* This method is the one most widely in use today. It is based on the assumption that the mortality of a substandard risk is a constant multiple of the basic mortality throughout the term of assurance. Let α be the rate of excess mortality, q_x the mortality rate of a standard risk, then the mortality rate of the substandard risk is $q_x' = (1 + \alpha)q_x$.

* H. JECKLIN in „Versicherungsmathematik" by W. Saxer, second part, page 201. Berlin: Springer 1958.

For practical considerations it is not usual to let α assume every possible value, but several groups are formed, for instance,

	Interval of α	Percentage of excess mortality used for calculation
Class 1.	up to 37%	25%
Class 2.	38— 62%	50%
Class 3.	63— 87%	75%
Class 4.	88—124%	100%
Class 5.	125—174%	150%
Class 6.	175—224%	200%

c) *Method of constant increase in mortality.* By this method the mortality rate of the substandard risk q'_x is expressed as $q'_x = q_x + \delta$ where δ is a constant addition.

Combinations of the above methods are possible in order to allow for an increasing or decreasing excess mortality. Extensive statistics are necessary to show in each case which of the above methods is the most suitable.

Abbreviated list of 50 causes for tabulation of mortality

Number	Cause groups
B 1	Tuberculosis of respiratory system
B 2	Tuberculosis, other forms
B 3	Syphilis and its sequelae
B 4	Typhoid fever
B 5	Cholera
B 6	Dysentery, all forms
B 7	Scarlet fever and streptococcal sore throat
B 8	Diphtheria
B 9	Whooping cough
B 10	Meningococcal infections
B 11	Plague
B 12	Acute poliomyelitis
B 13	Smallpox
B 14	Measles
B 15	Typhus and other rickettsial diseases
B 16	Malaria
B 17	All other diseases classified as infective and parasitic
B 18	Malignant neoplasms, including neoplasms of lymphatic and haematopoietic tissues
B 19	Benign and unspecified neoplasms
B 20	Diabetes mellitus
B 21	Anaemias
B 22	Vascular lesions affecting central nervous system
B 23	Non-meningococcal meningitis
B 24	Rheumatic fever
B 25	Chronic rheumatic heart disease
B 26	Arteriosclerotic and degenerative heart disease
B 27	Other diseases of heart
B 28	Hypertension with heart disease

Number	Cause groups
B 29	Hypertension without mention of heart
B 30	Influenza
B 31	Pneumonia
B 32	Bronchitis
B 33	Ulcer of stomach and duodenum
B 34	Appendicitis
B 35	Intestinal obstruction and hernia
B 36	Gastritis, duodenitis, enteritis and colitis, except diarrhoea of the newborn
B 37	Cirrhosis of liver
B 38	Nephritis and nephrosis
B 39	Hyperplasia of prostate
B 40	Deliveries and complications of pregnancy, childbirth and the puerperium
B 41	Congenital malformations
B 42	Birth injuries, postnatal asphyxia and atelectasis
B 43	Infections of the newborn
B 44	Other diseases peculiar to early infancy, and immaturity unqualified
B 45	Senility without mention of psychosis, ill-defined and unknown cases
B 46	All other diseases

Alternative classification of accidents, poisonings, and violence

	E = External cause	N = Nature of injury
BE 47	Motor vehicle accidents	BN 47 Fractures, head injuries and internal injuries
BE 48	All other accidents	BN 48 Burns
BE 49	Suicide and self-inflicted injury	BN 49 Effects of poisons
BE 50	Homicide and operations of war	BN 50 All other injuries

Special list of 50 causes for tabulation of morbidity for social insurance purposes

Number	Cause groups
C 1	Tuberculosis of respiratory system
C 2	Tuberculosis, other forms
C 3	Syphilis and its sequelae
C 4	Gonococcal infection
C 5	Dysentery, all forms
C 6	Other infective diseases commonly arising in intestinal tract
C 7	Certain diseases common among children
C 8	Typhus and other rickettsial diseases
C 9	Malaria
C 10	Diseases due to helminths
C 11	All other diseases classified as infective and parasitic
C 12	Malignant neoplasms, including neoplasms of lymphatic and haematopoietic tissues
C 13	Benign neoplasms and neoplasms of unspecified nature
C 14	Allergic disorders
C 15	Diseases of thyroid gland
C 16	Diabetes mellitus
C 17	Avitaminosis and other deficiency states
C 18	Anaemias
C 19	Psychoneuroses and psychoses
C 20	Vascular lesions affecting central nervous system
C 21	Diseases of eye
C 22	Diseases of ear and mastoid process
C 23	Rheumatic fever

Number	Cause groups
C 24	Chronic rheumatic heart disease
C 25	Arteriosclerotic and degenerative heart disease
C 26	Hypertensive disease
C 27	Diseases of veins
C 28	Acute nasopharyngitis (common cold)
C 29	Acute pharyngitis and tonsillitis, and hypertrophy of tonsils and adenoids
C 30	Influenza
C 31	Pneumonia
C 32	Bronchitis
C 33	Silicosis and occupational pulmonary fibrosis
C 34	All other respiratory diseases
C 35	Diseases of stomach and duodenum, except cancer
C 36	Appendicitis
C 37	Hernia of abdominal cavity
C 38	Diarrhoea and enteritis
C 39	Diseases of gallbladder and bile ducts
C 40	Other diseases of digestive system
C 41	Nephritis and nephrosis
C 42	Diseases of genital organs
C 43	Deliveries, complications of pregnancy, childbirth and the puerperium
C 44	Boil, abscess, cellulitis and other skin infections
C 45	Other diseases of skin
C 46	Arthritis and rheumatism, except rheumatic fever
C 47	Diseases of bones and other organs of movement
C 48	Congenital malformations and diseases peculiar to early infancy
C 49	Other specified and ill-defined diseases
C 50	Accidents, poisonings, and violence (external cause)

Metabolic causes of myocardial ischemia*

A. PLETSCHER

Among the many metabolic factors involved in the pathogenesis of myocardial ischemia two principal groups may be distinguished:

1 Disturbances leading to changes in the coronary arteries and in consequence to impairment of the coronary circulation. The most important alteration is sclerosis of the coronary arteries.

2 Primary metabolic disorders of the myocardium, not necessarily involving coronary circulation.

The purpose of the present communication is to review biefly certain important factors from each of the two groups (table I) with special attention to current concepts and to the findings of recent research.

Table I. *Metabolic causes of myocardial ischemia*

I *Metabolic causes of coronary sclerosis*
1. Changes in the blood lipids
   Total cholesterol
   Lipoproteins
   Fatty acids
   Clearing factor
2. Metabolic disturbances in the arterial wall

II *Primary metabolic disturbances in the mycocardium*
1. Catecholamines
2. Electrolyte shifts

I. Metabolic factors in the pathogenesis of coronary sclerosis

Although the biochemistry of coronary sclerosis is probably not essentially different from that of sclerosis of other arteries, the physiology and the metabolism of the coronary arteries show certain special features, such as being subject to greater mechanical strain, higher content of mucopolysaccharides in the arterial wall and a higher triglyceride fraction in the lipids. This may possibly explain why the degree of sclerosis in the coronary arteries does not always run parallel to that of other arteries.

The most important general factors in the production of coronary sclerosis may be classified into two groups: changes in the blood lipids and metabolic disturbances in the arterial wall.

---

* Published in Cardiologia 40, 97—112 (1962).

A. Changes in the blood lipids

Primary changes in the blood lipids are not the only cause of coronary sclerosis, but it is probable that they at least contribute to its onset and progression by, for example, causing lipid deposits in the arterial walls. In the following some possible relationships between blood lipids and coronary sclerosis will be discussed.

1. Total cholesterol. It is generally accepted that hypercholesterolemia may be a factor in the development of coronary sclerosis. This view is based on the following observations:

(a) Atheromatous lesions in man show a high content of free and esterified cholesterol.

(b) The incidence of coronary sclerosis is high in certain diseases accompanied by hypercholesterolemia, e.g. familiary xanthomatosis, essential hypercholesterolemia, diabetes mellitus, myxedema, status after bilateral ovariectomy.

(c) Statistical studies in patients, especially young men, with coronary sclerosis showed a correlation between high serum cholesterol levels and the incidence of the disease. Comparative studies in different population groups revealed a similar relationship.

(d) In experimental cholesterol atheromatosis, e.g. in rodents, a correlation exists between the degree as well as the duration of the high cholesterol level in blood and the incidence of atheromatous lesions. Until recently there was some doubt as to whether atheromata induced purely by feeding cholesterol could be taken as a model for human coronary sclerosis. It was found almost impossible to produce arteriosclerotic changes in omnivorous mammals, and the histology of cholesterol atheromata in rodents was found to differ in some respects from that of arteriosclerosis in man. Later work, however, has shown that cholesterol feeding can produce generalized arteriosclerosis for example in dogs, provided certain experimental conditions are fulfilled (e.g. suppression of thyroid function, renal hypertension); furthermore that cholesterol induced atheromatous changes in rabbits undergo gradual transformation into arteriosclerotic lesions of the human type [*1*].

2. Transport of cholesterol. Cholesterol, phospholipids and triglycerides of the blood are bound in part to the α- and β-globulins (lipoproteins) (table II).

Table II. *Plasma lipoproteins*

Alpha-lipoproteins			Beta-lipoproteins
	free cholesterol		
	esterified cholesterol	fatty acids	
Alpha-globulins —	phospholipids	fatty acids	— beta-globulins
	triglycerides	fatty acids	
	other lipids		

These globulin complexes may be regarded as transport forms of cholesterol. The α- and β-lipoproteins differ in their protein fractions (α- and β-globulins) and in the ratio of their protein and lipid content. The lipid fraction is larger in the β- than in the α-lipoproteins.

The importance of the transport form for cholesterol atherogenesis may be seen from the following findings:

(a) The possibility of inducing experimental arteriosclerosis in different animal species increases with the proportion of the total cholesterol that is transported in association with the β-lipoproteins. The proportion may range from about 10% in rats to about 50% in rabbits. In humans with spontaneous arterio- and coronary sclerosis 75% or more of the serum cholesterol is present in the β-lipoprotein fraction.

(b) In coronary sclerosis there exists in general a shift in the ratio between β- and α-lipoproteins towards the former.

(c) Extensive statistical studies in man have shown a significant correlation between the blood content of lipoproteins with low Svedberg flotation values (S_f 12—100) and coronary sclerosis. An equally close correlation has been found, however, between an increase in the total cholesterol and the frequency of coronary sclerosis.

(d) Ultracentrifugation of hypercholesterolemic rabbit plasma has provided direct evidence that the size of the lipoprotein particles is important. Of two fractions with the same cholesterol and phospholipid content only the one with the higher sedimentation rate was found to be atherogenic in rabbits [2].

3. Unsaturated fatty acids. The main fatty acids present in the plasma are the saturated stearic and palmitic acids and the unsaturated oleic, linoleic, linolenic and arachidonic acids (table III). Certain poly-unsaturated acids (linoleic, lino-

Table III. *Unsaturated fatty acids*

Oleic acid
$CH_3(CH_2)_7CH{=}CH(CH_2)_7COOH$
Linoleic acid
$CH_3(CH_2)_4CH{=}CHCH_2CH{=}CH(CH_2)_7COOH$
Linolenic acid
$CH_3CH_2CH{=}CHCH_2CH{=}CHCH_2CH{=}CH(CH_2)_7COOH$
Arachidonic acid
$CH_3(CH_2)_4CH{=}CHCH_2CH{=}CHCH_2CH{=}CHCH_2CH{=}CH(CH_2)_3COOH$

lenic and arachidonic), the so-called essential fatty acids, necessary for normal growth as well as for normal formation of the skin, cannot be synthetized in sufficient amounts by the animal organism. Whether they are essential for adult humans has not been definitely established, but it is probable that they are in children. Animal fats contain mainly saturated, and vegetable oils in addition unsaturated fatty acids.

Serum cholesterol levels are probably related to the degree of saturation of the fatty acids. Fats and oils poor in unsaturated fatty acids generally raise the serum cholesterol in man and animals, even when the diet contains no cholesterol. Oils rich in unsaturated fatty acids either lower the serum cholesterol or have no effect. In blood of patients with hyperlipemia the relative fractions of saturated and mono-unsaturated fatty acids are larger, and those of the poly-unsaturated fatty acids (linoleic and arachidonic) smaller than in subjects with normal blood lipid levels. This is true for the fractions of esterified cholesterol, phospholipids, triglycerides and free fatty acids [*3*].

The significance of fatty acids in the pathogenesis of *coronary artery sclerosis* is not clear. The intracellular deposition of cholesterol in cultures of endothelial cells from human aorta is inhibited by the addition of linolenic acid and increased by the addition of stearic acid [*4*]. Experimental work on the influence of unsaturated fatty acids on *atheromatosis induced by cholesterol feeding* in dogs and chickens has, however, given contradictory results. Corn oil rich in linoleic acid was found to have no effect on the onset and course of *spontaneous arteriosclerosis* in hens (table IV) [*5, 6*]. In the arteriosclerotic human aorta, moreover,

Table IV. *Influence of saturated fatty acids and of linoleic acid on spontaneous arteriosclerosis in the aorta of old hens*

Saturated fatty acids in the form of 5% lard + coconut fat and linoleic acid in the form of 5% corn oil (content of linoleic acid 54%) were fed for 20 months [*6*].

The figures indicate average values ± mean error for eight animals fed saturated fatty acids and ten animals fed linoleic acid.

Fatty acids in diet	Macroscopic lesions	Total lipids	Total cholesterol	
	Percentage of total aorta	Percentage of dry weight	Percentage of dry weight	Percentage of total lipids
Saturated	18 ± 3	14.2 ± 1.6	1.55 ± 0.13	12.25 ± 6.55
Linoleic acid	15 ± 4	14.3 ± 1.5	1.62 ± 0.09	11.83 ± 1.96

the poly-unsaturated fatty acids in free form as well as in the cholesterolester and glyceride fractions are increased at the expense of the saturated fatty acids; only the unsaturated fatty acids (especially arachidonic) of the phospholipid fraction being decreased [*7, 8*]. These findings are not in agreement with the theory that coronary sclerosis is due to deposition in the arteries (as the result of a deficiency of essential fatty acids) of cholesterol esters, which are not easily metabolized because they are rich in saturated fatty acids.

4. Clearing factor and triglycerides. The clearing factor, a lipoprotein lipase, is released from various tissues into the blood and possibly activated by heparin. In triglycerides of the chylomicrons and lipoproteins with high fat content (low density lipoproteins) the clearing factor causes hydrolysis; the liberated fatty acids form soluble complexes with plasma albumin, whereby the turbid emulsion is cleared. The fatty acid complexes are rapidly metabolized in the tissues and thus removed from the blood.

A relationship exists between clearing factor and coronary sclerosis. For example, in the plasma of patients with coronary sclerosis a lack of co-factors for the lipoprotein lipase and a decreased heparin level have been found. Both spontaneous and heparin-induced clearing following alimentary lipemia takes place more slowly and is less intensive in arteriosclerotic than in normal subjects. Similarly, in the blood of patients with coronary infarction there is a significant increase in triglycerides which may be higher than that of cholesterol.

Whether a reduction of the clearing effect is a causal factor in the pathogenesis of arteriosclerosis has still to be elucidated.

B. Metabolic disturbances in the arterial wall

It seems unlikely that passive infiltration of blood constituents into the arterial wall is alone responsible for the development of coronary sclerosis. Primary metabolic changes in the arterial wall itself are perhaps of equal or even greater importance. Numerous studies indicate that the walls of the arteries (even when arteriosclerotic) have a very active metabolism.

1. Lipids. Strong evidence exists that the arterial wall is capable of synthesizing lipids. Thus, for example, ^{32}P is actively incorporated into the phospholipids of the normal and arteriosclerotic arterial wall, and experiments with labelled acetate have shown that even fatty acids are synthesized in the walls of vessels [*9—11*]. It has been shown by electron microscopy that the lipids of human arteriosclerotic lesions are essentially intracellular (especially in the cells of smooth muscle), which is regarded as the result of metabolic activity of the cells [*12*]. Additional evidence for an active metabolism of the arterial wall derives from the observation that the composition of free fatty acids, glycerides and phospholipids in the arteries differs from that in blood [*7*]. That the aorta can synthesize cholesterol and even liberate it into the plasma has been demonstrated by experiments with isolated perfused aorta of young animals (calves) [*13*]; this capability seems to diminish with increasing age. The greater part of the cholesterol of atheromatous lesions derives probably from the blood [*7, 10, 14*].

2. Mucopolysaccharides. Disorders of the metabolism of mucopolysaccharides appear to be important in arteriosclerosis. Unfortunately the chemistry and metabolism of these substances is so complex that little is known about their physiopathology. Two groups, the acid and the neutral mucopolysaccharides, can be distinguished of which only the former have been studied more closely. The acid mucopolysaccharides are anionic polymers, which contain hexosamines, hexuronic acids and sulfate, but their structure is not uniform. The main representatives of the group known at present are shown in table V [*15*].

In connective tissue the mucopolysaccharides are located in the form of a gel between the collagen and the elastic fibrils and appear to be easily damaged. Their concentration is especially high in coronary arteries [*16*].

The former assumption that connective tissue is bradytrophic, i.e. that its metabolism is extremely slow, has been disproved. By measuring the rate of incorporation of ^{35}S-sulfate, ^{14}C-acetate and ^{14}C-glucose it could be shown that mucopolysaccharides have a relatively rapid turnover. Thus, the chondroitin sulfate of the rabbit aorta has a half-life of 14 days [*17*]; the half-life of other mucopolysaccharide fractions is perhaps even shorter. In coronary sclerosis of pyridoxine-deficient monkeys and dogs, and also in other types of experimentally induced atheromatosis, changes in the mucopolysaccharides can be demonstrated histologically by an increase of metachromatic substances in the arterial wall [*18, 19*]. This presumably corresponds to an increased turnover of the sulfate of the mucopolysaccharides, which has been demonstrated in rabbits with cholesterol atheromatosis, in rats with ACTH-induced atheromatosis and in cockerels fed with high doses of cholesterol and fat [*20—23*]. *In vitro* measurements in the human aorta have, however, shown that the uptake of sulfate decreases with increasing degree of arteriosclerosis and age [*24*]. Reports concerning quantitative changes of the mucopolysaccharide components in arteriosclerosis are also controversial.

Table V. *The acid mucopolysaccharides of the connective tissue*

I. *Polyuronides*
  1. Hyaluronic acid
  2. Chondroitin

II. *Sulfated polyuronides*
  1. Chondroitin sulfate A, B, C
  2. Heparitin sulfate (heparin monosulfate)

III. *Polysulfates*
  1. Keratosulfate

The contradictory results obtained up to now in this field of research is no doubt principally due to difficulties and variations in methods. The experiments, however, show that the metabolism of the mucopolysaccharides, an important constituent of the arterial wall, is alterated in arteriosclerosis. Anatomopathologists have suggested for several decades that changes in the mucopolysaccharides, in combination with edema of the intima, are perhaps the primary disturbances in arteriosclerosis. This view, however, has not been fully corroborated until now by biochemical research, and still requires further elucidation.

The role of metabolic factors in the pathogenesis of coronary sclerosis can thus be *summarized* as follows:

Statistical studies in man and animals have shown that changes in total serum cholesterol and in serum lipoproteins are related to the incidence of both coronary artery sclerosis and general arteriosclerosis. Experimental work supports the view that the relationship is causal. Saturated fatty acids generally cause hypercholesterolemia in man and animals. Poly-unsaturated fatty acids cause no essential increase of serum cholesterol and counteract the increase in serum cholesterol induced by saturated fatty acids. It remains to be elucidated whether a deficiency of essential fatty acids is directly involved (apart from raising the serum cholesterol) in the pathogenesis of coronary sclerosis. The role of the clearing factor in the development of this disease is also not yet known.

Recent research has shown that the arterial wall has an intensive metabolism and can synthesize phospholipids, fatty acids and cholesterol. The most important metabolic changes in coronary sclerosis appear to concern the mucopolysaccharides. Whether metabolic disturbances in the arterial wall are a primary cause of arteriosclerosis remains to be elucidated.

II. Primary metabolic disorders of the myocardium

A. Catecholamines

There exists experimental evidence that catecholamines may be primarily responsible for alterations in cardiac metabolism. Catecholamines in large quantity increase myocardial oxygen consumption, but this is not accompanied by a corresponding increase in the mechanical performance of the heart (= product of minute volume and blood pressure). The mechanical efficiency of the heart decreases in consequence [*25—27*], and the catecholamines are therefore said to cause a "wastage" of oxygen. The healthy heart compensates for this catecholamine-induced increased oxygen consumption by a corresponding increase of the coronary flow. Even in the normal heart, however, large doses of catecholamines may give rise to ischemic changes, as occurs, for example, in phaeochromocytoma. Necrosis and fatty infiltration of the myocardium have also been produced by catecholamine infusions in healthy animals. In man, too, myocardial necrosis has been observed following prolonged infusions of noradrenaline, even in the absence of coronary disease [*28—30*] (fig. 1).

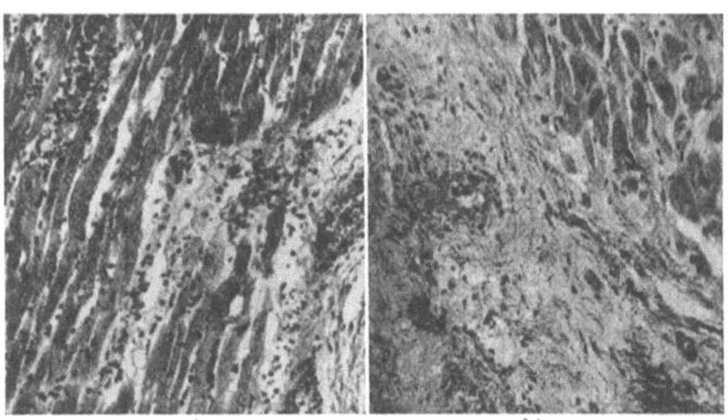

a) b)

Fig. 1a and b. Myocardial necrosis. (a) 28-year old patient, treated for eight hours with l-noradrenalin. (b) 33-year old man with phaeochromocytoma. (28)

The described effects of the catecholamines are probably more harmful in hearts with coronary sclerosis than in normal hearts. The increased oxygen consumption can no longer be compensated by an enhancement of coronary flow, so that relatively small quantities of catecholamines will cause ischemia. This hypothesis has been confirmed experimentally. Thus, for example, the dose of noradrenaline causing anoxic changes in the electrocardiogram has been found to be lower in rabbits with atheromatosis (induced by feeding cholesterol) than in normal animals [*31*].

Catecholamines are possibly responsible for precipitating attacks of angina pectoris as these often take place in conditions in which the catecholamine content of the blood is raised, e.g. physical exercise, emotional upset, crisis of pheochromocytoma. A significant increase of adrenaline and noradrenaline has been found in the plasma of patients with angina pectoris following exercise (Master's two step test). A similar increase was observed in acute myocardial infarction, but not in healthy subjects after exercise or in patients with pain of extra-cardiac origin. Increase in the total catecholamine content of the blood following cigarette smoking has also been observed in patients with angina pectoris [*32*].

Several investigators have noted that the heart is able to take up catecholamines from the blood. The noradrenaline content of the heart, for example, rises markedly after intraperitoneal or subcutaneous injections of catecholamines (fig. 2). This "avidity" for catecholamines may be partially responsible for the

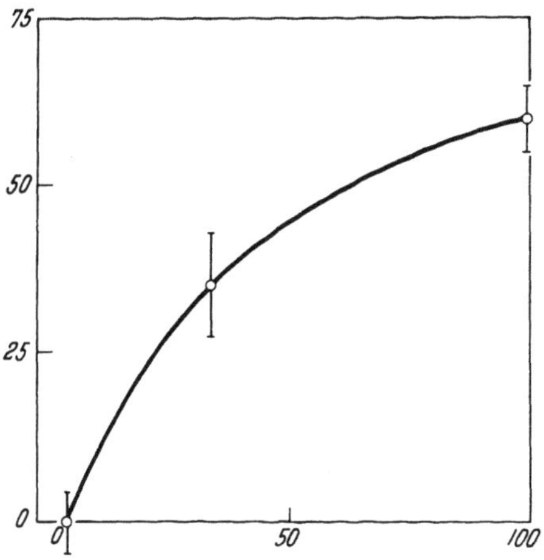

Fig. 2. Effect of iproniazid on the noradrenaline-content of the guinea pig heart. *Ordinate:* Noradrenaline-content of the myocardium 16 hours after intraperitoneal injection of iproniazid in percentage of untreated controls. *Abscissa:* Dose of iproniazid in mg/kg. The points indicate average values ± standard error of 4—32 determinations. (40)

catecholamine-sensitivity of the heart. It is not, however, proven whether all the catecholamines present in the heart are biologically active or whether they are largely stored in an inactive form. Function and metabolism of the heart are possibly influenced only by those amines which circulate in the blood or which have been liberated from cardiac stores. Support for this view comes from the work of Bing *and his group* and appears to indicate that the pharmacodynamic and metabolic action of the catecholamines in the heart-lung preparation depends on their concentration in the perfusion fluid and not in the heart itself [*33—35*]. Further research is needed to prove or disprove this theory.

Biological inactivation of the stored catecholamines might also explain to some extent the effect of *monoamine oxidase inhibitors*, which — paradoxically, in the light of present knowledge — relieve the symptoms of angina pectoris and at the same time increase the noradrenaline content of the heart (fig. 3). Certain

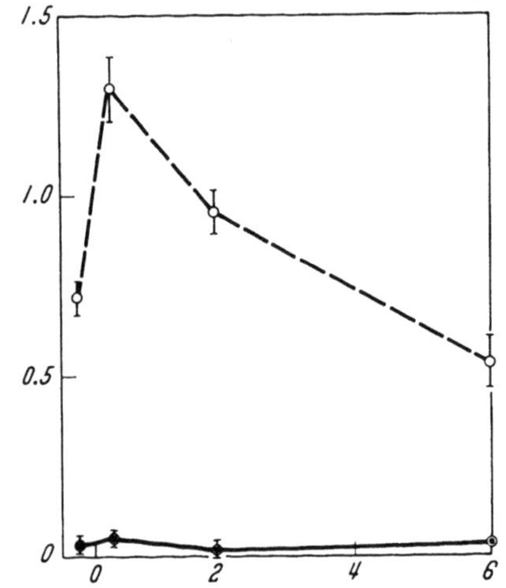

Fig. 3. Noradrenaline-content in the myocardium and blood of rats after intraperitoneal injection of noradrenaline bitartrate (corresponding to 2.5 mg/kg of noradrenaline base). *Ordinate:* Noradrenaline-content in γ/g. *Abscissa:* Time after injection of noradrenaline. — — — Heart, ——— Blood. The points indicate mean values ± standard error of 4—6 experiments. (Author's own trials)

studies (histochemical examination of the adrenal medulla, experiments with isolated blood platelets, fractionated centrifugation of organ homogenates) suggest that monoamine oxidase inhibitors probably raise the storage capacity of certain tissues for monoamines [*36*], and this in turn may lead to biological inactivation of the amines. Another point in favour of an inactivating mechanism is the fact that myocardial necrosis following injection of isopropylnorepinephrine can be diminished or prevented by previous administration of the monoamine oxidase inhibitor isocarboxazid [*37*].

B. Changes in electrolyte metabolism

Myocardial necrosis may be induced experimentally by combined administration of sodium salts (phosphates, sulfates, chlorates, but not chlorides) and corticosteroids. The distribution of the necrotic zones is somewhat similar to that in myocardial infarction of man. Potassium and magnesium salts as well as chlorides have a protective effect [*38*]. Prior administration of sodium salts plus corticosteroids in doses which per se are harmless promotes the occurrence of myocardial necrosis induced by various factors such as adrenaline, vasopressin, fluoroacetate, hot and cold baths, neuromuscular stress and surgical trauma [*38*]. Experiments with the isolated perfused heart also point to a relationship between the action of electrolytes and catecholamines. Decrease in the potassium concentration of the perfusion fluid, for example, is accompanied by an increase in the sensitivity of the heart to noradrenaline and to adrenaline. Thus, the potassium level appears to act as a trigger mechanism for the action of the catecholamines [*39*]. These findings justify the assumption that changes in electrolyte metabolism (such as occur in stress) facilitate the action of potential cardiotoxic factors, such as the catecholamines. To what extent these factors are involved in the development of myocardial anoxemia and necrosis in man and whether potassium and magnesium salts have a therapeutic effect are of course still open questions.

The present knowledge on disturbances leading to myocardial ischemia without impairing coronary circulation primarily may thus be *summarized* as follows:

It is probable that primary disorders of myocardial metabolism can be induced or promoted by catecholamines and electrolyte shifts. The catecholamines interfere with the oxygen economy of the myocardium because they increase the oxygen consumption of the heart more than its mechanical performance. Possibly only the free catecholamines exert this action whereas the ones stored in the heart may be biologically inactive. In experimental conditions electrolyte shifts either lead to myocardial necrosis (e.g. administration of sodium + corticoids) or increase the sensitivity of the heart towards anoxia-producing agents such as adrenaline. There are reasons to assume that catecholamines may be a factor in producing myocardial ischemia in man. As regards the clinical significance of electrolyte shifts no definite conclusions can be drawn at present.

Summary

Many factors are involved in the pathogenesis of myocardial ischemia. Until now interest has been focussed chiefly on changes in the blood constituents (cholesterol, lipoproteins, fatty acids etc.). There is, however, increasing evidence that metabolic changes in the arterial wall and in the myocardium are also important. It seems unlikely that myocardial ischemia due only to primary interference with myocardial metabolism (by, for example, catecholamines) is of clinical significance. It is none the less possible that catecholamines and electrolyte shifts may be additional or precipitating factors in the development of myocardial ischemia, in the presence of a damaged coronary circulation such as occurs in coronary sclerosis.

References

[*1*] Constantinides, P., J. Booth and G. Carlson: Advanced atherosclerosis of the human type in the rabbit: A new experimental tool. Internationales Symposium über „Drugs affecting lipid metabolism", Mailand, Juni 1960.

[*2*] Bragdon, J. H.: Transfusion transfer of experimental atherosclerosis. Circulation **4**, 466 (1951).

[*3*] Schrade, W., R. Biegler and E. Böhle: Fatty acid distribution in the lipid fractions of healthy persons of different age, patients with atherosclerosis and patients with idiopathic hyperlipidemia. J. Arteriosclerosis Res. **1**, 47 (1961).

[4] RUTSTEIN, D. D., E. F. INGENITO, J. M. CRAIG and M. MARTINELLI: Effects of linolenic and stearic acids on cholesterol-induced lipoid deposition in human aortic cells in tissue culture. Lancet 1, 545 (1958).

[5] FISHER, H., and A. S. FEIGENBAUM: Essential fatty acids of normal and atherosclerotic aortas from chicken receiving differently saturated fats for three years. Nature 186, 85 (1960).

[6] GEY, K. F., and A. PLETSCHER: Inability of refined corn oil to influence spontaneous arteriosclerosis of old hens. Nature 189, 491 (1961).

[7] BÖTTCHER, C. J. F., F. P. WOODFORD, C. CH. TER HAAR ROMENY-WACHER, E. BOELSMA-VAN HOUTE and C. M. VAN GENT: Fatty acid distribution in lipids of the aortic wall. Lancet 1, 1378 (1960).

[8] —, and C. M. VAN GENT: Changes in the composition of phospholipids and of phospholipid fatty acids associated with atherosclerosis in the human aortic wall. J. Arteriosclerosis Res. 1, 36 (1961).

[9] ZILVERSMIT, D. B., and E. L. MC CANDLESS: Independence of arterial phospholipid synthesis from alterations in blood lipids. J. Lipid Res. 1, 118 (1959).

[10] — —, P. H. JORDAN, W. S. HENLEY and P. F. ACKERMAN: The synthesis of phospholipids in human atheromatous lesions. Circulation 23, 370 (1961).

[11] NEWMAN, H. A., and D. B. ZILVERSMIT: Origin of various lipids in atheromatous lesions of rabbits. Circulation 20, 967 (1959).

[12] GEER, J. G., H. G. MCGILL, J. P. STRONG and R. L. HOLMAN: Electron microscopy of human atherosclerotic lesions. Fed. Proc. 19, 15 (1960).

[13] WERTHESSEN, N. T., M. A. NYMAN, R. L. HOLMAN and J. P. STRONG: In vitro study of cholesterol metabolism in the calf aorta. Circulat. Res. 4, 586 (1956).

[14] SCHWENK, E., and D. F. STEVENS: Deposition of cholesterol in experimental rabbit atherosclerosis. Proc. Soc. exp. Biol. 103, 614 (1960).

[15] MEYER, K.: Struktur und Biologie der Polysaccharidsulfate im Bindegewebe. In: Struktur und Stoffwechsel des Bindegewebes, Symposium an der Med. Universitätsklinik Münster (Westfalen). Stuttgart: Thieme 1959, S. 12.

[16] GILLMAN, T., M. HATHORN and J. PENN: Micro-anatomy and reactions to injury of vascular elastic membranes and associated polysaccharides. In: Connective Tissue (herausg. R. E. Turnbridge). London: Blackwell 1957, S. 120.

[17] ODEBLAD, E., and H. BOSTRÖM: A quantitative autoradiographic study on the uptake of labelled sulphate in the aorta of the rabbit. Acta chem. scand. 7, 233 (1953).

[18] KIRK, J. E.: Mucopolysaccharides of arterial tissue. In: The Arterial Wall (herausg. A. I. Lansing). Williams and Wilkins Company, 1959, S. 161.

[19] BUCK, R. C., and F. C. HEAGY: Uptake of radioactive sulphur by various tissues of normal and cholesterol-fed rabbits. Canad. J. Biochem. 36, 63 (1958).

[20] HILZ, H., und D. USTERMAN: Der Sulfatstoffwechsel der Gefäßwand in Beziehung zur Arteriosklerose und seine Beeinflussung durch Sexualhormone. Biochem. Z. 332, 376 (1960).

[21] KOWALEWSKI, K.: Uptake of radiosulphate by mucopolysaccharides of aorta in cholesterol-fed cockerels. Proc. Soc. exp. Biol. 101, 356 (1959).

[22] RINEHART, J. F., and L. D. GREENBERG: Arteriosclerotic lesions in pyridoxine-deficient monkeys. Amer. J. Path. 25, 481 (1949).

[23] MUSHETT, C. W., and G. A. EMERSON: Arteriosclerosis in pyridoxine-deficient monkeys and dogs. Fed. Proc. 15, 526 (1956).

[24] DYRBYE, M. O.: Studies on the metabolism of the mucopolysaccharides of human arterial tissue by means of S^{35}, with special reference to changes related to age. J. Gerontol. 14, 32 (1959).

[25] RAAB, W.: The adrenergic-cholinergic control of cardiac metabolism and function. In: Fortschritte der Kardiologie (herausg. R. Hegglin), Vol. 1. Basel: Karger 1956, S. 65.

[26] GEROLA, A., H. FEINBERG and L. N. KATZ: Role of catecholamines on energetics of the heart and its blood supply. Amer. J. Physiol. 196, 394 (1959).

[27] BERNE, R. M.: Effect of epinephrine and norepinephrine on coronary circulation. Circulat. Res. 6, 644 (1958).

[28] SZAKÁCS, J. E., and A. CANNON: l-Norepinephrine myocarditis. Amer. J. clin. Path. 30, 425 (1958).
[29] —, and B. MEHLMAN: Pathologic changes induced by l-norepinephrine: quantitative aspects. Amer. J. Cardiol. 5, 619 (1960).
[30] MALING, H. M., B. HIGHMAN and E. C. THOMPSON: Some similar effects after large doses of catecholamines and myocardial infarction in dogs. Amer. J. Cardiol. 5, 628 (1960).
[31] MELVILLE, K. I., and H. E. SHISTER: Cardiac responses to epinephrine and norepinephrine during prolonged cholesterol and high fat feeding in rabbits. Amer. J. Cardiol. 4, 391 (1959).
[32] GAZES, P. C., J. A. RICHARDSON and E. F. WOODS: Plasma catecholamine concentrations in myocardial infarction and angina pectoris. Circulation 19, 657 (1959).
[33] KAKO, K., J. D. CHOUDHURY and R. J. BING: Possible mechanism of the decline in mechanical efficiency of the isolated heart. J. Pharmacol. exp. Therap. 130, 46 (1960).
[34] DANFORTH, H., F. B. BALLARD, K. KAKO, J. D. CHOUDHURY and R. J. BING: Metabolism of the heart in failure. Circulation 21, 112 (1960).
[35] KAKO, K., A. CHRYSOHOU and R. J. BING: Storage of catecholamines in the heart. Effect of amine oxidase inhibitors. Circulation Res. 9, 295 (1961).
[36] PLETSCHER, A., K. F. GEY und P. ZELLER: Monoaminoxydase-Hemmer: Chemie, Biochemie, Pharmakologie, Klinik. In: Fortschritte der Arzneimittelforschung (herausg. E. Jucker), Vol. 2. Basel: Birkhäuser 1960, S. 417.
[37] ZBINDEN, G.: Inhibition of experimental myocardial necrosis by the monoamine oxidase inhibitor isocarboxazid (Marplan). Amer. Heart J. 60, 450 (1960).
[38] SELYE, H.: Elektrolyte, Stress und Herznekrose. Basel: Benno Schwabe & Co. 1960.
[39] MELVILLE, K. I., and B. KOROL: Cardiac drug responses and potassium shifts. Studies on the interrelated effects of drugs on coronary flow, heart action and cardiac potassium movement (part I and II). Amer. J. Cardiol. 2, 81, 189 (1958).
[40] PLETSCHER, A.: Einfluß von Isopropyl-isonikotinsäurehydrazid auf den Katecholamingehalt des Myokards. Experientia 14, 73 (1958).

Ethnological and clinical considerations on the relationship between body weight and arteriosclerosis*

G. Schettler

An alarming increase in the so-called degenerative cardiovascular disorders is reported from all highly developed countries. The undoubted absolute increase in the number of sufferers from vascular disease is partly attributable to the general rise in the expectation of life, but the younger and middle age groups are affected as well as the elderly. In countries with a high standard of living, cardiovascular disease ranks with cancer and traffic accidents as one of the principal causes of death. It is therefore not surprising that study of arteriosclerosis has been intensified in every field of medical research, one of the most important of which is the relationship between body weight and degenerative vascular disease. While insurance medical officers and statisticians regard it as an established fact that body weight is an important contributory factor in the development of cardiovascular disorders, physiologists and clinicians are divided in their opinions. As long ago as 1901 Rogers established that the mortality of insured persons who were overweight was in general high. Further statistical studies (summarised by Marks, 1956) led to the following conclusion: "Overweight shortens life, is an etiological factor in several principal diseases, and hastens their downward course. Particularly important is the relationship between the accumulation of excess weight and the development of cardiovascular disease" (Armstrong *et al.*, 1951). On the other hand, the Study Group on Atherosclerosis and Ischaemic Heart Disease of the World Health Organisation concluded (WHO Technical Report Series, No. 117, p. 17, 1957) that "There is no convincing evidence that relative obesity (the proportion of the body mass made up of fat), of itself, is a major factor in atherogenesis or the production of ischaemic heart disease in man." The physiologists Brozek and Ancel Keys (1957) throw doubt, based on a survey of the literature, on the validity of conclusions drawn from insurance statistics. According to their observations, obesity is no more frequent in sufferers from coronary disease than in the rest of the population. The opinions expressed by pathologists and clinicians also differ widely.

One of the first difficulties is to establish what is the "normal" or the "average" weight in a population or population group. Thus for example the "average" male population of North America is in fact moderately obese, while the male

---

* Lecture delivered at the Symposium "The pros and cons of sport", 7—8 June, 1961, at Berne. Published in Schweiz. Z. Sportmed. Vol. 9, No 3, P. 74—89 (1961).

population of Mediterranean countries is somewhat underweight. "Average" weight tables for adults of different ages do not reflect weight distribution in the population, and in particular changes due to age are not considered. Another source of difficulty is the recording of the state of nutrition and of the proportion of body fat. Direct measurement of the latter by, for example, measuring skinfold thickness with calipers, is not generally practised at clinical or life insurance examinations. Body fatness can be assessed simply by calculation of the index: height minus abdominal girth, and such indices have been used in the compilation of various insurance statistics. Calculation of the "normal weight" of individuals on the basis of body length (body length in centimeters minus 100 = standard weight in kg) gives no indication of the distribution of the body fat. Here constitutional factors are important. The available data suggest that pyknic and athleto-pyknic types are especially liable to coronary sclerosis. This does not, of course, mean that even markedly leptosomatic individuals may not have a myocardial infarction. Overweight athleto-pyknic individuals may have a relatively low proportion of body fat, and this constitutes an obvious possible source of error in the so-called Brocca's count. In my opinion careful individual examination is therefore better adapted for investigation of the relationship between body weight and degenerative vascular disease than are general statistical studies. None the less, the results of the insurance statistics are so interesting and, in spite of all the objections, so striking in many respects, that we shall consider them first.

For determination of the relationship of obesity to longevity and cardiovascular disease, it is not the "average" population that should be taken as control; GUBNER has proposed that persons who in comparison with average population are significantly underweight should be the controls for assessing the various grades of overweight. Table I sets out the results of studies made by various American insurance companies (after GUBNER).

These studies show clearly that in proportion as the body weight rises over moderate limits the mortality ratios also rise. Grossly obese persons, whose mortality rate is even higher, have not been included in this Table. Although the expectation of life of the underweight is greater than that of the overweight in all age groups, the disparity increases with time. The mortality statistics of the insurance companies show more than half the policy holders to have died of cardiovascular disorders, the most prominent among these being coronary sclerosis and stroke. Mortality data, however, offer only an indirect indication of an association between overweight and these vascular diseases. The earlier investigations have to be accepted with considerable caution, since recognition of myocardial infarction before the days of the electrocardiogram was hardly possible. In a study by SYDENSTRICKER, for example, the diagnosis of "arteriosclerosis" was based chiefly on palpation of the radial artery.

More recent work leaves no doubt of the special frequency of coronary disease among the obese. In 1949 the Equitable Life Assurance Company made a study of policies issued between 1940 and 1948. This revealed that the mortality from

Table I. *Mortality ratios (actual/expected) among moderate underweights and moderate overweights*

Study	Years policies issued	Follow-up	Age at issue	Mortality ratio (actual/expected) Underweights	Mortality ratio (actual/expected) Overweights
Medico-actuarial Mortality Investigation . . .	1885—1908	to 1909		(minus 15 to 20 lbs.)	(plus 15 to 20 lbs.)
			50—56	92%	121%
			57—62	82%	125%
				(minus 10% or more)	(plus 10 to 29%)
Medical impairment study	1885—1927	1909—1928	40—49	80%	119%
			50—59	80%	115%
				(minus 8 to 22 lbs.)	(plus 8 to 22 lbs.)
Provident mutual study	1920—1945	1937—1947	15—34	87%	124%
				(minus 23 to 42 lbs.)	(plus 23 to 42 lbs.)
				90%	152%
				(minus 43 lbs. or more)	(plus 43 lbs. or more)
				74%	152%
				(minus 20 to 24%)	(plus 20 to 24%)
Equitable Life Assurance Soc. of U.S.	1930—1939	to 1950	30—39	71%	151%
				(minus 25 to 44%)	(plus 25 to 44%)
				72%	134% (+25 to 29%)
					212% (+30 to 34%)
					189% (+35 to 44%)
				(minus 10 to 29.9%)	(plus 10 to 29.9%)
Equitable Life Assurance Soc. of U.S.	1940—1948	to 1949	30—49	86%	107%
			50 and over	90%	117%
				(minus 15 to 24%)	(plus 15 to 24%)
Metropolitan Life (women)	1922—1936	to 1936	under 30	100%	100%
			50 and over	83%	116%

cardiovascular disease was three times higher in the 30—39.9% overweight group than in the 10—29% underweight group, some three-quarters of the deaths from circulatory disorders being due to angina pectoris and coronary disease. In underweight men coronary disease constituted 67% of the total deaths from circulatory disorders, while in men who were of "average" weight, and 10—29% and 30—39% overweight, it constituted respectively 76, 77 and 78% of such deaths. These figures concerned males. In the Metropolitan Life Study of younger women no difference in mortality between the underweight and the overweight was found, but in women beyond the menopause (those at age 50 years and over) there were distinct differences similar to those in males. Table II presents the results of the Equitable Life study.

Table II. *Deaths due to circulatory diseases (males) (actual/expected)*

Weight	Issue age		
	30–49	50 and over	All ages
—10 to 29%	69% (a/e)	81%	73%
—9.9 to +9.9%	114%	104%	110%
+10 to 29.9%	132%	136%	136%
+30 to 39.9%	260%		225%

In view of these data, it is not surprising that candidates for life insurance who are overweight are asked to pay extra premiums. In the individual case, of course, no assessment of life expectancy should be attempted without performing a thorough physical examination and taking a careful family history. Certain forms of familial obesity are not, as is well known, incompatible with a normal life expectancy. Here the state of the circulation and especially the blood pressure are important determinant factors.

The relationship between obesity and arteriosclerosis was studied from the point of view of morbid anatomy by Wilens in 1947. He found advanced degrees of coronary sclerosis to be almost as common in women of normal weight as in corpulent women (20% and 22.6% respectively of the cases studied), whereas in markedly undernourished women it was much more rare (12.1%). In males the difference between the obese and the underweight was more striking (40.8% as against 12.5%). Allowance must of course be made for the fact that the primary disease which causes death not infrequently impairs the nutritional state. After conducting a comparative study of hospital in-patients and visitors, however, Wilens abides by his conclusion that the nutritional state is of primary importance in the genesis of coronary sclerosis. It goes without saying that coronary sclerosis is not to be classified together with general arteriosclerosis, and above all not with aortic sclerosis. Thus although both Gubner (1950) and Holman and associates (1956) found more severe degrees of coronary sclerosis in overweight than in underweight persons, in neither group was there any significant difference as regards aortic sclerosis. No differences were detected in other arteries in a study made by CINTI and DE BIASE in 1953. FABER and LUND in 1949 found no differences, either pathological or biochemical, as regards aortic sclerosis in various weight groups. On the basis of morbid anatomical observations, DUFF and MCMILLAN (1951) and HOLMAN and associates (1956—1958) confirmed the fact, familiar to all morbid anatomists, that the arteriosclerotic process develops in a series of phases. Marked disorders of circulation, especially in the coronary region, are commonly precipitated and maintained by thrombotic processes. In the early phase of fatty streak atheroma and yellowish plaque formation the development and progression of the condition is apparently not affected by the body weight. It is only in the later phases, which develop after the process has been going on for 20—30 years, that these differences become evident.

The extreme complexity of the problem of body weight and arteriosclerosis or coronary sclerosis, emerges from the findings of German army pathologists working in prisoner-of-war camps in Russia. All are unanimous in reporting (for the literature see SCHETTLER, 1961), that arteriosclerosis and coronary sclerosis were exceedingly rare among German prisoners-of-war who died in Russia and came to autopsy. There is no doubt that many of these men were overweight because of faulty nutrition. It is generally recognized that the changes in the subcutaneous connective tissue, the sustentacular tissue and the parenchyma and the gross disturbances of water and mineral salt metabolism specific to malnutrition are primarily responsible for the increase in body weight of such patients. This type of weight gain should not, of course, be regarded as identical with obesity. On the other hand we have, like other workers (GIESE *et al.*, PIERACH *et al.*), repeatedly encountered coronary sclerosis of unusual severity and unusually rapid course in ex-prisoners of war during the period when food had again become abundant and they were eating to excess. The malnutrition had evidently left behind it a legacy of arterial damage involving persistent disorder of the intramural metabolism of the arterial wall. As to whether the rapid increase of myocardial infarction in the nations of western and northern Europe during the second world war and in Germany during the post-war period should be attributed to similar lesions in the vessel walls resulting from hunger, I would not venture an opinion. It seems to me rather improbable. It is certainly noteworthy that extensive pathological studies by MORRIS in England and by our own working group in association with WERTHEMANN (using the autopsy material of the Institutes of Pathology of Marburg and of Basle [1956]) have not revealed any definite alteration in the frequency and type of coronary sclerosis during the war and post-war years. Similar observations were made in Hamburg. During the same period, on the other hand, a most remarkable increase in the clinical manifestations of myocardial infarction was observed at these Institutes. This means that the degree and frequency of the advanced forms of coronary sclerosis are not to be identified with those of clinical myocardial infarction. According to the statistics of the causes of death in the northern countries and Germany, there was undoubtedly a fall in deaths due to atherosclerosis in the latter years of the war and in the early post-war period as compared with the pre-war years and the latter post-war period. Also worthy of mention is the decrease in number of thrombo-embolic cases, including myocardial and pulmonary infarction, during the lean years. Study of autopsy material at the Institutes of Pathology of Freiburg and of Frankfort-on-Main shows an astonishing regression in the incidence of pulmonary embolism during the early post-war years compared with the later years of return to full nourishment (HAMPERL). A similar phenomenon was observed after the first world war (NORDMANN, 1939). There is no doubt that there was a marked fall in the body weight of undernourished populations and population groups. In my opinion conclusions as to cause and effect should not, however, be reached too hastily. There has been a noteworthy and ever mounting increase in the incidence of myocardial infarction in recent years. In the German Federal Republic it rose continuously in all age groups between 1952 and 1958. The increase affected both sexes, but analysis of the individual age groups shows pronounced differences between men and women. The 1952—1958 coronary death rate showed no significant variation in the different age groups in women up to 45, but in the 45—50 group a gradual rise was noted. This became more definite in the later age groups, where the difference between the male and female rates, still very evident up to the 60th year, began to even out. The increase in deaths from coronary disease in young and middle-aged men was striking and alarming. There was no increase up to the age of 25, but in the 25—30 group it rose from 15 in 1952 to 55 in 1958; the death rate per 100,000 in the respective age groups rose correspondingly. This tendency becomes even more marked in the later age groups. In 1952 44 men aged between 30 and 35 died of coronary vascular disease, in 1958 113, the ratio per 100,000 rising from 3.4 to 6.9. The number of deaths in the succeeding age groups were as follows in 1952 and 1958 respectively; 35—40, 105 and 223; 40—45, 298 and 410; 45—50, 704 and 1234; 50—55, 1359 and 2554. Even more frightening is the situation in the 55—60 and the 60—65 groups, in which the absolute figures for 1952 are 1745 and 2241 respectively, and for 1958 4185 and 4524! The ratio per 100,000 for the respective age groups rose from 151.8 in 1952 to 263.0 in 1958, and from 234.3 in 1952 to 403.6 in 1958. The age-conditioned increase in coronary causes of death already mentioned has of course to be taken into account here, and the expected death rate, which in coronary disease is considerable, has also to be considered. It is not to be assumed that there was a steady increase in the body weight of those persons who died of myocardial infarction between 1952 and 1958, but whether the proportion of obese individuals among these deceased persons had increased is not known. It may further be assumed that the body weight of those who died between 1952 and 1958 was higher in comparison with the early post-war years.

As regards ethnological differences in the incidence of atherosclerosis, myocardial infarction and apoplexy, no exact data on body weight are available. For example the remarkable rarity of myocardial infarction in Japan compared with the U.S.A. or with the Anglo-Saxon or the nordic countries could be attributed to a whole host of extraneous or intrinsic factors. Amony these factors nutrition undoubtedly plays a most significant role, and I share the view of KEYS, BRONTE-STEWART, I. PAGE, MALMROS and BIÖRCK that of all the hypotheses of the etiology and pathogenesis of atherosclerosis the theory regarding nutrition, with special reference to fats, is the best founded. The fact that peoples and population groups with a fat-rich diet are in general more obese than those whose diet is poor in fat may be assumed to be due to the high caloric value of fat. General nutritional and economic statistics, such as have been reported by YUDKIN, do not, however, give any clear indication on the part played by the proportion of fat in the total calorie intake, or by the relative proportions of spezific kinds of fat, in the development of myocardial infarction or cerebral thrombosis. Such per capita distribution statistics based on trade figures have, in my opinion, no medical significance at all. The conclusions that have been drawn from them have given rise to considerable perturbation, as recent literature surveys (GLATZEL, 1960) have shown. Even from these economic statistics, however, emerges the fact that the incidence of myocardial infarction is low in peoples with a relatively low fat diet, such as the Japanese, the Italians and the French. This applies also to certain poorer population groups in the so-called underdeveloped countries and in some Mediterranean countries. The procedure adopted by KEYS, of obtaining representative cross-sections of whole populations based upon careful individual investigations and upon surveys of determined social and professional categories, promises useful results. Here I must refer readers to the relevant literature. Valuable information can also be obtained from observations made in clinical practice. A study, reported by STEIN from the Department of Medicine of the University of Marburg and from the Küppelsmühle Sanatorium, Bad Orb, of deviations from standard weight (as assessed on the basis of height) in patients with recent infarcts or with infarct scars compared with patients suffering from other heart disease, showed (see Table III) a high incidence of infarction in the overweight. Here too constitutional factors may well be involved.

Table III. *Underweight or overweight*

	under	−20	−15	−10	−5	−0	+5	+10	+15	+20	over
	−20	−15	−10	−5	−0	+5	+10	+15	+20	+25	+25
Recent infarcts (%)	2.2	—	3.2	6.1	30.1	15.2	12.1	9.9	15.2	3.0	3.0
Old infarcts (%)	—	0.3	1.1	6.5	12.7	25.5	22.0	21.8	5.9	1.7	2.5
Other cardiac diseases (%)	1.3	6.6	12.2	16.2	22.6	17.1	12.9	5.4	2.2	0.9	2.6

It is well known that certain constitutional types have a tendency not only to obesity, but also to other diseases, such as high blood pressure, diabetes mellitus and gout, which cause atherosclerotic vascular changes to develop earlier and more severely. It is then diffiicult to distinguish in the individual case which of the primary diseases had a decisive effect on the atherosclerosis and what rôle must be ascribed to obesity. It may nowadays be assumed that, in general, a tendency to raised blood pressure is inherent in obesity, if the latter is interpreted as a uniform clinical syndrome (for the literature see SCHETTLER, 1961). Sufferers from gout and from diabetes mellitus too are not infrequently overweight. The question of the intermediary metabolism in the organ and depot fat in diabetics and the significance of insulin cannot be discussed here (for literature, see GUBNER, 1957). The association of hypertension, obesity and metabolic disorders — essential hyperlipaemia and essential hypercholesterolaemia should also be mentioned here — carries an increased risk of the development of coronary sclerosis and myocardial infarction. Cerebral vascular accidents should certainly also be included in this group. On the other hand, no electrocardiographic evidence of coronary vascular deficiency was found in a group of 80 men aged between 45 and 60 whose weight was at least 10 kg (22 lb) over the average for their age and height and whose blood pressure was significantly below normal (cardiac insufficiency as a cause of the low B.P. was excluded). The group also included cases of cirrhosis of the liver, in which, as is generally recognized, coronary sclerosis is relatively rare and slight. Clearly, therefore, obese individuals with low blood pressure and no disorder of fat metabolism have no special tendency to coronary sclerosis.

Much has been published in recent years on the part played by *blood factors* in the development of degenerative vascular disease and especially of ischaemic heart disease. The most important literature was summarized in my monograph on arteriosclerosis (1961). According to the findings of most workers, and to the results of our investigations, *obesity* is *not* accompanied by corresponding changes in the *blood factors,* and particularly not by increase in the serum cholesterol and the other serum lipids. The serum lipoproteins and glucoproteins do not necessarily show pathological changes in obese individuals as compared with those of normal weight or with the constitutionally underweight. On the other side reduction of raised blood lipid and cholesterol or lipoprotein levels following certain dietetic measures is often associated with a regression of body weight. It is none the less noteworthy that several research groups have demonstrated that the prognosis in myocardial infarction is substantially better in slightly undernourished patients on low-fat diets than in well-nourished patients on high-fat diets (for literature see SCHETTLER, 1961). The significance of blood pressure, body weight and serum factors is illustrated in Fig. 1, which is based on work by DAWBER and co-workers (1957). It shows that underweight, low blood pressure and low serum cholesterol carry a very low expectancy of coronary artery disease (A). Where all three of these attributes are low to moderate (B), the expected disease rate approaches the average. Where one of the three is raised (C), the expected disease rate is above the average, where two are raised (D), the risk is still greater and where all three are raised (E), it is about 20 times higher than in the first group. It would be instructive for similar studies to be carried out in other countries and population groups, and in different professions and age groups. In the Framingham study, in which there was a follow-up of four years, the new coronary disease rate in men between 45 and 62 was three times higher in those who were 20 or more per cent. overweight than in those whose weight was under average. In the Albany study, in which the observation period was 31 months, the coronary disease rate was 19‰ in men who were up to 20% overweight, 24‰ in those who were 20—39% overweight and 65‰ in those 40% or more overweight. Increase of body weight of more than 20% above any weight level existing at the age of 25 doubled the risk of developing ischaemic heart disease! In another study carried out at Los Angeles over a period of observation of two to three years, the prevalence of coronary disease in men of 40—54 was found to be five times greater in those overweight than in those underweight. In the 40—70 age group the disease quota was three times greater in the overweight than in the underweight. In the clinical material of CURTIUS, HARTWIG and SEHNERT obesity was more common than normal weight or overweight in patients with signs of coronary sclerosis or general arteriosclerosis.

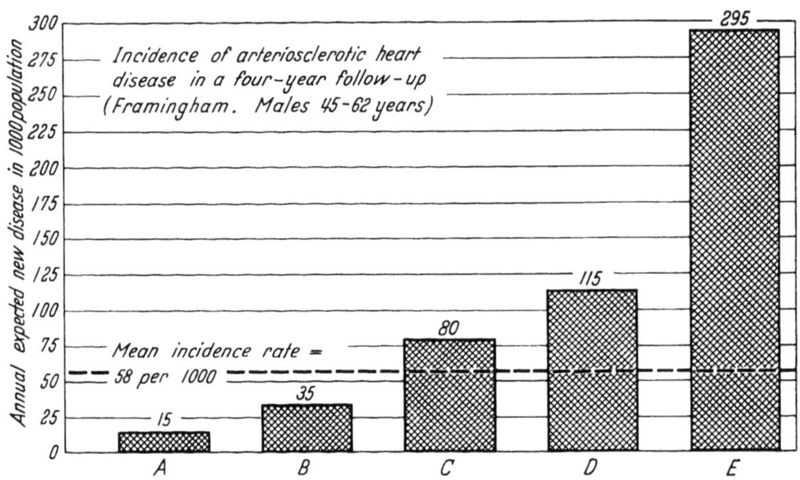

Fig. 1. The three principal factors in coronary disease.
A. Low or normal blood pressure, low body weight, low serum cholesterol level.
B. Low or normal blood pressure, low to moderate body weight, low to moderate serum cholesterol level.
C. One of the three factors is higher.
D. Two of the three factors are higher.
E. All three factors are higher.
(After Dawber et al., Amer. J. Public Health, 47, 4, 1957)

Current research results point to weight limitation as a desirable prophylactic and therapeutic measure in atherosclerosis. The greater the familial tendency to this disease, as ascertained by taking a careful history, the earlier should weight reduction be commenced and the more persistently should it be followed. All doctors are familiar with its usefulness in patients with circulatory failure, and experience has shown that these patients often suffer from coronary sclerosis and its sequelae. Any obese subject with signs of coronary sclerosis, or in whom this condition is even suspected, should endeavour to lose some weight in any case. The best way of doing this varies from case to case. Unfortunately, coronary patients who have given up smoking often become obese because they compensate by excessive indulgence in sweets or alcohol. Dock regards weight gain as extremly undesirable in these cases, and he prefers to allow his patients to resume smoking in moderation rather than to put on too much weight. Personally, I cannot subscribe to this view. Survivors of myocardial infarction should certainly keep their weight down, but it is also absolutely essential that they give up smoking. The latest report of the American Heart Association leaves no room for doubt as to the significance of smoking in the evolution of atherosclerosis.

Every physican appreciates that many factors contribute to the genesis of atherosclerosis in man and that any discussion of prophylactic or therapeutic measures must take them all into account. It would be a mistake to regard weight reduction alone as the keystone of the treatment of this condition. The doctor called upon to treat obesity must appreciate his patient's psychology, and this being absolutely essential if the patient has, or is regarded as probably having, coronary sclerosis.

That the problem of atherosclerosis is not a new one is seen from a lecture on calcification of the arteries which the Tübingen clinician OTFRIED MÜLLER delivered at Stuttgart in 1909 before a meeting of the German Women's Society for Care of the Sick in the Colonies. His words apply fully to present-day conditions and indicate in a truly prophetic way the situation which was to develop:

"Foremost among the diseases ascribed to wear and tear is atherosclerosis, one of the bugbears of our civilisation. Its predilection is for those members of society who are the most fitted for work and for creative effort — the important industrialist, the responsible official, the busy doctor or lawyer — snatching them prematurely from the midst of successful careers." MÜLLER further said:

"There can be no doubt that modern man wears himself out more rapidly than did his forbears. Competition is keener, work is more exacting, technical advances make increasing demands. There is little, alas, that we can do to change this state of affairs. The railway, the motor car, the aeroplane, the telegraph and telephone have contributed only in appearance to ease of living. This armed peace (sic! — Author) exerts slower but more continuous pressure than many a previous war. Men are grinding each other down gradually, instead of destroying each other suddenly. In spite of all humanitarian efforts these times are inflexible. If this trend continues, we may expect the speed of attrition to rise and the age limit for working capacity to fall. We must attempt to readjust the balance of our lives by creating rational, extra-professional activities, by attaching greater importance to recreation and above all by developing sources of interest within ourselves which will compete at least in some measure with the greatly increasing interests which assail us from without. Concentration of effort instead of the all too common dispersion, turning our interests inwards instead of ever more outwards, simplification of our mode of living, especially of our food, instead of ever greater luxury, re-establishment of contact with Nature, which has been lost to a large extent, and continuous medical supervision — these might well be the most effective weapons for conducting this struggle against death."

References

ARMSTRONG, D. B., u. Mitarb.: J. Amer. med. Ass. **147,** 1007 (1951).
BIÖRCK, G.: Zit in: World trends of cardiology, 1. Cardiovascular epidemiology. A. Keys u. P. H. White, New York: Hoeber-Harper 1956.
BRONTE-STEWART, B., u. Mitarb.: Lancet **1,** 521 (1956).
BROZEK, J., and A. KEYS: Publ. Health **47,** Suppl. April 1957.
CINTI and DE BIASE: Arch. Vecchi anat. pat. **19,** 857 (1953); zit. nach R. S. Gubner. Nutr. Rev. **15,** 353 (1957).
CURTIUS, F., K. HARTWIG und H. E. SEHNERT: Der Arthritismus. Lübeck 1956.
DAWBER, T. R., u. Mitarb.: Amer. J. Publ. Health **47,** 4 (1957).
DOCK, W.: Bull. Schweiz. Akad. med. Wiss. **13,** 5 (1957).
DUFF, L., and MCMILLAN: Am. J. Med. **11,** 92 (1951).
FABER, M., und F. LUND: Arch. Path. **48,** 351 (1949).
GIESE, u. Mitarb.: Die Dystrophie. Arbeit und Gesundheit neue Folge, S. 65. Stuttgart 1958.
GLATZEL, H.: Die Arteriosklerose des Adipösen. Ärztl. Praxis X, 3, 58 (1958).
GUBNER, R. S.: Nutr. Rev. **15,** 353 (1957).
HAMPERL, H.: Klin. Wschr. 1956; Ibid, **40,** 86 (1956).
HOLMAN, R. L., u. Mitarb.: Amer. **34,** (1950), 20; 40, 86 (1956).
YUDKIN, J.: Progress in cardiovascular diseases. **I,** 116 (1958).
KEYS, A.: Symposium III: Council on Foods and Nutrition, A.M.A. Chicago **77,** (1957).
MALMROS, H.: Acta med. scand. (Suppl.), **246,** 137 (1950).
MARKS, H.: Hum. Biol. **28,** 217 (1956).
MORRIS, J. N.: Lancet **1,** 687 (1956); Med. Offr **94,** 251 (1955).
MÜLLER, OTFRIED: Arterienverkalkung. Stuttgart: Strecker und Schröder 1909.
NORDMANN, O.: Chirurg **1930,** 913.
PAGE, I. H.: Chicago: Year Book Publishers 1946; weitere Lit. s. unter G. Schettler.
PIERACH, A.: Bad Nauheimer Fortbild.-Lehrg. **21,** 77 (1956); Klin. Wschr. **100,** 1527 (1958).
SCHETTLER, G.: Arteriosklerose. Stuttgart: Thieme 1961.
STEIN, E.: Der Herzinfarkt. Naegeli-Matis. Stuttgart: Schattauer Verlag 1960.
WILENS, S. L.: Arch. intern. Med. **79,** 129 (1947).

An appraisal of the exercise electrocardiogram test

R. GUBNER, M. D.

I. Applications, significance, and criticisms

Development of our knowledge of coronary heart disease during the past generation has occurred concurrently with, and indeed has been largely due to, the broadened application and understanding of electrocardiography. Beyond the clinical syndromes of myocardial infarction and angina pectoris, it is recognized that there is a vast substratum of asymptomatic coronary disease which is not readily detected by conventional diagnostic techniques. Even in patients with angina pectoris, the standard resting electrocardigram is normal in one-third to one-half the instances [*1, 2*]. Accordingly, various stress test have been developed to detect latent impairment of coronary flow reserve, i.e., coronary insufficiency. Of these, the best known, safest, most readily applicable and standardized is the Master double two-step exercise test [*3*].

Applications

The electrocardiographic response to exercise was employed as early as 1931 by WOOD and WOLFERTH [*4*] as a diagnostic aid in angina pectoris, and a similar study was carried out at about this time by GOLDHAMMER and SCHERF [*5*]. Since its introduction, the exercise test has been used clinically chiefly for objective verification of angina pectoris, although as pointed out below, it has many other applications. WOOD and WOLFERTH subjected 24 patients with angina pectoris to varying amounts of exercise and stopped exertion at the first suggestion of pain. Electrocardiograms were recorded before, several times during, and several times after the induced attacks of angina, as well as in an additional six cases with spontaneously occurring anginal attacks. Although changes in the ST segment and T waves were observed in 50% of their cases, even with only the three standard limb leads that were then employed, and although there were no untoward occurrences, WOOD and WOLFERTH stated that they were not prepared to recommend the procedure as a diagnostic aid. GOLDHAMMER and SCHERF noted transient changes in the electrocardiogram after exercise in 30 of 40 patients (75%) with angina pectoris they studied.

The standard two-step exercise electrocardiogram test to detect coronary insufficiency was first applied by MISSAL [*6*] in 1938. MISSAL adapted this procedure from the standardized two-step test of cardiac function of pulse and blood pressure responses, introduced by Master and OPPENHEIMER [7] in 1929. Subsequently, MASTER popularized the standard two-step electrocardiogram test, and since 1942 he, and others as well, have employed the double two-step test, in which the same rate of exercise is maintained for a three-minute, rather than a minute and a half, period, the amount of standard two-step ascents determined by age, weight, and sex. MASTER still employs the single two-step test initially, and if the response is negative, repeats the test as a double test after a period of rest. Most investigators who employ standardized exercise carry out the double two-step test directly.

Either because of unfamiliarity with the procedure, or because of reluctance to carry it out, the exercise electrocardiogram test is still not generally performed. Thus, in a survey of electrocardiographic practice in the United States conducted by the author [8], an analysis was made of electrocardiograms of 500 insurance applicants recorded by as many physicians throughout the United States, prior to and unrelated to application for insurance. In 99 of the 500 cases, electrocardiograms had been made because of a history of chest pain, but exercise tests for coronary insufficiency were performed on only 13 of the 99 patients complaining of chest pain.

It may be stated categorically that an exercise test should be carried out as a diagnostic aid on all persons complaining of chest pain whose resting electrocardiograms do not show evidence of myocardial disease, when patients are able to perform effort, except when acute or impending myocardial infarction is suspected. The scope of application of the electrocardiogram stress test extends far beyond its use in the differential diagnosis of chest pain. Since it the most sensitive clinically available technique for the recognition of impaired coronary flow, it should be applied in the diagnostic and prognostic investigation of all circumstances which are known to be attended by a heightened incidence of coronary heart disease. These include hypercholesteremia and all other serum lipid abnormalities, hypertension, and obesity. The rate of development of clinical coronary heart disease as a complication in persons with these conditions, as well as in persons with diabetes and those who exhibit arcus senilis, is three to five times as great as the incidence in the normal population [9]. Since coronary heart disease is a prime cause of death in men beyond the age of 40 and in postmenopausal women, it appears desirable to employ this procedure whenever cardiovascular surveys are conducted in these groups.

The electrocardiogram exercise test is being increasingly employed in underwriting evaluation of insurance applicants, not only persons with a history of chest pain but also persons who exhibit equivocal electrocardiographic abnormalities in standard resting tracings, in the circumstances enumerated above which predispose to coronary heart disease, and in the case of an applicant for a large amount of insurance, particularly one in an older age group. Thus, at The Equitable Life Assurance Society of the United States, of 1,246 cases in which electrocardiograms were specifically ordered as part of the examination of insurance applicants during the first six months of 1959, double two-step exercise tests were requested in 634, or slightly more than 50%. A total of 3,863 cases with one or more electrocardiograms were analyzed at the Home Office of the Equitable during this period.

The electrocardiogram exercise test has been applied also in surveys of military personnel and in periodic employee health examinations [*10—12*]. Other areas of application of the electrocardiogram exercise test have been in the appraisal of functional recovery after convalescence from an attack of acute myocardial infarction to determine exercise tolerance [*13*], and in the pharmacological evaluation of the efficacy of drugs in augmenting coronary circulation [*14*]. The test has been used also as a functional test in heart disease of types other than coronary heart disease [*15*].

Significance of an abnormal exercise test

Admittedly, the endorsement of such broad indications for the exercise electrocardiogram test must be predicated on evidence that abnormal responses are truly indicative of coronary heart disease and have prognostic significance. In their early report, Wood and Wolferth intimated on the basis of a very small number of follow-up fatalities, that electrocardiographic abnormalities in patients with angina pectoris developing after exercise were an unfavorable prognostic omen, but they stated that a much larger experience would be required to draw conclusions as to its significance. Such experience has been provided by the long-term follow-studies of Mattingly and Robb at the Walter Reed Army Hospital [*16*], more recently amplified by Mattingly [*17*], and by a similar study of Robb at the Metropolitan Life Insurance Company [*18*]. In both series, double standard two-step exercise tests were performed: in the Walter Reed study among military personnel suspected clinically to have coronary disease, and in the Metropolitan Life study among insurance applicants in whom the test was carried out because of large amounts of insurance applied for, or because of a history of chest pain and suspicion of coronary heart disease.

Mattingly's study, begun in 1942 and continuing through 1959, comprised 1,920 cases, with an average follow-up period of more than fiv years; a total of 186 deaths occurred among persons who had had exercise tests, and autopsies were performed on 78. Among the fatal cases, 61 patients had shown abnormal ischemic ST segment changes in their exercise tests, and in this group 87% died of coronary episodes within an average six-year interval. This contrasted with 62.5% coronary deaths among patients with equivocal exercise tests exhibiting the junctional type of ST segment depression, and 44% coronary deaths among those with negative exercise tests. In every instance with definitely abnormal exercise tests severe generalized coronary narrowing of the Grade 3 to Grade 4 type was found at necropsy. Among the entire group with positive exercise tests, including nonautopsied cases, 50% died within a 10-year period.

ROBB [19] has recently reported a study of 922 insurance applicants, with an average follow-up of three and one-half years. Among 160 persons exhibiting ischemic ST segment depression, 11 deaths occurred, 10 due to coronary artery occlusion. The death rate among those with positive—i.e., abnormal—tests, was eight times that of those with negative tests. Persons who had the equivocal junctional type of ST depression (168 cases) had a death rate only slightly higher than those whose tests were negative.

These strikingly adverse findings corroborate the earlier joint study of ROBB and MATTINGLY of 836 exercise tests performed in the period 1942 through 1951, followed up to 1952. In this investigation, coronary disease death rates per 1,000 years of observation were 49.2 for those with ischemic ST changes, 23.2 for those with junctional ST changes, 6.6 in the group showing T wave abnormalities after exercise, and 5.0 with negative exercise tests. Similar striking differences prevailed when an analysis was made of first coronary occlusion rates per 1,000 years of observation. Among ischemic ST reactors, the rate was 79.1, in the junctional ST group 35.2, among those with T wave changes 13.3, and among negative reactors 8.9. In a simultaneously reported study at the Metropolitan Life Insurance Company of 492 persons studied in the period 1949 through 1956 and followed to 1957, the dearth rate per 1,000 person-years of observation was 22.2 in the ischemic ST segment group, 9.7 in the junctional ST group, and 8.0 in those with negative exercise tests. All deaths in those with ischemic ST segments changes were due to coronary disease.

A follow-up study by FRANCO [11] at the Consolidated Edison Company of New York revealed that in apparently healthy persons with abnormal exercise electrocardiogram tests, myocardial damage or coronary thrombosis subsequently developed in 20%, contrasting with only a 3% rate of development of vascular complications in the same period among those with a negative test. Another study similar to that of FRANCO was reported recently by BRODY [12], of the Greenbrier Clinic; in it the prognostic value of double Master two-step exercise tests performed routinely in the course of annual physical examinations on 756 business executives who had no history or symptoms suggestive of coronary heart disease was in vestigated. The average follow-up period was slightly more than four years, with a minimum follow-up of three years. Among 280 patients (mean age 53) with positive tests, 32, or 11.4%, developed classic angina pectoris, coronary insufficiency, or definite myocardial infarction within the 3- to 10-year follow-up period. Of 23 patients (mean age 54) who showed decided ischemic ST segment changes, 6 subsequently developed myocardial infarction and 10 developed classic angina pectoris; thus a total of 69.5% developed overt coronary heart disease. Of 476 patients who had negative exercise test results (mean age 49), 20, or 4.2%, developed classic angina pectoris, coronary insufficiency or definite myocardial.infarction in the 3- to 10-year follow-up period.

There can be little doubt from these investigations that a definitely abnormal ST segment exercise response has very real significance; that it portends a greatly abbreviated life expectancy, and a vastly increased likelihood of future overt coronary heart disease and death from this cause. Among persons complaining of chest pain, there is fairly general agreement in the literature that an abnormal exercise test offers a valuable clinical objective indication of coronary insufficiency, and that abnormal responses occur in a majority of those with organic pectoris.

Criticisms of the exercise test

Despite the abundant evidence that the exercise electrocardiogram test provides the most sensitive clinically applicable method for the detection of coronary heart disease and that it has important prognostic value, it has not received unqualified acceptance. Thus, GARDBERG [20] states that only rarely is the exercise electrocardiogram of any value unless an anginal attack is induced by the exercise, and HORLICK [21] suggests that there is very little point in performing a MASTER double two-step test unless there is a reasonable suspicion of angina on clinical grounds. Such expressions of skepticism derive largely from the circumstance that the criteria for abnormality initially proposed and popularized by MASTER led to the erroneous diagnosis of coronary insufficiency, due to false positive responses, in many normal persons. This is the most cogent criticism, and one which remains despite many attempts to refine criteria distinguishing abnormal from normal exercise responses. This question is considered in further detail below.

Other objections have been voiced to the standard double two-step exercise test. One, which experience has dispelled, is that the test is hazardous. This criticism was voiced in the early report of WOOD and WOLFERTH, but time has proved this fear unfounded. There have been very rare instances where performance of the exercise test has been followed shortly by an episode of frank myocardial infarction. In the few cases which have been reported, it appears obvious that the test should not have been carried out, for the patients had premonitory signs of myocardial infarction and the resting electrocardiograms suggested myocardial involvement. In patients who have a recent onset of chest pain and in whom impending infarction is suspected, it is amplicit that stress is to be avoided. However, in those whose chest pain is stable or in those who have recovered from the acute stage of myocardial infarction, no untoward results have occurred in the many thousands of cases collectively studied by MATTINGLY and ROBB, MASTER, the author, and others. There is, accordingly, no basis to interdict the test, which imposes no greater stress than is involved in the performance of the routine activities of most persons. Obviously, exercise should be halted if, and as soon as, the patient develops pain or other undue symptoms, and even if the full quota of the test is not performed, ischemic electrocardiographic abnormalities as a rule precede the appearance of pain.

The criticism has been raised that a negative double two-step exercise test does not exclude severe coronary disease or even impending infarction [21], but this does not in any sense vitiate the utility of the test. The objective clinical diagnosis of coronary insufficiency is a difficult one, and the fact is that the double two-step exercise test provides the best available method for the clinical detection of coronary insufficiency, with positive results, in the experience of most investigators, in the majority of persons with angina pectoris; and the test serves further to disclose coronary insufficiency in many asymptomatic persons.

The claim has been made—contrary to the general experience—that the test was found positive in 96.8% of 250 consecutive patients with definite coronary disease, and that negative single double two-step exercise electrocardiograms "practically exclude coronary insufficiency" [*22*]. Employing newer criteria to eliminate false positive responses, MASTER and ROSENFELD [*23*] state that they have observed only one false negative response (and four false positives) in 163 males with coronary disease. Such a high degree of specificity exceeds the experience of others, but complete specificity is too much to hope for in any biological test. It is probably specious to draw too absolute a distinction between negative and positive test results, not only because of the difficulty in evaluating the considerable number of borderline responses in distinct positive or negative categories, but also because the presence or absence of coronary disease cannot be stated in absolutes, since, in fact, major degrees of coronary artery narrowing are present in fully two-thirds of men above the age of 50 years [*24*].

Some controversy has centered on the question of whether the exercise test should be standardized, as MASTER particularly has recommended, or whether, as advocated by SCHERF [*25*], the amount and type of exercise should be carried out individually according to the patient's tolerance. GARDBERG and ROSEN [*20*] have made the incisive statement that "the extremely bad practice of following the highly popularized criteria for the so-called 'standardized' exercise tests have caused a great many healthy people to be told that they have heart disease. Exercise cannot be standardized and the evaluation of *individual* electrocardiographic findings purely upon a statistical basis is open to serious question".

The careful long-term follow-up studies of MATTINGLY and ROBB, cited in detail above, using the double two-step test, refute the criticism of the validity of statistical evalution. While it must be acknowledged that there are many factors other than the foot-pounds of work in a unit of time which determine the manifestations of angina pectoris and electrocardiographic evidence of coronary insufficiency, this does not constitute a valid criticism of the electrocardiogram exercise test, any more than criticism levelled at similarly standardized loading tests in evaluating various organ functions, such as tests of liver, renal, or pulmonary function. In evaluating the individual patient with angina pectoris, it may be desirable to perform more or less exercise than is called for by the double two-step test or to introduce other variables, such as exercising after a meal or at cold temperatures to help elicit abnormalities. However, when stress electrocardiogram tests are individualized, it becomes difficult even in the same patient to evaluate changes in successive tests unless the identical procedures are followed.

Varying the amounts of exercise when tests are carried out in large groups, such as periodic health examinations, or insurance applicants, makes data assembled utterly meaningless. Not only is it imperative that the amount of exercise be standardized, but it is essential that the tests be performed under reasonably controlled circumstances (see discussion of technique on page 115). It is even more essential that serial tracings of particularly significant electrocardiographic leads be made at stated intervals after performance of the tests with identical location of precordial electrodes in the successive tracings. Only if such conditions of uniformity are observed can interpretation be made of tests carried out by different observers. Admittedly, such conditions may not be essential, or at times desirable, in the case of a particular patient seen in private practice, but in the investigation of groups, particularly when more than one person carries out the tests, as much uniformity as possible is essential.

II. Determinants of ischemic electrocardiographic abnormalities and chest pain

In a previous report [26] the applications, significance, and criticisms of the exercise electrocardiogram test in detecting coronary insufficiency were surveyed. The most direct method for demonstrating coronary artery disease, and one which has rapidly gained clinical status, particularly in context to potential surgical intervention such as endarterectomy, is contrast coronary arteriography using cineangiographic techniques. However, general clinical employment dictates a simpler method, for which the double two step exercise test serves quite adequately. Indeed, the electrocardiographic response to stress in many ways bears more closely on the problems of coronary insufficiency and angina pectoris than do morphologic changes in the coronary arteries, such as may be elegantly visualized by coronary arteriography. It is well recognized, that no necessary, or at times even close correlation obtains between organic changes in the coronary arteries and myocardial involvement or between these and electrocardiographic changes and anginal pain [27].

Nature of ischemic electrocardiographic abnormalities and chest pain

S-T segmental changes in the electrocardiogram after exercise, properly interpreted, are pathognomonic of myocardial ischemia, and are determined by the same factors responsible for chest pain, which is a frequent but not invariable concomitant of coronary insufficiency. Anatomically the portion of the heart muscle most vulnerable to ischemia is the subendocardial layer of the left ventricle including the papillary muscles, where the efficiency of coronary flow is lower than it is to the atria, right ventricle, and outer wall of the left ventricle. Intramural pressure in the left ventricle during systole, which is highest in the inner layer of the left ventricle, impedes coronary flow to the deeper layers of the left ventricle; but not to the outer left ventricular wall, right ventricle or atria, where intramural pressures are lower than coronary artery perfusing pressure.

Accordingly, during the systolic portion of the cardiac cycle—and this becomes more significant the more rapid the heart rate—blood flow to the inner left ventricle is relatively compromised, explaining the predilection of this area to ischemic myocardial involvement [*28*]. Particularly is this the situation when significant coronary artery narrowing exists, and the coronary artery perfusion pressure is accordingly lowered. Involvement of the subendocardial portion of the left ventricle is reflected in the electrocardiogram as depression of the S-T segment. Depression of the S-T segment is produced experimentally [*29, 30*] as well as clinically by injury to the subendocardial region of the left ventricle, and this is the locus of the predominant biochemical as well as morphological lesion in coronary insufficiency and angina pectoris [*31*].

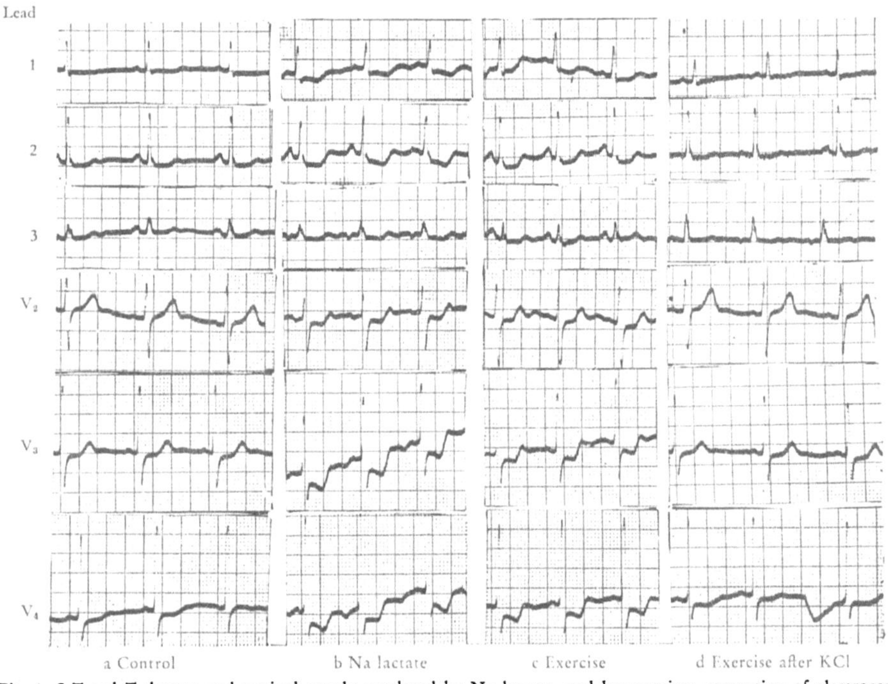

Fig. 1. S-T and T changes and anginal attacks produced by Na lactate, and by exercise; prevention of electrocardiographic changes and pain by pretreatment with potassium chloride before exercise: (a) control; (b) Na lactate produced marked S-T and T changes and severe anginal attack, requiring six 1/150 grain glyceryl trinitrate (nitroglycerin) pills over 20 minutes before pain abated; (c) exercise test (single Master test) produced marked S-T and T changes and anginal attack; and (d) exercise test after pretreatment with KCl (30 mEq in 500 cc. 5% G in W in 40 minutes) did not produce electrocardiographic changes or pain (woman, 52, severe angina pectoris)

Functionally (and the myocardial lesion of coronary insufficiency and angina pectoris is, except when severe and protracted, a reversible biochemical one rather than structural), the specific cause of the S-T depression abnormalities in the electrocardiogram, and also the determinant of anginal pain, is an acute potassium efflux from myocardial cells caused by ischemia. If this potassium shift is minimized by preloading patients with coronary insufficiency with an infusion of potassium chloride prior to performance of exercise, S-T segmental depression and development of pain both may be prevented, as illustrated in Fig. 1. Conversely, if exercise is carried out after depleting myocardial potassium by infusion of sodium lactate, S-T segment abnormalities and pain on performance of exercise are both greatly enhanced. Indeed, infusion of sodium lactate may be used as a substitute for the exercise test when exercise cannot be carried out, and rapid infusion of 120 cc of molar sodium lactate will frequently produce anginal attacks and S-T segmental changes identical with those produced by exercise (Fig. 2). Since the factor of anoxia is not involved in this procedure, and similar ischemia prevails if exercise is carried out with or without pretreating with potassium chloride or sodium lactate, oxygen lack cannot be the cause of electrocardiographic abnormalities and pain sui generis.

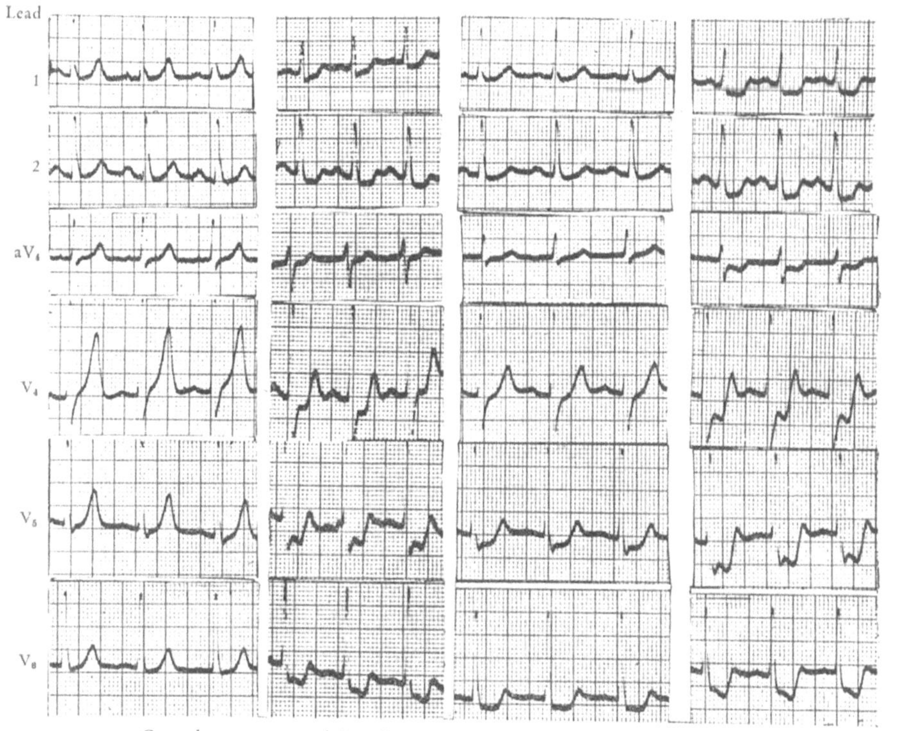

Fig. 2. Intensification of ischemic S-T changes produced by exercise by infusion of Na lactate prior to exercise: (a) control; (b) exercise (double 2-step) produced anginal pain and S-T abnormalities typical of acute coronary insufficiency; (c) Na lactate infusion produced S-T changes similar to those induced by exercise; (d) exercise performed after Na lactate infusion produced extreme S-T depressions, exceeding those resulting from exercise or Na lactate alone (man, 61, old posterior infarct, severe angina pectoris)

The "P", or pain substance postulated by Sir Thomas Lewis, appears to be not an organic metabolite such as lactic acid, as has commonly been assumed, but rather the potassium ion. Efflux of potassium from the myocardial cell, which is the immediate and prime biochemical change to follow anoxia [*34, 35*], leads to depletion of intracellular potassium [*36—38*]. Since the augmented extra cellular potassium is not promptly washed away owing to decreased coronary flow, the result is a greatly increased extracellular to intracellular potassium ratio. This is the physiological determinant of muscle contracture (treppe), i.e., sustained contraction, which occurs in heart muscle as well as in skeletal muscle [*39*].

In this sense then, spasm of the affected myocardium occurs, and there is a substantive basis for the concept of myocardial spasm as the cause of angina pectoris, an early view which has not been held in repute for over a hundred years. There are relatively few pain fibers in the myocardium directly, and a further factor contributing to the sensation of pain may be spasm of the coronary veins, since a large outpouring of potassium occurs into the coronary veins from the myocardium immediately after the onset of ischemia [*34, 35*]. When total coronary occlusion occurs, there is a very large piling up of extracellular and coronary venous potassium, due to tissue release and failure of flow to wash it away, and prolonged pain, which characterizes acute myocardial infarction, results. This large accumulation of extracellular potassium is an important factor in causing ventricular arrhythmias and sudden death in coronary occlusion [*35*]. Electrocardiographically, extracellular potassium accumulation is reflected in abnormally tall pointed T waves which may be seen as the very earliest electrocardiographic changes in acute coronary artery occlusion. An increased T wave amplitude is also commonly seen in tracings made immediately after exercise, at a time when increased potassium efflux, which is an accompaniment of increased work of the heart, has not yet been washed away by coronary flow. The effect of potassium in causing vascular spasm may be easily demonstrated by antecubital intravenous injection of potassium chloride at a flow rate exceeding 2 mEq per minute, which causes immediate spasm and pain along the subclavian vein.

Although the locus of electrocardiographic changes and pain appears to lie in myocardial electrolyte changes, the primary lesion of myocardial ischemia which produces these changes is, of course, a serious compromise in coronary artery flow. Here too, however, functional factors superimposed on the morphologic lesions of narrowed coronary arteries are at play. A mechanistic view is generally held that coronary insufficiency results when there is a disproportion between myocardial oxygen needs and coronary artery oxygen supply; and augmented cardiac work with effort which cannot be compensated by a commensurate increase in coronary flow is generally held responsible for coronary insufficiency and angina pectoris. While this is doubtless true, the factor of increased cardiac work alone does not explain all the provocative factors in angina pectoris [*40*]. Notably may be mentioned the almost immediate occurrence of pain in some persons with acceleration of the heart rate and, conversely, the abrupt abatement of pain when the heart rate is slowed by carotid sinus pressure during an anginal attack (Fig. 3).

When the velocity of blood flow is accelerated, as happens immediately with tachycardia, lateral pressure against the arterial wall is decreased according to the Bernoulli principle, and if a coronary vessel is narrowed its opposing sides may be brought into apposition by the phenomenon of flitter. The hydraulic studies of Rodbard [*41*] on flow through collapsible tubes may be cited to illustrate this effect. "The presence of a partial constriction in the tube introduces new characteristics which markedly affect the conditions of flow ... with stroboscopic illumination or high speed cinematography the smooth stream can be seen to be converted from an intact continuous column into a series of discreet drops ... The production of an area of narrowing of a rubber segment sets the stage for an increased velocity and a consequent fall in lateral pressure, in the narrowed region. With the fall in lateral pressure, the walls of the rubber segment tend to collapse and this creates the conditions for a higher velocity, a further drop in lateral pressure, and progressive closure. When the tube is almost completely collapsed by this process, flow ceases and the total head becomes available as lateral pressure. This force blows tube open, flow begins again, and the flitter cycle is repeated."

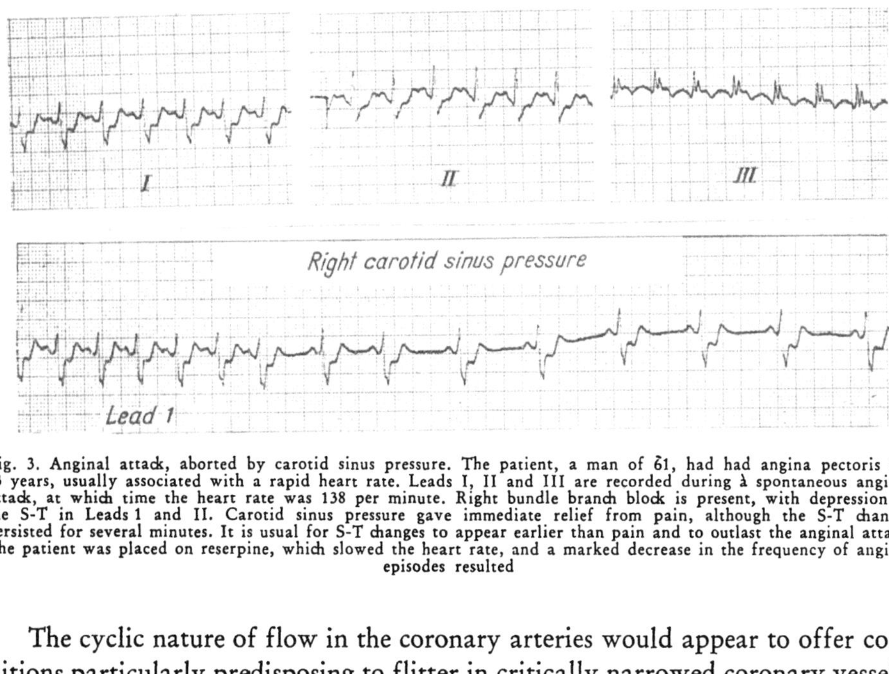

Fig. 3. Anginal attack, aborted by carotid sinus pressure. The patient, a man of 61, had had angina pectoris for 23 years, usually associated with a rapid heart rate. Leads I, II and III are recorded during a spontaneous anginal attack, at which time the heart rate was 138 per minute. Right bundle branch block is present, with depression of the S-T in Leads 1 and II. Carotid sinus pressure gave immediate relief from pain, although the S-T changes persisted for several minutes. It is usual for S-T changes to appear earlier than pain and to outlast the anginal attack. The patient was placed on reserpine, which slowed the heart rate, and a marked decrease in the frequency of anginal episodes resulted

The cyclic nature of flow in the coronary arteries would appear to offer conditions particularly predisposing to flitter in critically narrowed coronary vessels. Accordingly, transient complete obstruction of a partially obstructed coronary artery may result. The cause of this transient abstruction lies in the accelerated flow rate within the vessel, rather than an active vascular constriction, but the effect is similar to that which would be produced by active coronary artery "spasm", a long mooted and improbable occurrence, since under conditions of anoxia coronary vasodilatation rather than constriction occurs. Reducing the rate of flow by slowing the heart rate, or by enlarging the entire vascular bed with glyceryl trinitrate (nitroglycerin) ends the flitter effect, allowing return of coronary flow. Relief from angina pectoris which may follow induced hypothyroidism also may be attributed to a slowed velocity of blood flow eliminating flitter.

That coronary flow in a narrowed artery may actually be totally suspended during an anginal attack is illustrated in a case studied by Sones [*42*]. In this patient who had an attack of angina pectoris during coronary cineangiography transient complete shutdown of flow occurred through a diseased right coronary artery. The heart rate was considerably accelerated during the episode and a flitter phenomenon rather than active spasm may be presumed to have occurred. Patients with coronary artery disease extract more oxygen from their coronary circulation than do normal subjects, as reflected by more complete desaturation of coronary venous blood sampled from the coronary sinus [*43*]. A noteworthy exception, observed in two patients with angina pectoris who developed anginal attacks during effort studied by Gorlin [*43*], was that both failed to demonstrate a fall in coronary venous oxygen content at the time of their pain. This may be explained by the interpretation offered above that total coronary artery flow cut-off occurred in the diseased vessels during the anginal attack and consequently the coronary sinus was not receiving blood from the affected portion of the myocardium.

There are other determinants of angina pectoris and coronary insufficiency that a straightforward mechanistic view of cardiac work in relation to coronary flow does not explain. Notable is the effect of blood and insulin in potentiating or producing angina and ischemic electrocardiograph abnormalities. This may be attributed to a depletion of potassium from the heart [*44*] and serum produced by postprandial potassium movement and deposition in the liver. A common denominator of other factors which augment angina and electrocardiographic abnormalities also lies in their effect in depleting myocardial potassium, among them epinephrine, digitalis, and cold. Conversely, quinidine, which augments intramyocardial potassium [*45, 46*], has been reported to ameliorate angina pectoris [*47*].

The absence of pain in many persons with frank coronary insufficiency and even acute infarction, particularly in older persons, in women, and in persons with heart failure, finds an explanation in the considerably decreased myocardial potassium in women as compared with men [*48*], in older age groups [*48*] of both sexes, and in persons with heart failure. With the myocardium thus depleted of potassium, ischemia cannot provoke the acute marked potassium efflux which is the cause of pain, although the electrocardiographic abnormalities of ischemia are still evident in the form of S-T changes.

False positive exercise tests and criteria of abnormality

The above consideration of the determinants of S-T segmental changes in the electrocardiogram and angina pectoris are pertinent to a discussion of the exercise test, for they help to explain the close association between the S-T changes and angina pectoris, which the exercise test is primarily used to authenticate. Futhermore, the observations concerning the basic role of potassium bear importantly on the question of false positive tests, which are frequently invoked as a criticism of the test. Any circumstance which depletes the myocardium and particularly the inner wall of the left ventricle, of potassium, be it tachycardia, a meal, age, female sex, digitalis, anxiety with epinephrine release, hypertension, or myocardial disease, will tend to lower the S-T segment. The pattern of the S-T segment in the resting electrocardiogram shows characteristic differences in older persons, particularly in women in whom total body and myocardial potassium are most lowered, compared with the younger population. This may be recognized as a slightly depressed and relatively prolonged flat S-T segment, in contrast to the S-T in young persons, which is shorter and slopes upward into the T wave at a more obtuse angle (Fig. 4). When exercise is performed, these changes become

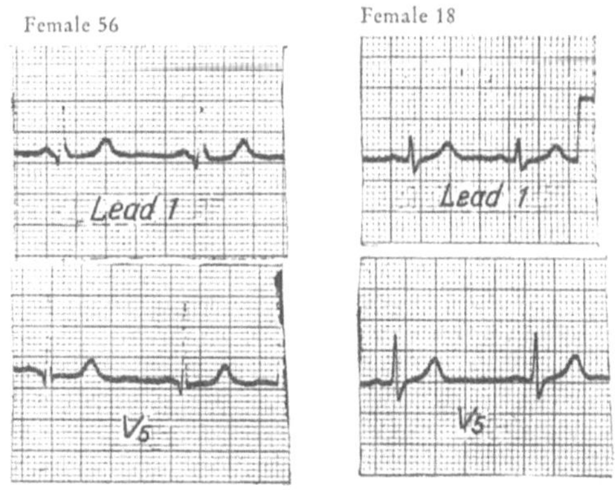

Fig. 4. "Older female" electrocardiogram. Leads I and V_5, are shown in a normal woman of 56, and a normal young woman of 18. Note that the S-T segment is flattened, prolonged, and very slightly depressed in the older female, whereas in the younger woman the S-T tends to take off above the isoelectric line, with a rising and shorter limb. This difference presumably is due to decreased total body and myocardial potassium in older persons, particularly women. Exercise tests in older women very frequently exhibit "false positive" responses. Similar patterns and abnormal S-T changes with exercise may be observed in hypertension

more evident and a "positive" test is more readily elicited. Consequently, one cannot hope for specificity in the exercise test, however refined the criteria employed, in older persons and particularly in women much above the age of 40. Since coronary disease is a problem only in postmenopausal women, the test is of limited value unless striking changes result. Another important area of false positive tests, first pointed out by the author many years ago [*49*], is in persons who hyperventilate, in those of asthenic build, and in those who are anxious and may exhibit tachycardia [*50*]. In such situations S-T changes may occur which are of functional rather than organic origin, but they may ordinarily be distinguished from those of ischemic nature by their upward slope, to which the term junctional S-T has been applied, in contrast to the flat or sagging S-T segmental changes of ischemic nature [*51*]. Such functional S-T changes tend to be maximal in the immediate postexercise tracing, whereas those of ischemic origin usually are maximal in the two- to three-minute postexercise electrocardiogram. Positive exercise tests are also frequently elicited in persons with hypertension [*52*], particularly those who have been on a salt-depleting regimen with thiazide diuretics causing potassium depletion. Digitalis likewise tends to favor a positive exercise test and it is of little value to carry out an exercise test in persons who have been receiving digitalis. Factors provoking "false positive" tests and features distinguishing such responses from true positive tests have been surveyed by LEPESCHKIN and SURAWICZ [53].

In general the more marked the S-T changes, the longer they persist (usually they are maximal in the two- to three-minute post-exercise period and tend to disappear by six minutes), the greater the number of leads exhibiting definite changes, the severer the degree of coronary insufficiency [54]. It ist pointless, and in fact undesirable, to take 12 lead electrocardiograms after exercise, since it is essential to take tracings periodically for many minutes following exercise, and Leads I and II, and precordial leads V_4, V_5 and V_6 usually exhibit the most striking changes (Fig. 5).

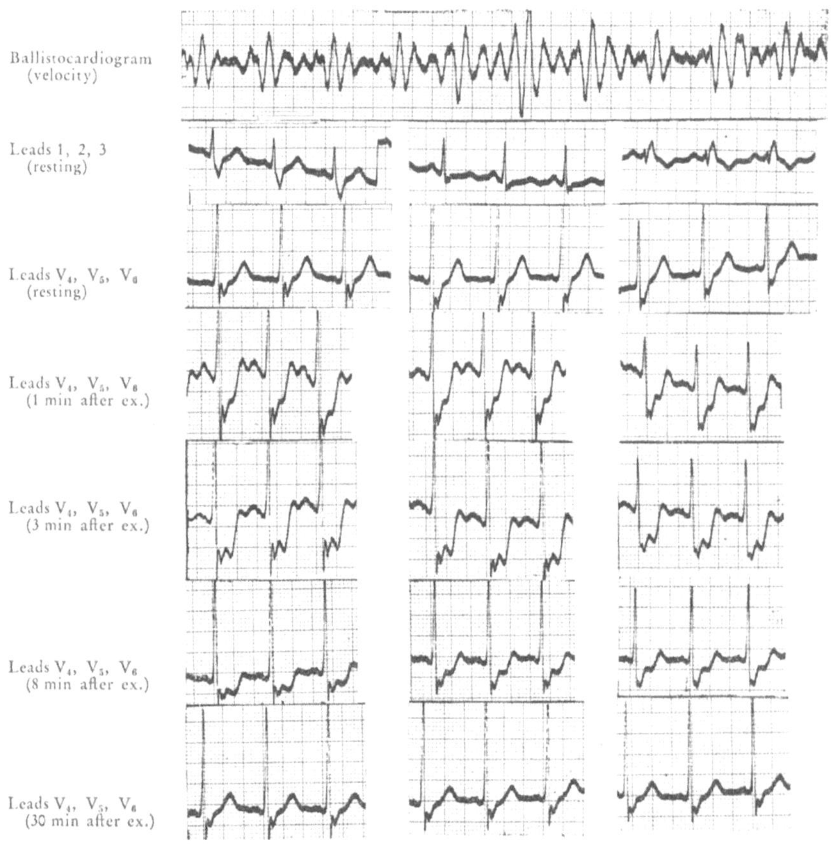

Fig. 5. Severe coronary insufficiency with marked S-T changes after exercise. The patient, a man of 57, had had chest pain on effort, and at times at rest, for five weeks. Resting tracing shows right bundle branch block. After 32 ascents chest pain developed and exercise was stopped. Chest leads V_4, V_5, and V_6 exhibit marked S-T abnormalities, which did not diseappear until a half-hour after exercise. The patient was hospitalized and given anticoagulants because of concern over an impending infarct. The further course was uneventful. Tracings after exercise reveal coronary insufficiency in the presence of right bundle branch block, but are not informative with left bundle branch block. The ballistocardiogram (shown in top strip) was normal in all respects, with minimal respiratory variation. It is apparent that in this patient with severe coronary insufficiency resting ballistocardiogram gave no clue to the presence of disease

A good correlation obtains between abnormal S-T changes in the electrocardiogram exercise test and direct demonstration of abnormal coronary flow dynamics studied by direct measurement of coronary flow and oxygen utilization in man [*43*], as well as by correlation with operative findings at coronary endarterectomy [*55*].

Robb and Marks have shown clearly that the type and degree of ischemic S-T segment depression (the only truly positive criterion) after exercise reflects the severity of the coronary disease [*54*]. It should be stressed that significant S-T segment depression reflects widespread myocardial ischemia. The development of major T wave inversions, runs of ectopic beats replacing normal rhythm, and transient bundle branch block are less specific changes but nevertheless suggestive of coronary insufficiency (Fig. 6).

The anatomic studies of Blumgart [*56, 57*] have shown that in patients with organic angina pectoris multiple coronary closures are usually found at autopsy

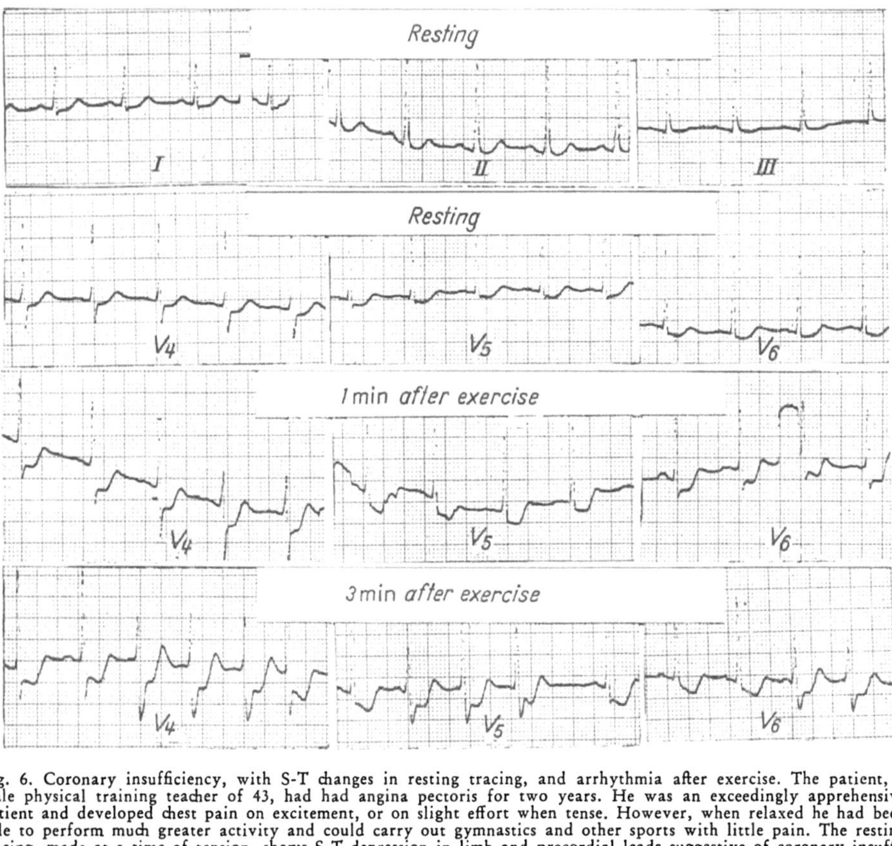

Fig. 6. Coronary insufficiency, with S-T changes in resting tracing, and arrhythmia after exercise. The patient, a male physical training teacher of 43, had had angina pectoris for two years. He was an exceedingly apprehensive patient and developed chest pain on excitement, or on slight effort when tense. However, when relaxed he had been able to perform much greater activity and could carry out gymnastics and other sports with little pain. The resting tracing, made at a time of tension, shows S-T depression in limb and precordial leads suggestive of coronary insufficiency. Tracing after double two-step exercise test shows marked increase in S-T segment abnormalities, and runs of supraventricular ectopic beats. Death occurred suddenly three weeks after this record. The presence of S-T changes in a resting tracing, marked increase in abnormalities with exercise, and increasing frequency of anginal attacks, all of which were present in this patient, are suggestive of impending infarction. Because of the history of peptic ulcer, anticoagulants were not employed. Similar fatal outcome in other patients observed by the author where anticoagulants were withheld because of a history of ulcer has suggested that prophylactic anticoagulants should be used despite such history

with diffuse myocardial involvement. It is not surprising therefore that after recovery from myocardial infarction normal exercise tests are often observed, for the ischemia in such instances be localized to a confluent area particularly in persons who have suffered their initial attack. However, it is useful to perform exercise tests in evaluating ability to resume physical activity after an attack of myocardial infarction [13]. If no electrocardiographic signs of ischemia or pain develop with exercise, early and relatively full return to activity may be encouraged. Conversely, if decided evidence of ischemia appears (Fig. 7) caution is necessary in allowing resumption of an active life. This is an application of the exercise test which deserves more widespread employment.

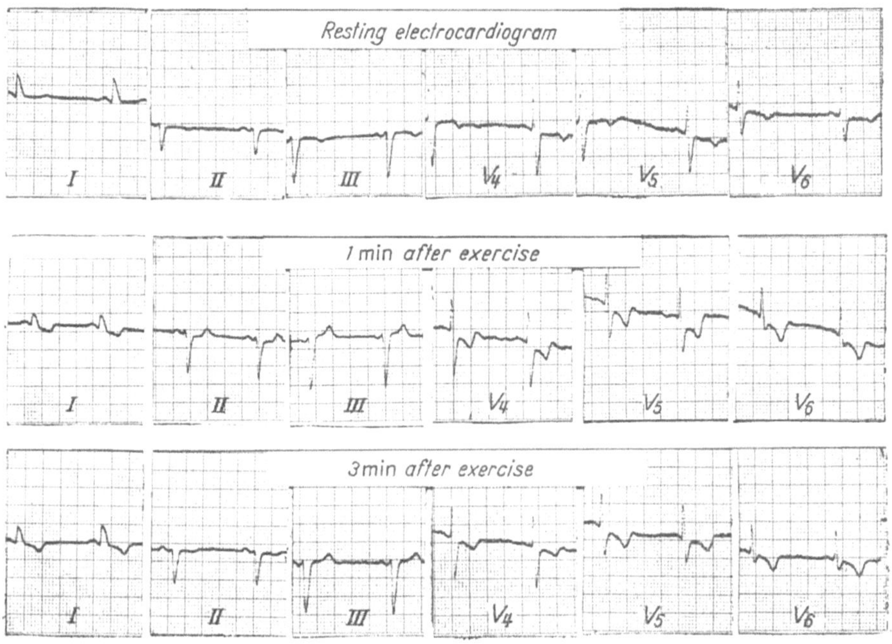

Fig. 7. Functional evaluation with exercise test after myocardial infarction. The patient, a male building superintendent of 64, had suffered an attack of acute posterior wall infarction two months previously, with an uneventful recovery. After 30 ascents transitory slight pain developed and exercise was stopped. Tracings made immediately and three minutes after exercise reveal marked S-T depression and T abnormalities in Leads I, V_4, V_5, and V_6; and the T waves initially inverted in Leads II and III became upright in the immediate postexercise tracing. Such changes indicate severe residual ischemia following recovery from acute infarction. The patient died suddenly one month later. When the exercise test is normal after convalescence from an acute attack of infarction, as is commonly the case, earlier and more complete return to full physical activity may be encouraged

Summary

The Master double two-step exercise test serves conveniently for the detection of coronary insufficiency, and for objective evaluation of chest pain, particularly since resting electrocardiograms are normal in approximately half of patients with angina pectoris. The test is useful also to detect latent coronary insufficiency in circumstances known to be attended by heightened incidence of coronary heart disease. These include hypercholesteremia and other serum lipid abnormalities, hypertension, obesity, diabetes, and arcus senilis. Since coronary heart disease is so widely prevalent and a prime cause of death, it appears desirable to employ the exercise test whenever cardiovascular surveys are conducted in adults, as in periodic health examinations. Another useful area of application is in the appraisal of functional recovery after convalescence from an attack of myocardial infarction.

A good correlation exists between abnormal S-T changes in the electrocardiogram exercise test and abnormal coronary flow dynamics studied by direct measurement of coronary flow and oxygen utilization in man. Postmortem studies on patients whose exercise tests had been abnormal regularly have shown severe generalized coronary artery narrowing. Death rates and subsequent attacks of myocardial infarction in those with positive tests are as high as 8 to 10 times that in persons with normal responses; hence abnormal findings have important prognostic significance.

The cause of S-T segmental depression in the electrocardiogram is not anoxia per se, but an abnormal potassium efflux from the myocardium provoked by ischemia. Electrocardiographic changes, and cardiac pain on performance of exercise, can be minimized or obviated by preloading patients with a potassium chloride infusion prior to the test. Conversely, depletion of myocardial potassium by prior intravenous infusion of sodium lactate greatly accentuates S-T abnormalities and pain on performance of exercise. The sodium lactate test may be employed as a substitute for the double two-step exercise test when exercise cannot be performed.

The dynamic factors responsible for cardiac pain in angina pectoris involve both myocardium and coronary arteries. In the myocardium potassium loss causes myocardial contracture and heightened potassium in the coronary veins causes venospasm. Heightened extracellular potassium, which is not washed away owing to impaird coronary flow, is responsible for protracted pain, arrhythmias, and sudden death in acute coronary artery occlusion. A dynamic factor in diseased coronary arteries contributing to the syndrome of angina pectoris is transitory total obstruction of coronary flow produced by a "flitter" effect, rather than coronary artery spasm. With an increased flow velocity, as occurs for example during tachycardia, lateral pressure is reduced and vessel walls are brought into apposition, transiently causing complete stoppage of flow. When the speed of flow is slowed by rest, carotid sinus pressure, or dilatation of the entire vascular bed by glyceryl trenitrate (nitroglycerin), "flitter" is terminated and flow is restored, with prompt abatement of pain as the accumulated potassium is washed away.

The factor of potassium loss from the myocardium bears importantly on the problem of false positive exercise tests. Where the myocardial potassium content is relatively low, as in older persons—particularly women—or persons with hypertension, myocardial disease, and heart failure, S-T changes are more readily induced by exercise. Similarly, food intakte, insulin, anxiety with epinephrine release, tachycardia, and digitalis all lower myocardial potassium and favor the appearance of S-T segment changes on performance of exercise.

In general, the more marked the S-T depression and the longer these changes persist, the severer the degree of coronary insufficiency. The development of other abnormalities, such as major T wave inversions, significant arrhythmias and transient bundle branch block, are suggestiv but less specific of coronary insufficiency than depression of the S-T segment. Leads I and II, and precordial leads V_4, V_5, and V_6 usually exhibit the most striking changes. These suffice for serial tracings which should be taken periodically for several minutes following exercise. Properly performed and interpreted, and with recognition of limitations as to specificity, the double two-step exercise test is a most useful clinical index of the functional adequacy of the coronary circulation.

References

[1] BURNETT, C. J.: Pain and pain equivalents in heart disease. Ann. intern. Med. **10**, 1156 (1937).

[2] MASTER, A. M., and I. ROSENFELD: The Master "2 step" electrocardiographic test brought up to date. Trans. Amer. Life Ins. med. Dir. **43**, 70 (1959).

[3] —, R. FRIEDMAN and S. DACK: The electrocardiogram after standard exercise as a functional test of the heart. Amer. Heart J. **24**, 777 (1942).

[4] WOOD, F. C., and C. C. WOLFERTH: Angina pectoris: The clinical and electrocardiographic phenomena of the attack and their comparison with the effects of experimental temporary coronary occlusion. Arch. intern. Med. **47**, 339 (1931).

[5] (a) SCHERF, D., und S. GOLDHAMMER: Zur Frühdiagnose der Angina pectoris mit Hilfe des Elektrokardiogramms. Z. klin. Med. **124**, 111 (1933).

(b) HAUSNER, E., und D. SCHERF: Über Angina pectoris-Probleme. Z. klin. Med. **126**, 166 (1933).

[6] MISSAL, M. E.: Exercise tests and the electrocardiograph in the study of Angina pectoris. Ann. inter. Med. **11**, 2018 (1938).

[7] MASTER, A. M., and E. T. OPPENHEIMER: Simple exercise tolerance test for circulatory efficiency with standard tables for normal individuals. Amer. J. med. Sci. **177**, 223 (1929).

[8] GUBNER, R. S., and H. E. UNGERLEIDER: Survey of electrocardiographic practice in the United States. Circulation **14**, 947 (1956).

[9] DAWBER, T. R., F. E. MORRE and G. V. MANN: Coronary heart disease in the Framingham study. Amer. J. publ. Hlth **47**, (Suppl.) April 1957.

[10] FEINBERG, G. L., M. SCHWARTZ and R. J. MANSFIELD: Screening program among key personnel in industry: Emphasis on routine Master two-step exercise test. N. Y. med. J. **56**, 3162 (1956).

[11] FRANCO, S. C.: Conference on heart in industry. Med. Sci. **6**, 468 (1959).

[12] BRODY, A. J.: Master two-step exercise test in clinically unselected patients. J. Amer. med. Ass. **171**, 1195 (1959).

[13] GUBNER, R. S., and H. E. UNGERLEIDER: Newer aspects of clinical electrocardiography. N. Y. med. J. **48**, 2491 (1948).

[14] RUSSEK, H. I.: The electrocardiographic Master exercise test in the evaluation of the drug therapy in Angina pectoris. Seminar on the electrocardiographic exercise test, Vermont Heart Association, Burlington, 20. Sept. 1959.

[15] HELLERSTEIN, H. K.: Significance of an abnormal exercise test. Seminar on the electrocardiographic exercise test, Vermont Heart Association, Burlington, 20. Sept. 1959.

[16] ROBB, G. P., H. H. MARKS and T. W. MATTINGLY: Value of double standard two-step exercise test in detection of coronary disease. Trans. Amer. Life Ins. med. Dir. **40**, 52 (1957).

[17] MATTINGLY, T. M.: Criteria and significance of a two-step exercise test as determined by clinical evaluation of patients on long time follow-up. Pathology studies of coronary arteries in patients dying after the test and studies in normals. Seminar on the electrocardiographic exercise test, Vermont Heart Association, Burlington, 20. Sept. 1959.

[18] ROBB, G. P., H. H. MARKS and T. W. MATTINGLY: Stress tests in the detection of coronary disease. Postgrad. Med. **24**, 4 (1958).

[19] ROBB, G. P.: Value of the electrocardiographic Master exercise test as determined from a follow-up of one-thousand consecutive tests in military personnel and in life insurance applicants. Seminar on the electrocardiographic exercise test, Vermont Heart Association, Burlington, 20. Sept. 1959.

[20] GARDBERG, M., and I. L. ROSEN: Electrocardiogram of the mont. Curr. med. Dig. Sept. 1959, p. 75.

[21] HORLICK, L.: A clinical re-evaluation of Master's two-step test. Canad. med. Ass. J. **80**, 9 (1959).

[22] (a) MASTER, A. M., L. E. FIELD and E. DONOSCO: Coronary artery disease and "two-step exercise test". N. Y. med. J. **57**, 1051 (1957).

(b) MASTER, A. M.: The "two-step" exercise electrocardiogram: Its use in heart disease, including valvular heart disease of adults. Bull. St. Francis Hosp. (Roslyn) **10**, 1 (1953).

[23] (a) MASTER, A. M., and I. ROSENFELD: The Master "2-step" electrocardiographic tests brought up to date. Trans. Amer. Life Ins. med. Dir. **43**, 70 (1959).

(b) ROSENFELD, I., E. DONOSO and A. M. MASTER: Interpretation of the Master "2-step" exercise electrocardiogram by quantitative analysis of RS-T segment. Proc. Soc. exp. Biol. (N. Y.) **103**, 320 (1960).

[24] WHITE, N. K., J. E. EDWARDS and T. J. DRY: The relationship of the degree of coronary atherosclerosis with age in man. Circulation **1**, 645 (1950).

[25] SCHERF, D., and A. T. SCHAFFER: Electrocardiographic exercise test. Amer. Heart J. **43**, 927 (1952).

[26] GUBNER, R. S.: An appraisal of the exercise electrocardiogram test. Part I: Applications, significance and criticisms. J. occup. Med. **2**, 57 (1960).

[27] —, and H. E. UNGERLEIDER: Long term prognosis and insurability in coronary heart disease. Amer. Heart J. **58**, 436 (1959).

[28] — — Electrocardiographic criteria of left ventricular hypertrophy: Factors determing the evolution of the electrocardiographic patterns in hypertrophy and bundle block branch. Arch. intern. Med. **72**, 196 (1943).

[29] WOLFERTH, C. C., S. BELLET, M. M. LIVEZY and F. D. MURPHY: Negative displacement; an experimental study. Amer. Heart J. **29**, 220 (1945).

[30] HELLERSTEIN, H. H., and L. N. KATZ: The electrical effects of injury at various myocardial locations. Amer. Heart J. **36**, 184 (1948).

[31] MASTER, A. M., R. S. GUBNER, S. DACK and H. L. JAFFE: Differentiation of acute coronary insufficiency with myocardial infarction from coronary occlusions. Arch. intern. Med. **67**, 647 (1941).

[32] GUBNER, R. S., and D. J. BEHR: Role of electrolytes in origin of ischemic cardiac pain and associated electrocardiographic abnormalities. Circulation **16**, 889 (1957).

[33] — — Effect of sodium lactate and potassium chloride on electrocardiogram and exercise tolerance in coronary disease. Clin. Res. Proc. **5**, 163 (1957).

[34] KREUZIGER, H., H. ASTEROTH und K. ZIPF: Kaliumveränderungen nach Herzinfarkt im Tierexperiment. Z. Kreisl.-Forsch. **43**, 385 (1954).

[35] HARRIS, A. S., A. BISTENI, R. A. RUSSELL, J. C. BRIGHAM and J. E. FIRESTONE: Excitatory factors in ventricular tachycardia resulting from myocardial ischemia — potassium a major excitant. Science **119**, 200 (1954).

[36] HERLES, F., and S. DAUM: Abnormalities of electrolyte distribution in the myocardium with myocardial infarcts and coronary changes in the electrocardiogram. Čas. Lék. čes. **96**, 1050 (1957).

[37] JENNINGS, R. B., J. R. CROUT and G. W. SMETTERS: Studies on distribution and localization of potassium in early myocardial ischemic injury. A.M.A. Arch. Path. **63**, 586 (1957).

[38] RUSSEL, R. A., J. CRAFOORD and A. S. HARRIS: Ventricular myocardial composition after experimental coronary occlusion. Fed. Proc. **17**, 138 (1958).
[39] HAJDU, S.: Mechanism of staircase and contracture in ventricular muscle. Amer. J. Physiol. **174**, 371 (1953).
[40] LEVINE, S. A.: Some notes concerning Angina pectoris. J. Amer. med. Ass. **171**, 1838 (1959).
[41] RODBARD, S., and H. SAIKI: Flow-through collapsible tubes. Amer. Heart J. **46**, 715 (1953).
[42] SONES, M.: Personal communication to the author.
[43] GORLIN, R., J. V. MESSER, H. J. LEVINE, W. A. NEILL and R. J. WAGMAN: Coronary circulation in health and disease. Med. Clin. N. Amer. **44**, 1181 (1960).
[44] LAVEQUE, P. E.: Atrial arrhythmias and myocardial potassium. Fed. Proc. **17**, 388 (1958).
[45] GERTLER, M. M.: Effect of digitoxin and quinidine on intracellular electrolytes of the rabbit heart. Proc. Soc. exp. Biol. **92**, 629 (1956).
[46] CONN JR., H. L., and J. C. WOOD: Acute effect of quinidine on potassium exchange and distribution in the dog ventricle. Amer. J. Physiol. **199**, 151 (1960).
[47] FREEDBERG, A. S., J. E. F. RISEMAN and E. D. SPIEGEL: Objective evidence of the efficiency of medicinal therapy in Angina pectoris. Amer. Heart J. **22**, 494 (1941).
[48] ANDERSON, E. C., and W. H. LAUGHAM: Average potassium content of the human body as a function of age. Science **130**, 713 (1959).
[49] UNGERLEIDER, H. E., T. F. DUHIGG and R. S. GUBNER: Examination of the heart in navy applicants. U. S. nav. med. Bull. **41**, 441 (1943).
[50] HOLMGREN, A., B. JONSSON, M. LEVANDER, H. LINDERHOLM, SJÖSTRAND and G. STRÖM: Electrocardiographic Changes in vasoregulatory asthenia and the effect of physical training. Acta med. scand. **165**, 259 (1959).
[51] WOOD, P., M. MCGREGOR, O. MAGIDSON and W. WHITTAKER: The effort test in Angina pectoris. Brit. Heart J. **12**, 363 (1950).
[52] MANTERO, O., E. LONGHINI et P. TOSSI: De l'importance diagnostique de l'épreuve de l'hypoxémie dans l'evaluation clinique de l'hypertrophie myocardique. Arch. Mal. Coeur **52**, 912 (1959).
[53] LEPESCHKIN, E., and B. SURAWICZ: Characteristics of true-positive and false-positive results of electrocardiograph Master two-step exercise test. New. Engl. J. Med. **258**, 511 (1958).
[54] ROBB, G. P., and H. H. MARKS: Evaluation of type and degree of change in post-exercise electrocardiogram in detecting coronary artery disease. Proc. Soc. exp. Biol. **103**, 450 (1960).
[55] KATTUS, A., W. P. LONGMIRE, J. A. CANNON, M. E. WINFIELD and J. H. DAVIS: Diagnostic and functional evaluation of candidates for coronary endarterectomy. A.M.A. Arch. intern. Med. **104**, 870 (1959).
[56] BLUMGART, H. L., M. J. SCHLESINGER and D. DAVIS: Studies on the relation of the clinical manifestations of Angina pectoris, coronary thrombosis, and myocardial infarction to the pathologic findings. Amer. Heart J. **19**, 1 (1940).
[57] ZOLL, P. M., S. WESSLER and H. L. BLUMGART: Angina pectoris: A clinical and pathologic correlation. Amer. J. Med. **11**, 351 (1951).

The prognostic implications of the electrocardiogram

HARRY E. UNGERLEIDER, M. D.

The electrocardiogram as applied in clinical practice is used primarily as a diagnostic instrument. Prognosis is a prediction of future events from present signs. In forecasting the probable future of the patient with heart disease the electrocardiogram provides us with objective signs which have remote as well as immediate diagnostic application.

Those, like myself, who are engaged in life insurance medicine are concerned principally with the problem of prognosis, in other words, the ultimate mortality experience of the various impairments to which the human mechanism is subject. In evaluating the outlook in cardiovascular diseases, the electrocardiogram has assumed a most important role. During the past twenty-nine years, we have accumulated electrocardiograms of over 35,000 persons in the diagnostic laboratory at the Equitable Life Assurance Society of the United States and for the past several years we have been reviewing about 6,000 electrocardiograms annually submitted on applicants for insurance policies. The availability of long range follow up has made it possible for us to carry out a number of studies on mortality experience with various cardiac abnormalities, and particularly electrocardiographic abnormalities, some of which are reviewed here. Basically, there are three categories which fall within our scope: coronary disease, hypertrophy and cardiac irregularities.

It should appear a simple matter to catalog a list of electrocardiographic abnormalities and study these individually for the mortality experience. In certain instances, we have in fact been able to do this as will be indicated. However, it is not possible to treat the entire range of electrocardiographic abnormalities in this fashion. Some years ago, one of the large insurance organizations [*1*] undertook a mortality rating of each electrocardiographic finding separately, but it rapidly became evident that this was not only impractical, but thoroughly fallacious. The reasons for this are manifold. First, many electrocardiographic abnormalities occur, not as isolated findings, but rather as patterns. As one example we may cite the pattern of right ventricular hypertrophy in which right axis deviation is associated with T wave changes in leads II and III, and in which one must also consider multiple precordial leads. Another cause of difficulty is that many findings are of no consequence individually, but are non-specific and must be related to the general clinical picture. Such is the case with low voltage of the QRS complex which may be due to a large variety of causes, some entirely extracardiac in origin. In addition, there is a lack of unanimity in the definition of what constitutes an abnormality, as for example, slurring and notching of the QRS complex. Other abnormalities are difficult to identify with precision, as we learned from personal experience in attempting to carry out a study on the Q-T interval. The variations in the Q-T interval reported by the same trained analyst in reading the same electrocardiograms on successive occasions proved so great as to vitiate a study of the significance of variations in this interval. These unrelated examples illustrate the difficulties in any comprehensive studies, and indicate the necessity of approaching electrocardiographic interpretation statistically, as well as in clinical medicine, from the individual aspect, keeping clinical correlations constantly in mind. It must be remembered that the electrocardiogram reflects only one segment of the clinical picture, and that prognosis is not determined by the electrocardiogram as such, but by the underlying disease.

Coronary artery disease

Although changes in the coronary arteries are not a necessary or an integral part of advancing years, they are, in fact, almost universal. In a study carried out on 320 applicants for insurance policies a few years ago, employing roentgenographic and electrocardiographic criteria, we found evidence of arteriosclerotic changes in half of the men between the ages of fifty-one and fifty-five years and in 75 per cent of those above fifty-five years of age [2]. This accords well with the extensive pathologic studies of WHITE, EDWARDS and DRY [3], who demonstrated the presence of a severe grade of coronary artery sclerosis in over two-thirds of subjects above the age of fifty years. Viewed in this light, isolated electrocardiographic abnormalities in people above the age of fifty years become almost fortuitous findings. The clinical incidents which may punctuate changes in coronary arteries, such as coronary occlusion, are but the surface visible strata which may portend danger at the time of occurrence. Yet, as the work of BLUMGART and co-workers [4] has shown, coronary occlusion often occurs unheralded by any clinical signs of illness. In either event, having once recovered from the acute and frequently critical phases of the attack, the future of the patient in respect to life expectancy and usually in relation to functional capacity as well, is not compromised by and dictated by the attack he has sustained but rather by further fortuitous changes in his coronary arteries. Within the past few years, two important studies [5] on life expectancy after attacks of coronary occlusion have been carried out in life insurance organizations. In both, the average life expectancy following the attack was approximately ten years. These cases are weighted adversely in comparison with the average case encountered in clinical practice, as data for these studies were drawn exclusively from disability experience; in other words, persons who were considered totally and permanently disabled three months following their attack. Certainly the outlook must be considerably more favorable when rapid functional recovery ensues, as is the situation in the vast majority of instances, and when patients are placed on a therapeutic regimen which may favorably influence their further course.

Acute phases of coronary disease

It is well to inquire specifically how the electrocardiogram does and does not bear on the outlook in coronary artery disease. This is best viewed by individually surveying the several clinical syndromes of coronary disease.

Impending myocardial infarction. This is a relatively unappreciated but nevertheless important syndrome. On careful inquiry, a surprisingly large number of persons sustaining coronary attacks will give a history of vague and indefinite pain in the chest for some days or weeks antedating the actual attack. More important are patients who actually present themselves for examination with this complaint. The pain is by no means regularly typically anginal in nature, and unfortunately the electrocardiogram is usually normal. Although one might anticipate *a priori* that in such instances a provocative exercise test for evidence of coronary insufficiency would be informative, in our experience this has proved sadly disappointing. This is a situation in which the electrocardiogram more commonly than not fails prognostically even in predicting an immediately imminent event. Recognizing this, we may not rely too heavily on the electrocardiogram when our clinical judgment leads us to suspect that a coronary attack is impending. I digress to remark that in my opinion the prophylactic use of anticoagulants in this situation is probably more useful than when an attack already has occurred.

Acute coronary occlusion. When an attack of coronary occlusion occurs the electrocardiogram is our prime diagnostic instrument, but it does much more. It helps us prognostically in appraising not only the location but also the extent and severity of the attack and its evolution. Although clinical judgment is paramount and we have many signs to go by, the electrocardiogram is a useful guide to immediate mortality at the time of the acute attack. Sometime ago, we carried out a study comparing electrocardiographic features in 100 patients with acute myocardial infarction without known antecedent heart disease of whom fifty survived and fifty died. There was a striking difference in the electrocardiographic patterns among the survivors as compared with those who died [6]. In brief, the majority of survivors exhibited an uncomplicated typical pattern either of anterior or posterior infarction; whereas among the group who died, forty-five of the fifty showed some complicating electrocardiographic abnormality in addition to the characteristics of anterior or posterior involvement.

Chief among these complicating features were the following: (1) evidence of combined anterior and posterior involvement; (2) presence of bundle branch block indicating septal involvement in addition to anterior or posterior infarction; (3) presence of Q waves across the entire precordium, indicative of extensive anterior infarction; (4) presence of a deep Q wave in lead I indicative of high anterior infarction in addition to the usual involvement of the apical area of the left ventricle; (5) marked deviations of the S-T segment beyond what is usually observed in acute anterior or posterior infarction; (6) progressive abnormality rather than improvement of the S-T segment; and (7) presence of major arrhythmias. Arrhythmias were found to be of graver consequence in anterior infarction. In posterior infarction they occur commonly and are often transitory.

Additional features observed more commonly in patients who died included tachycardia, very low voltage, progressive electrocardiographic changes other than the usual serial evolution, a predominantly upright QRS in lead aVR, electrical alternans, significant prolongation of the Q-T interval, very prominent P waves and abnormal depression of the P-R segment indicating auricular infarction. It is evident then that the electrocardiogram serves prognostic as well as diagnostic purposes in acute coronary occlusion. As has been observed repeatedly, there is no decided difference in outcome between infarction of the anterior and posterior wall.

Functional recovery in acute coronary occlusion. The electrocardiogram is serviceable prognostically in coronary occlusion not only at the time of the attack but also in evaluating recovery and ability to resume functional activity. For this purpose, the resting electrocardiogram is of no value, for it may be months before the typical serial changes in the electrocardiogram after an attack of acute infarction evolve to a stable pattern and it is unwarranted to keep the patient incapacitated while the changes are slowly evolving. We have applied the electrocardiographic response to exercise prognostically in assessing the degree of functional recovery following convalescence from acute myocardial infarction. If any considerable ischemia still remains, exercise will cause the reappearance of changes similar to those observed in the initial phases of the attack. However, if the patient has made a good functional recovery, the electrocardiogram will show no such marked changes following a moderate amount of effort. This seems a sensible procedure to employ in appraising the fitness to return to physical activity rather than to use arbitrary advice as is generally practiced. While it may appear that there is some element of risk in exposing a patient to exercise after recovery from a coronary attack, certainly it is much better to do this under supervision and actually observe what effects exercise has on the myocardium rather than allow him to undertake full activity without knowledge of its consequences.

Mild myocardial infarction. A distinctive syndrome which may be attended by a good immediate prognosis as well as a somewhat more favorable long term outlook comprises those patients, forming a not inconsiderable number, whose acute attacks are very mild. After an initial episode of pain in the chest which, although initially severe, may not be protracted, the clinical course may be entirely benign and laboratory data such as temperature, sedimentation rate and transaminase, may be inconclusive. Electrocardiograms are apt to exhibit only T wave changes which may not be major in degree or involve multiple leads, and such abnormalities as occur may regress completely within a few days or weeks. In a series of patients hospitalized with this pattern, presumably reflecting minor or focal infarction, the most common age group comprised persons in the late thirties and in the forties [7]. There were no deaths and functional recovery was uniformly good. However, the long term outlook cannot be considered benign, however minimal the acute attack. In one series of sixty-nine such patients [8] hospitalized with a slightly more severe pattern, but less than the classic attack of acute myocardial infarction, there were four deaths within the first month and three to four deaths annually over a five-year follow up. Forty-seven of sixty-five patients (72.3 per cent) survived for five years. The majority of deaths in the follow-up period were due to heart disease.

Ballistocardiogram in coronary occlusion. The ballistocardiogram is almost universally recorded with electrocardiographic apparatus, and has become a common adjunct in the examination of cardiac patients, particularly those with coronary disease. However, although the ballistocardiogram provides interesting physiologic information, in our experience, its actual clinical value has been limited.

Abnormal grades of ballistocardiograms occur so commonly beyond the age of forty-five to fifty years that very little diagnostic value can be attached to such abnormalities unless they be extreme. When there is any considerable tachycardia, the ballistocardiogram cannot be properly interpreted. Left ventricular activity, which is what interests us in coronary disease, is reflected only in the expiratory phase of respiration and if the ballistocardiogram is recorded with respiration suspended in inspiration the complexes almost invariably appear normal, for we are recording right rather than left ventricular activity. In patients with coronary occlusion, we have generally found the ballistocardiogram to be abnormal in older people after coronary attacks and we have generally found it to be substantially normal in younger people who have had coronary attacks [9]. This reflects the general age trend we observe in the population at large. The fact that the ballistocardiogram so frequently remains normal after coronary attacks in younger persons serves to indicate that in most instances attacks of myocardial infarction do not greatly decrease the force or power of the heart. This affirms our clinical recognition that physical activity and performance are not generally severely compromised by coronary attacks.

Chronic coronary disease

An even more important problem than the use of the electrocardiogram in prognosis of the acute phases of coronary artery disease is the evaluation of electrocardiographic abnormalities in chronic coronary disease which may be totally asymptomatic or may be attended by the symptoms of angina pectoris. In this situation, so common as we have already indicated in persons above the age of fifty years, the electrocardiogram usually provides the sole abnormality on examination. It is from the electrocardiogram that we must decide not only as to diagnosis but also the probable pattern of the patient's future (Table I).

Table I. *Mortality ratios (actual: expected) in coronary heart disease*[1]

	Mortality (%)
Coronary occlusion (myocardial infarct)-good functional recovery, with minimal residua	
Under 60 years of age at time of attack	
0 to two years	Over 500
2 to 5 years	500
5 to 10 years	300
More than 10 years	200
Over 60 years of age at time of attack, or questionable or minimal episode of infarction	
1 to 5 years	300
5 to 10 years	200
Pain in the chest	
Anginal type	
Onset within one-year period, or severe in degree producing functional limitation or requiring frequent use of nitroglycerin, major electrocardiographic abnormality	500
Evidence of coronary insufficiency in exercise test	
Under 60 years of age	500
Over 60 years of age	300
No evidence of coronary insufficiency on double two-step exercise test	200 to 300
Atypical pain in the chest	
Not having anginal characteristics; results of electrocardiographic exercise test negative	100 to 200
Asymptomatic coronary disease (electrocardiographic abnormalities)	
Pattern of old infarction without history (Q wave abnormalities, etc.)	
Under 60 years of age	500
Over 60 years of age	300
Major T wave abnormalities	
Under 60 years of age	300 to 500
Over 60 years of age	200 to 300
Abnormal double two-step exercise test	
Ischemic S-T segment changes	
Under 60 years of age	300
Over 60 years of age	200
Junctional S-T segment or atypical changes	150 to 200
Minor T wave abnormalities	100 to 200
Bundle branch block	
Incomplete right, or other conduction anomaly	150 to 200
Complete right or left bundle branch block	200

[1] The term mortality ratio (ratio of actual: expected deaths) is infrequently used in clinical parlance, but serves the useful purpose of expressing the prognostic significance of a particular disorder in relation to another population, the standard of similar age and sex. This population may be insured persons charged the standard rate of premium, or the general population of a specified area and time. A mortality ratio of 100 per cent indicates that within a fixed period of time the proportion of deaths among those with the disorder in question is equal to the proportion expected to die according to the rates of mortality of the standard population. A mortality ratio of 150 per cent indicates that one and a half times the proportion of deaths expected in the standard population have occurred among those with the specified disorder. Insurability is generally limited to persons whose impairments are such that it is anticipated that they will not experience an long term mortality ratio exceeding 500 per cent, that is, will not exceed five times as many deaths as would occur in a similar group of standard lives.

Asymptomatic coronary disease: Some data on survival in asymptomatic coronary disease have been gathered from mortality studies in patients with isolated electrocardiographic abnormalities presumably due to coronary disease, such as bundle branch block and T wave changes. In right or left bundle branch block as an isolated impairment, mortality was found to be surprisingly low, not greatly exeeding the expected mortality in a study at the Equitable Life Assurance Society of the United States. Experience with major T wave abnormalities is somewhat less favorable, as indicated by a long term follow up among employees at the Prudential Life Insurance Company [*5*]. Among a small number of persons with major T wave abnormalities the mortality ratio was approximately three and a half times that of a control group. A larger experience among persons with isolated minor T wave abnormalities (such as low amplitude in leads I, II, and left precordial leads) revealed a mortality twice that of the control group.

Prognostic value of exercise test. An important prognostic, as well as diagnostic, aid in coronary disease is provided by the double two-step exercise test properly performed and interpreted. A follow-up study of 836 military personnel and 379 applicants for insurance policies in whom this test was carried out because of suspicion of coronary disease has been reported by Robb, Marks and Mattingly [*5 b*]. In both groups the death rate in those who exhibited ischemic electrocardiographic changes after exercise was almost three times greater than in those whose test had given negative results, and there were more than six times as many deaths subsequently from acute coronary occlusion in those whose test had given an abnormal result. Persons with pain in the chest whose exercise tests gave negative results had virtually the same mortality experience as that for adult men of comparable age in the general population. Similar observations have been reported in studies employing the anoxemia test, in which there was a six- to seven-year follow up, although in another study more reserved conclusions were drawn concerning the prognostic value of this test.

Prognostic significance of Bundle Branch Block. Several studies have been carried out on certain electrocardiographic abnormalities associated with chronic coronary disease, namely, bundle branch block and the Q wave in lead III. Some preliminary studies also have been carried out on the prognostic significance of other isolated findings such as T wave abnormalities.

Abnormalities in the ventricular complex are of several types. Widening of the QRS beyond 0.10 second is a definitely abnormal finding except in the precordial leads in which the QRS duration may normally attain 0.11 second. A more advanced expression of this abnormality is bundle branch block in which the width of the QRS exceeds 0.12 second, but within the past few years it has been recognized that not all types of bundle branch block carry an equally poor prognosis. A not uncommon type of atypical bundle block is encountered in which the widening is in the S wave, the so-called S_1 type of bundle branch block. This is indicative of organic heart disease, but apparently does not signify as extensive myocardial disease as the typical pattern of bundle branch block usually associated with considerable cardiac enlargement and diffuse myocardial disease. Another type of widened QRS pattern exists, which is presumably due to aberrant conduction from auricle to ventricle, the Wolff-Parkinson-White syndrome or bundle branch block associated with short P-R interval. Patients with this anomaly are subject to attacks of paroxysmal ventricular tachycardia, but are otherwise normal and do not have organic heart disease. Nevertheless, we have observed several patients with a short P-R interval and widened QRS (confirming to the Wolff-Parkinson-White pattern) in whom definite hypertensive heart disease existed, and we are therefore reluctant to dismiss this abnormality lightly. Admittedly, it is a rare finding.

Some time ago we reported a study on the mortality of bundle branch block, comprising an analysis of 193 persons studied in the diagnostic laboratory of the Equitable Life Assurance Society [*10*]. The type of bundle branch block was classified as right in 131 patients, left in fifty-two, atypical in five and of the WPW type in five. It is of interest that the incidence of right bundle branch block is more common than that of left bundle branch block in the general population, particularly in younger age groups. The most significant finding in our study was the unexpected observation that bundle branch block in the absence of other cardiovascular abnormalities is not attended by a high mortality rate. In the past, bundle branch block has been regarded as of ominous portent, but our own study indicates that this is far from the truth and indeed we have now opened the possibility of insurance to such patients, properly selected.

Prognostic significance of a deep Q_3 wave: A most important problem in regard to the QRS is the ever recurring question of the Q_3 wave. Although numerous studies have confirmed the pathologic significance of the Q wave in lead III as first described by Pardee, this sign still remains a subject of inquiry and some uncertainty. Occuring preponderantly in patients with organic heart disease, particularly coronary artery disease, Q waves conforming to PARDEE's criteria of abnormality are seen also in certain normal persons, particularly in those whose heart lies transversely. In order to distinguish normal from pathologic Q waves in lead III, various modifications of PARDEE's criteria have been recommended. Unipolar extremity leads, simultaneous registration of multiple limb leads and esophageal leads have been employed for this purpose.

Other problems complicate the interpretation of the Q wave in lead III. Among these are its anatomic basis, the significance of Q_3 waves when marked respiratory variation occurs, the significance of the small Q_3 wave not fully meeting PARDEE's criterion of equaling or exceeding 25 per cent of the greatest amplitude of the tallest QRS in the limb leads, the propriety of accepting as an abnormal Q_3 complexes preceded in some beats by a small initial upward deflection, and the significance of the QS pattern in lead III and its relation to the Q_3 wave.

Recently we carried out an investigation in an attempt to resolve some of these questions by reviewing a large source of material which appeared uniquely suitable for such an analysis [*11*]. A total of 1,355 patients were studied in all of whom the records of history, physical examination and teleoroentgenogram were reviewed in addition to the electrocardiogram. A limited mortality study suggests strongly that the Q_3 wave deflection is a significant abnormality which should not be dismissed simply because of associated overweight and transverse position of the heart. Fifteen of seventeen patients with no cardiovascular abnormalities other than the abnormal Q_3 wave deflection succumbed to coronary disease with an average survival period for the entire seventeen patients of 5.7 years.

Significance of S-T and T abnormalities: As already indicated, abnormalities of the S-T segment and T wave can be due to a great diversity of causes which do not necessarily signify organic heart disease. It is beyond the scope of this paper to consider these individually. However, in our opinion, the generally accepted abnormalities of this complex should be regarded as indicating organic myocardial involvement unless there is adequate proof to the contrary. A frequent problem is the differentiation of positional effects on the S-T segment and T wave from organic changes, e.g., asthenic persons who in the erect position may demonstrate low T waves in lead I and inverted T in leads II and III, and also inversion of the T wave in lead aVL and some precordial leads. The fact that abnormalities of the T wave can be made to disappear with position or vary with respiration should give us cause to dismiss such findings; even though from time to time all of us see bizarre cases with inversions of the T wave in any lead which we cannot explain or correlate with organic disease.

Adequate data on the ultimate prognosis, i.e., life expectancy with persons of various T wave abnormalities, are not available. For such studies to be carried out, a breakdown into a great number of groups becomes necessary involving consideration of the type of T wave abnormalities, the leads in which they occur, the age and body build, and the presence or absence of associated abnormalities. These necessarily dilute sampling so that ultimate mortality experience in adequate numbers becomes difficult to obtain. Some indication that T wave abnormalities, even when not marked, are significant is provided from a study conducted among employees of the Prudential Insurance Company [*5*]. So minor a change as notching of the T wave was considered in this study to be indicative of a life expectancy category not much better than those of patients who had recovered from an acute myocardial infarction. Excluding notching of the T waves in the transitional zones of leads V_2 and V_3 it was found that more than three-quarters of the persons with definite notching of the T wave above the age of forty years had evidence of cardiovascular disease, and there were several fatalities in a limited follow up averaging slightly over four years in this group.

Another borderline finding, i.e., low T waves in leads V_5 and V_6 was similarly found to have an unfavorable outlook. Again, three-quarters of the persons with this abnormality had evidence of organic heart disease, which was two and a half times higher than the incidence of cardiovascular abnormalities among a control group with normal electrocardiograms. In this group, too, there were several fatalities in a follow-up period of four years whereas none occurred among the control group. A third borderline abnormality, inversion of the T wave in lead aVL, provided almost identical adverse experience in persons above the age of forty years. When the inverted T wave in lead aVL was associated with an upright QRS complex greater than 5 mm., not only was the evidence of organic heart disease much greater in this group than in the control subjects, but the fatalities in an average three-year follow-up period were also significantly higher.

In view of the unfavorable aspect of these borderline types of T wave abnormalities, it is evident that one must regard greater degrees of T wave abnormalities, such as inversion in leads I and II, and in the precordial leads, with greater concern. It is fair to regard persons with such abnormalities who are above the age of forty years in the same category as those who have recovered from myocardial infarction. Both have coronary artery disease and the future of such patients depends on the further progression of changes in their coronary arteries.

The mortality rate from coronary artery disease may be assessed from Table I.

Cardiac arrhythmias

Some arrhythmias of themselves carry an evidently poor prognostic import since they are of themselves hazardous. Others are important in that they provide a clue to the presence of organic heart disease and in such circumstances the prognosis must be appraised from whatever associated condition is present. In the first category are ventricular fibrillation and tachycardia, heart block, and under certain circumstances, auricular flutter and fibrillation. In the second category the most common arrhythmia is extrasystoles.

Extrasystoles. Some years ago we carried out an analysis of 1,142 applicants for insurance policies with extrasystoles or premature contractions [*12*]. In 58 per cent of the applicants with extrasystoles or premature contractions, no objective evidence of heart disease was found. In addition to physical examination and the electrocardiogram, fluoroscopic study or a teleoroentgenogram of the heart was made in most patients. Brachial pulse sphygmograms synchronous with the electrocardiogram were also recorded in a large number.

Analysis of this large series indicates that ventricular extrasystoles occur with considerably greater frequency than supraventricular premature contractions, and that in the presence of heart disease there is still greater preponderance of ventricular premature contractions. Several factors were found to increase the significance of premature beats. Among these are (1) occurrence of premature beats of multifocal origin; (2) frequent and persistent premature beats, particularly if they occur successively in short runs interrupting the regular rhythm; (3) a definite increase in the number or a "shower" of extrasystoles immediately following exercise; (4) occurrence of premature contractions in the presence of a rapid heart rate, i.e., over 90 per minute; (5) inversion of the T wave in the next regular beat which follows the extrasystole; and (6) postextrasystolic pulsus alternans. Any of these findings strongly suggest that extrasystoles are caused by organic heart disease.

A study carried out at the Prudential Life Insurance Company which comprised 476 patients with unifocal ventricular extrasystoles, 237 with unifocal supraventricular premature beats and eighty with multifocal premature beats, led to the conclusion that persons above the age of forty years with extrasystoles should be viewed conservatively from a prognostic viewpoint. In this study it was found that 71 per cent of those above the age of forty years with extrasystoles had other indications of organic heart disease whereas in a comparable age group without ectopic beats only 32 per cent had evidence of cardiovascular abnormalities. There was a high incidence of cardiovascular deaths in an average follow up to 5.1 years, totaling 29 per cent of 372 patients with extrasystoles and other cardiovascular abnormalities, compared to a mortality rate of 2 per cent in a control group of comparable age. When multifocal extrasystoles were present, the mortality experience was also highly unfavorable. It was concluded on the basis of this study that the present of extrasystoles, especially in older age groups, dictates a careful cardiovascular study.

Sinus arrhythmias and prolonged P-R interval: A surprisingly high incidence of heart disease was also found in older persons with marked sinus arrhythmia and in both young and older persons who exhibited a wide P wave exceeding 0.11 second or abnormally high P waves, and also in persons with a prolonged P-R interval. It is evident that arrhythmias, which may be of themselves innocent, nevertheless often reflect the presence of organic heart disease. Particularly in older people one cannot, in view of this experience, dismiss cardiac irregularities lightly.

Cardiac hypertrophy

Electrocardiographic criteria for left ventricular hypertrophy. It is not generally appreciated that the electrocardiogram is more sensitive than roentgenologic methods in detecting left ventricular hypertrophy. The electrocardiographic pattern of left ventricular hypertrophy or strain has long been recognized, but specific criteria indicating the point of departure from normal were not established prior to the analysis of 940 patients carried out in our laboratory. On the basis of this study, left ventricular hypertrophy may be considered to be present when left axis deviation occurs in association with any of the following changes: (1) increase in amplitude of the QRS complex, best expressed by the sum of R_1 and S_3. Hypertrophy is present if this sum exceeds 2.5 mv. and is probably present if it is over 2.2 mv. The increase in voltage is the earliest electrocardiographic change in hypertrophy. Subsequent to our study, electrocardiographic criteria for left ventricular hypertrophy have been elaborated by SOKOLOW and LYON using QRS amplitude in unipolar extremity and precordial leads. These are somewhat more sensitive than the limb lead criteria of voltage, but less specific and sometimes are falsely positive. (2) Any perceptible depression of the S-T segment in lead I, even of as slight degree as 0.5 mm. (3) Lowering of T_1 below 1 mm. or further degree of abnormality of T_1.

The changes in the S-T segment and the T wave may develop in the absence of left axis deviation, and left axis deviation is not an invariable or necessarily integral part of the electrocardiographic pattern of left ventricular hypertrophy. The usual occurrence of left axis deviation with left ventricular hypertrophy in hypertension is due largely to predominant obesity with transverse position of the heart, which in itself causes left axis deviation. In slender subjects with left ventricular hypertrophy left axis deviation is not so frequently observed.

Electrocardiographic signs of left ventricular hypertrophy in hypertension. Employing our criteria we found that evidence of left ventricular hypertrophy in the electrocardiogram was present considerably more often than roentgenologic changes in 100 subjects with advanced hypertensive disease [*13*]. Electrocardiographic and roentgenologic changes do not necessarily parallel one another. While electrocardiographic abnormalities occur relatively more frequently than roentgenologic changes, there also may be definite evidence of left ventricular enlargement in the roentgenogram while the electrocardiogram is normal. This is particularly the case when concurrent right ventricular enlargement is present, the opposite electrical effects of those chambers balancing one another. In analysis of 100 patients with advanced hypertensive disease, it was found that combined roentgenographic and electrocardiographic study revealed hypertrophy or arteriosclerotic changes in 90 per cent. The advantage of employing both procedures, therefore, is evident.

Electrocardiographic signs of left ventricular hypertrophy and prognosis. The electrocardiographic patterns of left ventricular hypertrophy are of considerable prognostic importance. A few years ago we carried out a mortality study in an effort to determine whether electrocardiographic criteria for the detection of left ventricular hypertrophy and arteriosclerotic changes would allow classification of subjects with elevated deviations from normal blood pressure into distinct groups, regardless of actual blood pressure levels, and thus provide an index of the duration and stage of the hypertensive disease. This study was carried out with reference to the electrocardiographic findings and without consideration of the teleoroentgenogram, although the latter would have contributed much to the investigation.

The material for the study comprised 424 applicants for insurance policies who were examined in the diagnostic laboratory of the Equitable home office. In practically all applicants, the primary impairment which led to examination in the diagnostic laboratory was hypertension, but not of sufficient degree to cause declination as a single factor. Higher readings which, in themselves, would have dictated declination without further study were found, however, in a number of cases at the time of home office examination.

The electrocardiograms of those 424 subjects with hypertension were divided into four groups: (1) normal electrocardiogram; (2) borderline electrocardiogram; (3) pattern of left ventricular hypertrophy; and (4) evidence of myocardial disease with or without left ventricular hypertrophy. The data were tested for homogeneity as to age, build and blood pressure. They were found to be homogenous with regard to age and build, and reasonably homogenous with regard to blood pressure. The average blood pressure reading was 160/100 mm. Hg.

In view of the relative homogeneity of the factors of age, build and blood pressure, the increase in mortality from 186 per cent in those with normal electrocardiograms to 344 per cent in those with the pattern of hypertrophy must be considered as correlated with the conditions which caused the electrocardiographic changes which formed the criteria for the study. It is evident that in patients with hypertension who present the pattern of left ventricular hypertrophy, as defined by the criteria established in this study, the mortality becomes quite excessive and high extra premiums for insurance policies are necessary. Even the group with normal electrocardiograms has a mortality of 186 per cent, but these people are insurable with a relatively low extra premium. The conclusion appears warranted that the evaluation of the duration of hypertension based on the electrocardiogram is a valuable and important consideration in the prognosis and insurability of patients with hypertension.

The findings abundantly justify the employment of more detailed study in the presence of hypertension. Since the electrocardiogram was normal in only 44 per cent of 424 applicants with hypertension, it would appear worthwhile to record electrocardiograms routinely whenever the blood pressure is over 140 mm. Hg systolic and 90 mm. Hg diastolic.

Summary

The electrocardiogram has definite value prognostically as well as diagnostically in its major spheres of application, coronary disease, cardiac hypertrophy and the arrhythmias.

This paper reviews the prognostic significance and the effect on mortality statistics of these types of heart disease.

References

[1] Bonnet, E. C.: Notes on one method of underwriting electrocardiogram. Proc. Life Ins. M. Dir. **26**, 120 (1940).

[2] Ungerleider, H. E., and R. Gubner: Blood lipids and human arteriosclerosis. J. Mich. med. Soc. **1**, 1360 (1938).

[3] WHITE, N. K., J. E. EDWARDS and T. J. DRY: Relationship of the degree of coronary arteriosclerosis with age, in men. Circulation 1, 645 (1950).
[4] (a) BLUMGART, H. L., M. J. SCHLESINGER and D. DAVIS: Studies on relation of clinical manifestations of angina pectoris, coronary thrombosis and myocardial infarction to pathologic findings, with particular reference to collateral circulation. Amer. Heart J. 19, 1 (1940).
(b) BLUMGART, H. L., M. J. SCHLESINGER and P. M. ZOLL: Angina pectoris, coronary failure and acute myocardial infarction. J. Amer. Med. Ass. 116, 91 (1941).
[5] (a) KEESLING, C. E., R. S. SCHAAF and A. M. LYLE: Mortality studies of isolated electrocardiographic T wave changes. Proc. Life Ins. M. Dir. 39, 5 (1955).
(b) ROBB, G. P., H. H. MARKS and T. W. MATTINGLY: Detection of coronary artery disease. Proc. Life Ins. M. Dir. 40, 52 (1956).
[6] Unpublished data.
[7] Unpublished data.
[8] Unpublished data.
[9] GUBNER, R., M. RODSTEIN and H. E. UNGERLEIDER: Ballistocardiography. Circulation 7, 268 (1953).
[10] RODSTEIN, M., R. GUBNER, J. P. MILLS, J. F. LOVELL and H. E. UNGERLEIDER: A mortality study in bundle branch block. Arch. Int. Med. 87, 663 (1951).
[11] UNGERLEIDER, H. E., and R. GUBNER: The Q_3 and QS_3 deflection in the electrocardiogram. Arch. Intern. Med. 72, 196 (1943).
[12] UNGERLEIDER, H. E., and R. GUBNER: Extrasystoles and the mechanism of palpitation. Trans. Amer. Therap. Soc. 42, 169 (1942).
[13] GUBNER, R. S., and H. E. UNGERLEIDER: Electrocardiographic criteria of left ventricular hypertrophy. The factors determining the evolution of the electrocardiographic patterns in hypertrophy and bundle branch block. Arch. Intern. Med. 72, 196 (1943).

Cancer — the challenger

Eugene V. Higgins, M. D.

The title of this article has several applications to the day by day problems of medical underwriting faced by Medical Directors in their evaluation of the cancer history life insurance applicant.

First, cancer challenges in the sense of runner-up, next in succession, the competitor fighting for a chance to displace the champion. In fact, in one mortality grouping it has taken over first place and has become the leading cause of death for women between the ages of thirty and sixty. In 1900 cancer ranked eighth among the ten leading causes of death in the United States and today is aggressively placed second in the ranking, being led only by diseases of the heart. This advance up the scale is due, of course, to the successful control research and clinical medicine have achieved over the infectious diseases — pneumonia, influenza, tuberculosis and enteritis — which headed the list only fifty years ago.

Another factor of great influence, based on the observation that cancer is particularly an upper age group disease, is our growing population with its ever increasing percentage of individuals in the older ages. In this regard it would be well to keep in mind that while the older individuals are the primary victims of cancer a very significant number of cancer deaths, over 15 per cent of the annual total, are reported in young people under twenty-five years of age. In fact, cancer kills more children in the three to fifteen year age group than any other disease.

With the constantly reported progress in the field of cardiovascular disease therapy, from the still almost unbelievable open heart surgery to the fundamental studies on arteriosclerosis and atherosclerosis, we are probably justified in concluding that the neoplastic diseases will continue to contribute an increasing percentage of deaths for some years to come. However, on that score no one can look very far ahead. There are ideas, concepts and theories being advanced and investigated today which could prove explosively successful and make all projection of past experience curves completely valueless.

Then, cancer challenges in the sense of the insidious, pervasive, disruptive and destroying blight which we in medicine see most vividly. It challenges the normal structures and functions of any of our body tissues from blood stream to brain, from most solid bone to most delicate gland, it can lay low the infant and it can make a torment of old age's final days. It is no wonder that such a multifaceted horror has been regarded as insoluble as the mystery of life itself not only by the uneducated but even by serious students in the past.

This challenge of cancer which defies us to define its genesis and reveal its cure is one of the most stimulating spurs which nature has applied to man. Fortunately, the spur gores each and every one of us and there is hardly anyone so ignorant or indifferent but what he will contribute something, be it brain, brawn or bottom dollar, to blunt its raking slash.

Our response to the challenge is evident in part in the work being done at the National Cancer Institute and in the extensive activities of the American Cancer Society. It is not the best method of showing this activity, but it is significant to note that in 1938 the National Cancer Institute worked on a budget of $400,000 while in 1961 it had an appropriation of $111,000,000 with over one-third of this being used by the research program of the Institute itself and the remainder being distributed as grants to private institutions and individuals all over the United States. The American Cancer Society received contributions of $4,000,000 in 1945 for its work; while in 1960, its contributions came to almost $34,000,000. Approximately 60% of this amount is devoted to a cancer research and education program, 25% to cancer patient services.

It is not possible in this paper to list the privately endowed medical research centers and clinics at grips with the cancer problem and to name a few would not be fair to the many omitted. A recent addition to the attacking forces in action against cancer has been the United States Atomic Energy Commission. Its reports deal with the use of radioactive materials in therapy, their dangerous aspects as causative agents and their value to research in biochemical cell structure and function.

The insurance industry has contributed both men and money to these activities, but it has been on an individual basis, not to be compared with the well-organized, united effort made in setting up the Life Insurance Medical Research Fund. It should take a positive position on the need for and the value of a more definite contribution to the work being done toward the solution of the cancer problem.

Finally, cancer challenges those in the field of Insurance Medicine in the sense of being a most serious mortality evaluation problem. As physicians we understand fully, from having seen many times, the shock and disruption of living patterns which a cancer diagnosis can produce. As Medical Directors we are well aware that one of the ways an individual attempts to remedy this disruption and restore some stability to his planning is by applying for life insurance protection for those dependent on him. We have the responsibility for issuing or declining this protection to these medically impaired men and women. The way we meet that responsibility, the accuracy of our evaluation of the mortality problem presented in the history, the examination, the attending physicians' reports and the laboratory data before us will be our answer to "Cancer — the Challenger" as it presents itself daily to us.

The obligation we have today is the same old one our honored predecessors in the work of Insurance Medicine accepted. It is a twofold obligation which requires us in conscience to make judgments which will protect that statistical entity known as company mortality and which will make insurance protection available to as many individuals as possible who apply for it. The individuals who present the underwriting mazes such as cancer are seldom "sold" insurance because the agents in the field know only too well the hazards and heartbreaks associated with such an application to compete very strongly for it. These people come and ask the company to set a price so that they may buy. Nowhere more than in this particular problem of cancer underwriting is anyone better fitted than the Medical Director to do the thinking and accept the responsibility for setting the price on the insurance issued. It is his problem from preliminary inquiry through the whole case to final notation of rated issue or declination. And this is exactly as it should be.

Obviously, declination is the safest answer in protecting company mortality, but it certainly does not contribute to company growth or service, nor does it satisfy the other obligation to make insurance available when sought. To quote from a Rating Manual of 1915: "The history or existence of a cancer of any variety in the applicant is cause for absolute rejection". In the years since 1915 we have progressed considerably from that iron curtain position.

Rarely is a case rejected without some feeling of dissatisfaction over such a decision. The only constant exception to this reaction is the lack of candor problem. Therefore, in the case of the applicant presenting a history of cancer, the Medical Director will do his best to determine conditions on which his company can make an offer of a kind that shall satisfy the double obligation to insurer and to insured.

Let us now consider the basis for the offer of life insurance to the applicant with a cancer history. Conferences with the members of the medical staff of the North American Reassurance Company and others, as well as correspondence with Dr. James C. Cooney of the American Cancer Society, Dr. John Heller of the National Health Institute and Dr. Matthew H. Griswold, Chief of the Division of Cancer, Connecticut State Department of Health, leaves us with the opinion that review and revision of current cancer underwriting rules and classifications are constantly needed to provide more selective, individually evaluated insurance protection for these applicants. "Selective" is used here in the sense of identifying those cancer risks which are explosively unpredictable as well as those which give good grounds for possibly more favorable underwriting action than any accepted as risks in the past.

The next part of this report will be an outline of the facts on which this opinion is based. The material outlined prompted a revision of the Cancer Section of the North American Reassurance Company's Rating Manual. The action our company has taken in the field of cancer underwriting over the past thirty years is interesting and is outlined in Table I (a, b, and c).

This course of action, directed in past years at the North American Reassurance Co. by Dr. James T. Montgomery and Dr. Edgar W. Beckwith, follows the numerical guidance of the Life Insurance Impairment Studies and also reflects appreciation of the fact that when a significant amount of work is obviously being done and immense amounts of money are being spent to solve the cancer problem, vital knowledge will be uncovered concerning its nature, even if the problem itself is not completely solved and shelved.

Table I(a). *Changes in cancer underwriting*
North American Reassurance Company, 1925 to 1961
Extra premiums in dollars per thousand to be charged the specified number of times according to the number of years after treatment regarded as curative.

	Carcinoma and sarcoma				
	1925	1936	1946	1952	1955
Within 1 year . . .	Decline	Decline	Decline	Decline	Decline
Within 2 years . . .	Decline	Decline	Decline	Decline	Decline
Within 3 years . . .	Decline	Decline	Decline	Decline	Decline
Within 4 years . . .	30.00 5x	Decline	Decline	Decline	15.00 6x*
Within 5 years . . .	30.00 4x	Decline	30.00 6x	20.00 6x	15.00 5x
Within 6 years . . .	30.00 3x	30.00 5x	30.00 5x	20.00 5x	15.00 4x
Within 7 years . . .	30.00 2x	30.00 4x	30.00 4x	20.00 4x	15.00 3x
Within 8 years . . .	17.50 2x	30.00 3x	30.00 3x	20.00 3x	15.00 2x
Within 9 years . . .	15.00 1x	30.00 2x	30.00 2x	20.00 2x	15.00 1x
Within 10 years . . .	5.00 1x	30.00 1x	30.00 1x	20.00 1x	+30 to 0
Within 11 years . . .	0	+25	+30 to 0	+30 to 0	0

* Plus one extra premium of $ 15.00

A. Example: A cancer history applicant in the fifth year after curative treatment would be charged the usual life insurance premium appropriate to his age plus an extra premium of $ 15.00 annually for each of the next five years.

B. In 1956 the period of declination was changed from a fixed period of three years as shown above (1955) so that it ranged from two to four years, depending on the site and stage of the cancer and the individual evaluation of the applicant.

Table I(b). *Changes in cancer underwriting*
North American Reassurance Company, 1925 to 1961
Extra premiums in dollars per thousand to be charged the specified number of times according to the number of years after treatment regarded as curative.

	Epithelioma, squamous cell (epidermoid) carcinoma				
	1925	1936	1946	1952	1955
Within 1 year . . .	Decline	Decline	Decline	Decline	7.50 4x
Within 2 years . . .	Decline	Decline	Decline	7.50 4x	7.50 3x
Within 3 years . . .	Decline	Decline	Decline	7.50 3x	7.50 2x
Within 4 years . . .	20.00 5x	12.50 5x	10.00 6x	7.50 2x	7.50 1x
Within 5 years . . .	20.00 4x	12.50 4x	10.00 5x	7.50 1x	0
Within 6 years . . .	20.00 3x	12.50 3x	10.00 4x	0	0
Within 7 years . . .	20.00 2x	12.50 2x	10.00 3x	0	0
Within 8 years . . .	12.50 2x	12.50 1x	10.00 2x	0	0
Within 9 years . . .	10.00 1x	+20	10.00 1x	0	0
Within 10 years . . .	5.00 1x	+20	+20	0	0

Table I(c). *Changes in cancer underwriting*
North American Reassurance Company, 1925 to 1961
Extra premiums in dollars per thousand to be charged the specified number of times according to the number of years after treatment regarded as curative.

Epithelioma, basal cell carcinoma					
	1925	1936	1946	1952	1955
Within 1 year . . .	Decline	Decline	Decline	Decline	0*
Within 2 years . . .	Decline	10.00 4x	7.50 3x	5.00 3x	0
Within 3 years . . .	Decline	10.00 3x	7.50 2x	5.00 2x	0
Within 4 years . . .	10.00 5x	10.00 2x	7.50 1x	5.00 1x	0
Within 5 years . . .	10.00 4x	10.00 1x	0	0	0
Within 6 years . . .	10.00 3x	0	0	0	0
Within 7 years . . .	10.00 2x	0	0	0	0
Within 8 years . . .	5.00 2x	0	0	0	0
Within 9 years . . .	5.00 1x	0	0	0	0
Within 10 years . . .	5.00 1x	0	0	0	0

* With histologic diagnosis.

It is this significant knowledge and the methods devised to obtain it which make up the facts mentioned above. These facts may be analyzed as follows:

(1) study of the genesis of cancer;
(2) current methods for the diagnosis of cancer;
(3) progress in the treatment of cancer;
(4) statistical evaluation of the epidemiology of cancer including the Life Insurance Impairment Studies.

The genesis of cancer

Dr. William Boyd of Toronto used this phrase in a still most readable paper delivered before the Medical Section of the American Life Convention in 1941. By it, he indicated a consideration of the causes and beginnings of cancer. Because of the unrestrained growth pattern of cancer cells the problem has long been approached from the biological viewpoint in which efforts are made to determine what factor stimulates the abnormal growth or what factor is absent that restrains abnormal growth.

Today, there is a rather wide swing of opinion toward the theory that a virus-like agent is causative of all cancer. This virus-like agent is regarded not as an extrinsic or exogenous stimulus, but is conceived as a self-reproducing cell entity, latently present in the body cells and stimulated into reproduction by the many well-known carcinogenic agents. The late Dr. C. P. Rhoads has reported studies which confirm the similarity of cancer to disease known to be caused by parasitic micro-organisms.

Cancer has only recently been demonstrated to conform to the famous Koch postulates. The invading cancer cells are easily shown in the tissue affected.

Cancer cells can be cultivated outside the body — this has been accomplished with human cancer cells within only recent years. The disease can be induced by the cultivated organisms — again, demonstrated in human volunteers only a few years ago. The last postulate, the acquiring of resistance to medications, has also been shown to occur in cancer cells. As Dr. RHOADS said, these studies "have proved certain fundamental biological principles which establish as correct the analogy employed (i.e., between cancer and parasitic micro-organisms), which have given us feeble means for better control of cancer in man today and which promise much more for the future."

This theory of a latent virus in our body cells was also propounded by Dr. WENDELL M. STANLEY, a Nobel prize winner and Professor at the University of California, before the National Cancer Conference a few years ago. He cited the herpes simplex virus as an example of this cell virus symbiotic relationship. Cancer results when the virus undergoes activation or mutation under the stimulus of a carcinogenic agent. Obviously, with such basic concepts of causation being investigated, the direction of therapy can be much more successfully guided.

Dr. LOWELL T. COGGESHALL, when he was Special Assistant for Health and Medical Affairs to the Secretary of Health, Education and Welfare, as well as an active cancer research investigator, said: "Many of the best scientific minds of our country, indeed the world, are now attacking the problem with determination. From their efforts frequent advances are being made on virtually every front which lead us to believe that control of cancer is a possibility not too remote from accomplishment."

The diagnosis of cancer

The essential dictum in this phase of cancer work is the catch-phrase: "Early Cancer is Curable". It covers a multitude of possibilities and was the subject of a short essay in a recent issue of "Cancer Research". In ordinary usage we usually accept the phrase, "early cancer", as meaning having only recently produced signs and symptoms. Among these, however, there are going to be some incurable cancers because of factors involving inaccessibility of site or essential nature of the structure involved or a minimal premetastatic stage. However, statistics demonstrate that the earlier cancer is found and treatment instituted, the better the survival rate. Statistics also demonstrate that in a well operated Cancer Detection Center, such as that at the University of Minnesota, the number of cancers found will be almost equally divided between symptomatic and asymptomatic.

No adequate general diagnostic test for cancer has been found as yet, despite considerable study and trial. Mass cancer screening projects are being studied and in some areas, such as Memphis, Tennessee, have been under way long enough for some evaluation of their results to be assessed. The vaginal smear or cytologic test for cancer of the cervix and corpus uteri developed by Dr. PAPANICOLAOU has been applied to over 100,000 women in the Memphis area with a report of 750 cancers found, 450 asymptomatic and not even suspected. The bottleneck in such studies was the lack of technicians trained to recognize the abnormal cells. An effort is being made to relieve this by use of an automatic electronic scanner which recognizes the unusual fluorescence shown by the cancer cells under ultraviolet light. A urine analysis indicating the degree of stomach acidity will be a fairly simple screening procedure for identifying persons with hypochlorhydria and additional x-ray examination of these individuals will then be done. With these newly devised approaches and the older methods of examination, reenforced by a continuation of the existing program of the American Cancer Society and the National Cancer Institute for education of the public and the medical profession in alertness to any and all indications of cancer, an increase in the number of cancers detected in all sites should easily be achieved.

The treatment of cancer

Extirpation surgery and radiation continue to be the two most successful means of treating cancer. It is generally accepted that radical surgery is near a peak of technical perfection and we should expect little progress in the direction of being able to do operative procedures in the future which are not undertaken today. The training in surgery which young men entering that field have received over the past ten or fifteen years will result almost certainly in a lessening of the difference in results of cancer surgery reported by the specialty hospitals and those of the local community hospitals. Research has produced much more detailed knowledge in recent years about the choice between surgery and radiation therapy or the proper combination of the two. New types of radiation therapy have been developed and still others are on the horizon. These modalities are also being used to create new concepts of tissue and cell activities and the isotopes indicate differences between normal and cancer cell activity which will furnish new methods of attack on cancer. The technical advances in the field of radiation treatment are as amazing as those achieved by the surgeons and they are far from complete.

The great increase in chemotherapy research has produced some startling results. A few words about the work reported concerning nucleic acid anabolism will give some idea of what is going on in the laboratories. Fundamental biochemical studies showed that nucleic acid, a constituent of both normal and cancer cells, underwent different anabolic processes in the two. Cancer cells were more basophilic and contained more nucleic acid. Nitrogen mustard, the first of the effective chemical agents against cancer, was known to be capable of destroying nucleic acid in very weak dilutions. Radiation therapy was demonstrated to depolymerize nucleic acid. Cancer cells have been shown to have chromosome abnormalities and nucleic acid is an essential part of the chromosome.

It is known that penicillin acts to prevent the reproduction of bacterial cells by changing nucleic acid function.

The patient and gifted laboratory men who recognized and assembled all these odds and ends of biochemical, bacteriological and radiation research are convinced they have opened a rational approach to the chemotherapy of cancer. To quote the late Dr. C. P. RHOADS: "At one time, and not so long ago, to dream of a pill for cancer was regarded as a sign of insanity. Now we have several pills. True, their effect is feeble, certain that it is transient, and obvious that only certain forms of cancer patients respond, but responses do occur. It is equally true, however, that several types of transplantable cancer in animals now can be wholly destroyed by systemic chemotherapy and cure effected. We hold that it is right to continue our work, to extend the basic principles already developed, in the hope for further cancer control in man."

The epidemiology of cancer

The epidemiology of cancer, that is, the statistical delineation of the cancer problem in the United States, has been worked on intensively over the past twenty and particularly the past ten years. Dr. JOHN HELLER has said: "When the National Cancer Institute was established in 1937 no information was available on the distribution of cancer morbidity in the population of the United States." Clinic and hospital reports were multitudinous and very helpful, but could not be related to a population base. A ten city study area was mapped out and with the help of State and County Medical Societies thousands of physicians contributed information to the Institute in 1937 and again in 1947. These cancer surveys have supplied us with knowledge of inestimable value.

In this field of cancer epidemiology extensive reports have been released during the past few years. One was "Some Observations on the Epidemiology of Cancer in the United States" from the office of Dr. JOHN HELLER of the National Cancer Institute, published in the December 25, 1955 issue of the Journal of the American Medical Association. Another was "Survivorship of Reported Cancer Cases in Northern New York State" from the office of Dr. PAUL R. GERHARDT, Director of the Bureau of Cancer Control, N. Y. State Department of Health, which appeared in the July, 1956 issue of the American Journal of Public Health. Still another, and a most impressive piece of work, was "Cancer in Connecticut, 1935—1951" from the office of Dr. MATTHEW H. GRISWOLD, Chief of the Division of Cancer, Connecticut State Department of Health, 1956.

Some additional publications of considerable import are: the 1956 report on "Cancer in Iowa" from the office of Dr. EDMUND G. ZIMMERER, Commissioner of the Iowa State Department of Health; the "Epidemiological and Vital Statistics Report" published in 1956 and in 1960 by the World Health Organization; "Cancer at Mid-Century" presented by Dr. MICHAEL SHIMKIN of the National Cancer Institute at the June, 1956, National Cancer Conference;

"Extent of Cancer Illness in the United States", Public Health Service, 1958; Sloan-Kettering Institute for Cancer Research, Report XIV, 1960; and "Survival Experience of Patients with Malignant Neoplasms", Public Health Service, 1960.

All who heard Dr. NEIL E. McKINNON at the 1954 Toronto meeting of the Association of Life Insurance Medical Directors, and those who did not but have read his paper on "Cancer Mortality", will have no trouble recalling the potent use he made of clinical statistics in his conclusion, and I quote: "The past twenty-five to thirty years have provided a vast experience which has demonstrated fallacy in our conceptions of the spread of cancer, fallacy and discrepancy in diagnosis, and fallacy thereby in appraisal of the results of treatment. In spite of earlier and more extensive treatment, they have not given any decisive reduction in mortality from metastasizing cancer."

Clinical data substantiate the following points in his paper:

1. The mortality pattern of a series of cancer cases is determined by the types of cases in that series; mixing the types leads to an unreliable set of conclusions.

2. The stage and character of the tumor present is the most important factor in prognosis.

3. In different series this factor will be evaluated by different clinics and differing values assigned by individual pathologists to such matters as anaplasia, differentiation and mitosis.

4. Microscopy cannot prognosticate the metastatic tendency of a particular tumor.

5. Duration and stage of a tumor have little demonstrable relationship.

6. These facts make the submitted evidence in many series doubtful, in others fallacious and in all subject to several reasonable interpretations.

This very logical report by Dr. McKINNON led to his discouraging observation that: "The past thirty years have not given any decisive reduction in mortality from metastasizing cancer." That refers, of course, to cancer on which it is not possible to place a reasonable mortality evaluation. Once the cancer case reaches the fourth or fifth year after treatment and later, however, we can hazard a fairly sound estimation as to the character of the cancer which was present. It is then possible to set some rational limits to the probabilities in the particular case with the assistance of laboratory reports, attending physicians' statements, medical examination and inspection reports.

In addition to that somewhat solacing thought, recent reports from sources which certainly must be regarded as being statistically reliable give a rather more optimistic evaluation of the work being done.

Dr. HELLER of the National Cancer Institute states: "Early diagnosis of cancer is generally recognized to offer the most hope for successful treatment. This principle of cancer control is supported by data collected through follow-up of patients with cancer." He presents a table based on over 80,000 observations of patients with cancer (Table II) which indicates the survival experience based on the stage of cancer development at the time of diagnosis. Dr. HELLER concludes: "For a number of sites of cancer origin, the data suggests that some progress has been made in the management of the cancer problem. Further substantial advances are within reach through fuller utalization of available technics."

Table II. *Cancer survivors, % by stage at diagnosis*

Stage at diagnosis	Years survived			
	1*	1**	5**	10**
All stages	64	54	27	16
Localized	84	72	43	26
Regional involvement	58	50	20	11
Remote metastases	28	14	3	1

* National Cancer Institute.
** Connecticut Cancer Register.

Dr. GRISWOLD, Chief of the Division of Cancer in the Connecticut Department of Health, in a report on more than 70,000 cancer cases observed from 1935, states: "The trend in five year survival rates indicates that the outlook for diagnosed cases is improving. Though stage at diagnosis is a controlling factor in prognosis, the observed improvement in the five year survival rates appears to be due to more effective utilization of available therapeutic technics." He presented a table which shows the basis for this opinion (Table III). He specifically considers one of the doubts raised by Dr. MCKINNON and says: "Since the higher survival rates for localized and regional cases were accompanied by higher rates for all stages combined, the increase in survival rates by stage cannot be attributed to changes in the classification of cancer by stage. This leads to the conclusion that therapy rather than a shift in stage at diagnosis was responsible for the improved survival experience."

Table III. *Five-year survival rates (%) by stage at diagnosis in different time periods* *

	1935–40	1941–46	1947–51
All stages	25	29	32
Localized	39	44	51
Regional involvement	18	20	22
Remote metastases	1	2	2

* Connecticut Cancer Register.

In the National Cancer Institute Report three items are of major importance: prevalence, incidence and mortality. As indicated in Table IV, incidence showed a 14 per cent increase and since this figure was reached after making an adjustment for the changed age composition of the study group between 1937 and 1947 the increase is most probably due to better diagnosis, more awareness of the significance of early lesions and more adequate laboratory studies to identify the condition if it is suspected.

Table IV. *Basic epidemiologic cancer classifications* *
prevalence — incidence — mortality

Prevalence:	the number of persons per 100,000 of population known to have had cancer at any time during the study year: 1937: 390 1947: 430 A 10% increase.
Incidence:	the number of persons per 100,000 of population first diagnosed as having cancer during the study year: 1937: 280 1947: 319 A 14% increase.
Mortality:	the number of persons per 100,000 of population dying during the study year with cancer as the primary cause: 1937: 144 1947: 149 A 3% increase.

* National Cancer Institute.

The 3 per cent increase in mortality when prevalence had increased by 10 per cent and incidence by 14 per cent, suggest that progress has been made in the management of the cancer problem — probably a combination of earlier case finding and more successful treatment. This thought is fairly well confirmed by the fact that in 1937 out of every 100 cancer patients seen, 68 were hospitalized, while in 1947 this number increased to 73. Also, in 1937 only 61 of every 100 had microscopic diagnosis, while in 1947 this figure went to 72.

The outstanding change between 1937 and 1947, as reported by Dr. HELLER in December 1955 when final tabulations were completed, was the large increase in cancer of the lung and bronchus. Both incidence and mortality rate more than doubled. This may have been due to improved case finding in part, but it appears too large not to include an appreciable real increase as well. The National Institute is continuing to collect and evaluate evidence in an effort to either prove or disprove the cause and effect relationship between smoking and lung cancer. As yet the evidence indicates multiple environmental factors, of which smoking is one, as probable carcinogenic agents.

Let us refer again to Table II, showing the number of survivors according to the stage of cancer when the diagnosis was made. Obviously, this table is an essential guide to any evaluation of insurability in the applicant with a cancer history. While we are looking at it, however, changes are taking place in it. This is because the statistics concerning cancer by site indicate that half of all forms of cancer (excluding skin) originate in organs accessible to direct examination by the physician in his office, i.e., cancer of the prostate, rectum, mouth and pharynx, thyroid, breast and uterus. Yet, only half of these are being diagnosed while localized at the site of origin.

Here, certainly, is a job for education. Education of the public and of the medical profession to a realization of the deadly importance of what they may be missing through indifference, carelessness or neglect. This is another field in which Medical Directors who control the physical examination of thousands of people every year, can do much to stimulate the examining staff to an awareness of the opportunity to be of invaluable service to the applicant for insurance who undergoes their questioning and examination. The life insurance sales representative and the examining physician would be proud to have an existing impairment of health such as cancer recognized and brought under care through our services. Granting the diagnosis and the completion of adequate treatment, the insurer can always approach such a man with confidence that he will appreciate the help rendered him and more than likely he will return for consideration as an applicant again.

Continuing this interesting and practical subject of cancer epidemiology and before taking up an evaluation of the 1951 Impairment Study, there are a few tables and graphs with which we should be familiar.

Table V(a) and (b) is a composite of the estimates made by the National Cancer Institute, the New York State Cancer Registry, the Connecticut State Cancer Registry, and the National Office of Vital Statistics, showing the estimated cancer incidence and mortality by sex and by site in percentage of total cancer incidence and mortality.

Table V(a). *Estimated current cancer incidence and mortality by sex and by site in percentage of total cancer incidence and mortality* *

1. Estimated cancer incidence by site in percent of total cancer incidence.
2. Estimated cancer mortality by site in percent of total cancer mortality.

Male			Female		
	1.	2.		1.	2.
Skin	14%	2%	Breast	22%	19%
Lung & Bronchus	11	17	Cervix uteri	11	12
Stomach	11	12	Skin	10	1
Prostate	11	11	Large intestines	9	12
Large intestines	9	9	Stomach	5	8
Buccal cavity & Pharynx	7	3	Rectum	5	4
Urinary organs	7	6	Ovary	5	6
Rectum	6	5	Corpus uteri	3	2
Lymphomas	4	2	Urinary organs	3	3
Leukemia & Aleukemia	3	5	Lymphomas	3	2
Pancreas	3	5	Liver & Biliary	3	5
Esophagus	3	3	Lung & Bronchus	2	3
Larynx	3	2	Leukemia & Aleukemia	2	4
Liver & Biliary	3	4	Pancreas	2	4
Brain & Nervous system	2	3	Buccal cavity & Pharynx	2	1
			Brain & Nervous system	1	2

* C. S. CAMERON, M. D.; Combination of U. S. Ten-city, N. Y. and Connecticut Cancer Reports, 1956.

Table VI(a) is derived from a report published in the June 1956 "Statistical Bulletin" of the Metropolitan Life Insurance Company and shows cancer mortality by sex and by site in two different age groups. The mortality is that experienced by industrial policyholders and arranged so that the highest mortality figures are at the top of each column. The figures are in terms of an average of annual death rates per 100,000. Table VI(b) presents a 1959 study of similar material from the United States Office of Vital Statistics.

Table V(b). *Estimated current cancer incidence and mortality by sex and by site in percentage of total cancer incidence and mortality*

1. Estimated cancer incidence by site in percentage of total cancer incidence.*
2. Cancer mortality by site in percentage of total cancer mortality.**

Male			Female		
	1.	2.		1.	2.
Skin	16%	2%	Breast	25%	19%
Lung & Bronchus	14	21	Cervix uteri	12	7
Prostate	12	10	Large intestine	10	13
Large intestine	9	9	Ovary	6	7
Rectum	9	4	Skin	4	1
Urinary organs	7	6	Corpus uteri	4	5
Stomach	6	10	Stomach	4	6
Buccal cavity & Pharynx	4	3	Rectum	4	4
Lymphomas	4	5	Urinary organs	3	3
Leukemia & Aleukemia	4	5	Pancreas	3	5
Pancreas	4	6	Leukemia & Aleukemia	2	4
Esophagus	2	3	Lung & Bronchus	2	4
Larynx	2	2	Liver & Biliary	2	4
Liver & Biliary	2	3	Lymphomas	2	4
Brain & Nervous system	2	3	Brain & Nervous system	1	2
			Buccal cavity & Pharynx	1	1

* Incidence estimates by American Cancer Society for 1961, for United States.
** National Office of Vital Statistics, 1959 Mortality, for United States.

Table VI(a). *Mortality from cancer of specified sites*
Whites by sex and in age groups 45—54, and 55—64 *

Males			Females		
	45–54	55–64		45–54	55–64
Respiratory system	33.3%	30.7%	Breast	24.9%	18.6%
Stomach	8.6	9.7	Uterus	16.5	14.2
Lymph. & Hemato.	8.5	6.9	Intestines	10.7	12.8
Intestines	7.8	9.1	Ovary	9.5	7.4
Urinary system	5.8	5.9	Lymph. & Hemato.	7.0	6.8
Pancreas	5.5	4.4	Stomach	3.9	5.8
Buccal & Pharynx	4.8	4.0	Rectum	3.8	4.7
Liver	3.6	3.9	Respiratory system	3.5	4.2
Rectum	3.4	5.4	Liver	2.8	5.7
Genitalia	1.8	5.1	Pancreas	2.7	4.5
Skin	1.7	.9	Urinary system	2.0	3.0
Prostate	1.3	4.7			

* Statistical Bulletin, Metropolitan Life Insurance Company, 1956.

Table VI(b). *Mortality from cancer of specified sites*
Whites by sex and in age groups 45—54, and 55—64 *

Males			Females		
	45–54	55–64		45–54	55–64
Respiratory system . . .	31.3%	33.0%	Breast	28.1%	21.6%
Lymph. & Hemato. . . .	11.5	8.6	Uterus	13.7	12.0
Intestines	7.9	8.8	Ovary	9.8	8.6
Stomach	7.1	7.8	Intestines	9.4	12.0
Pancreas	6.0	6.0	Lymph. & Hemato. . .	7.3	7.5
Urinary system	5.2	5.9	Respiratory system . . .	5.2	5.0
Buccal	4.8	3.8	Stomach	3.3	4.7
Rectum	3.8	4.4	Rectum	3.0	3.7
Liver	2.6	3.0	Pancreas	2.8	4.5
Skin	2.4	1.3	Liver	2.4	4.4
Genitalia	1.8	4.6	Urinary system	1.8	2.8
Prostate	1.2	4.3			

* United States Office of Vital Statistics, 1959 Mortality, for United States.

Table VII is a report from the National Cancer Institute showing the change in percentage of cancer incidence and mortality from 1937 to 1947 by major systems.

Table VII. *Percentage change in cancer incidence and mortality from 1937 to 1947* *

Primary site	Incidence	Mortality
Female genitalia	0%	—10%
Digestive system	0	— 8
Urinary organs	+16	— 8
Male genitalia	+16	— 2
Buccal cavity	+12	+ 2
Breast	+11	+ 9

* National Cancer Institute.

Table VIII is a Connecticut State report showing by sex and by site the percentage of cancer patients surviving for five years after diagnosis. These figures are divided so as to group them above and below an arbitrarily selected 20 per cent survival rate.

Figure 1 is a graph showing cumulative mortality in percentage of the cancer patients alive at stated time intervals after diagnosis. The figures for this graph were collected by the Connecticut State Cancer Registry where more than 75,000 cancer cases acted on in all stages of progression are tabulated. This graph is on semilogarithmic double phase scale, permitting direct comparison of rate change, and it indicates a mortality rate which decreases with time. See Appendix I for numerical data concerning these graphs.

Table VIII. *% Cancer patients surviving for five years after diagnosis*
By sex and by site: 1947 to 1951 *

Male		Female	
	%		%
All sites	25	All sites	38
Sites with a % survival lower than 20%		Sites with a % survival lower than 20%	
Pancreas	1	Pancreas	1
Esophagus	2	Stomach	7
Lung & Bronchus . . .	3	Esophagus	8
Stomach	5	Lung & Bronchus . . .	8
		Kidney	16
Sites with a % survival higher than 20%		Sites with a % survival higher than 20%	
Brain & Nervous system	20	Ovary	24
Prostate	21	Brain & Nervous system	25
Rectum	21	Rectum	31
Large intestines	24	Bone	32
Kidney	27	Large intestines	33
Bladder	28	Bladder	36
Bone	28	Buccal cavity & Pharynx	44
Buccal cavity & Pharynx .	35	Breast	46
Larynx	37	Cervix uteri	53
Breast	51	Corpus uteri	62
Skin	67	Skin	68

* Connecticut Cancer Register.

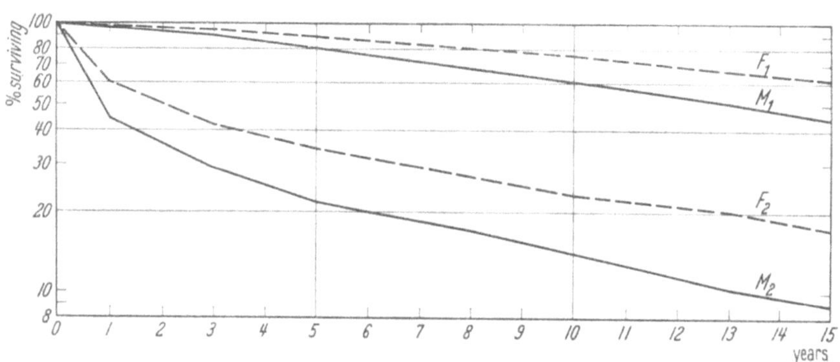

Fig. 1. M — Male
F — Female
1 — Normal life expectancy
2 — The % of all cancer cases surviving to 15 years after diagnosis
Data from "Cancer in Connecticut, 1935—1951" and "U. S. Life Tables, 1949—1951"

Across the top of each graph is plotted the curve of normal life expectancy. This was derived from the "United States Life Tables and Actuarial tables for 1949—1951" released in 1955. The curves for males and females are a weighed average of the life expectancy for five age groups: under 45, 45—54, 55—64, 65—74 and over. When compared with these graphs showing the expected mortality rate for the general population of equivalent age composition the cancer curves are seen to become nearly, but not quite, parallel with them after five years survival. It seems reasonable to conclude that the rate of depletion in the cancer group surviving five, ten, fifteen and more years is likely to remain somewhat elevated above that which will be shown by the population in general. Once again, these charts show the better mortality experienced by women.

Figure 2 shows the survivorship rates for cancer cases diagnosed when localized, after regional involvement has occurred and when distant metastases were reported. The upper curve, that of the localized cancer cases, parallels very closely the normal life expectancy graph and it is these cases we are trying to identify and underwrite properly. As in the preceding graph, the women survive longer.

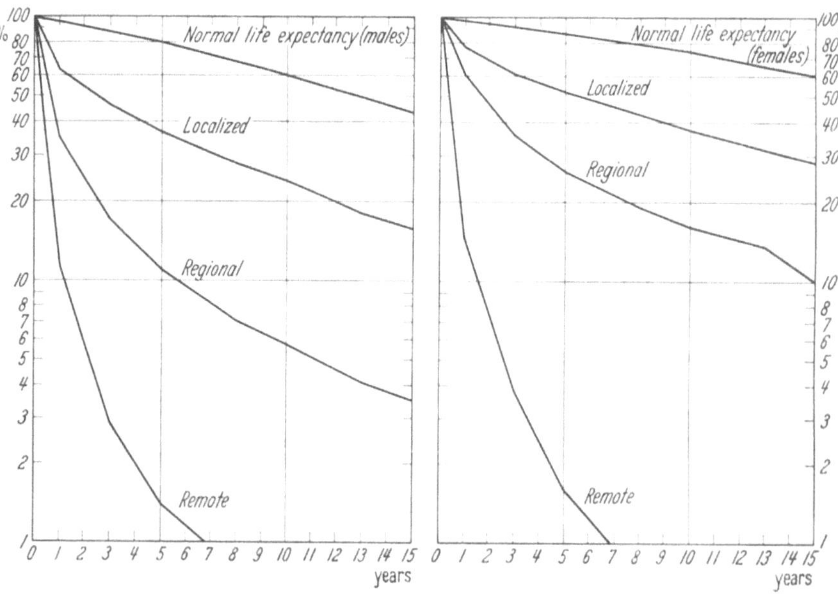

Fig. 2. % Cancer cases surviving 15 years by stage at diagnosis. Data from "Cancer in Connecticut 1935—1951" and "U. S. Life Tables, 1949—1951"

The life insurance industrywide study of neoplastic disease as reported in the 1951 Impairment Study is somewhat disappointing in the fact that its extent is so limited. There were only 970 entrants for carcinoma and sarcoma combined. This relatively small number prevents any exact projection of experience but does give some basis for calculations directed toward arriving at an acceptably sound extra premium to be applied for a history of cancer.

It seems quite reasonable that the cancer section of the 1951 Impairment Study should be relatively small, i.e., 970 entrants out of a total of 625,000 in the study. For one thing, the applicant with a cancer history has always been underwritten with considerable caution — and rightly so. For another, the extra premium assessed on the policy issued to this applicant has been quite high in the past — when the case was not immediately declined — and this acted as an efficient economic deterrent for many.

One of the most pertinent things learned from the 1951 Impairment Study is the confirmation of the shift in disease patterns from the formerly predominant infectious causes of death to the cardiovascular and neoplastic conditions which dominate our mortality studies today. In the cardiovascular field the insurance industry contributes most effectively through the Life Insurance Medical Research Fund to the resolution of the problems which abound in that field of medicine. Every medical underwriter tries to apply practically to daily underwriting problems the leads which clinical investigation furnishes him. The simple fact that many of us are now struggling with the underwriting of persons with a history of coronary disease, of hypertensive patients under treatment, or applicants who have recovered from cardiac surgery indicates that progress is continuing. Similar developments have taken place in cancer diagnosis, treatment and research. The past record shows that we have been aware of such changes and have adjusted our mortality thinking in terms of progress made.

Two sections of the 1951 Impairment Study should be kept in mind when we begin consideration of this problem. The first is the G 1—G 6 group, listing a total of 970 entrants made up of both carcinoma and sarcoma cases which had undergone one operation and on which insurance was issued from the third year post-operative, i.e., both standard and substandard issues combined. This group had 39 deaths with 32 expected, showing a mortality ratio of 148 per cent. The second is the G 3 group listing carcinoma cases with operation over ten years ago at the time of insurance issue. This group provides a mortality within standard limits.

At the 1955 New York meeting of the Association of Life Insurance Medical Directors, Mr. ANDREW WEBSTER, Vice President for Selection of the Mutual Life Insurance Company of New York, presented one of those reports which are always typical of his thinking — practical, analytical and basically helpful. He reviewed some of the methods used in arriving at the extra premiums assessed against medically impaired risks. He selected one of the important cancer categories of the study and considered the mortality ratios presented therein in terms of the confidence interval applicable to them and in terms of the additional deaths per thousand they represented. The confidence interval is, of course, a synonym for the possibly more familiar phrases, probable error or probable deviation.

The G 2 table of figures from the 1951 Impairment Study which Mr. WEBSTER analyzed, presented here as Table IX(a) and (b), considers carcinoma, with operation, once, within 6 to 10 years of application, substandard, by duration of exposure in years. The lower half of the table, marked Table IX(b), shows the 3 to 5 and 6 to 10 year exposures with their mortality ratios and the confidence intervals calculated for each.

As Mr. WEBSTER noted, the experience presented here is quite limited but it does indicate a decreasing mortality is to be anticipated and a temporary extra premium may be used to compensate for it. It is interesting to note how this small experience appears to be confirmed in the mortality curves of the two graphs presented in the earlier part of this report.

To approximate this temporary extra he adjusts the actual deaths according to the confidence interval range of the mortality ratio, taking the upper, or as he very frankly says, "pessimistic", limit to calculate the number of deaths with that higher mortality ratio. This adjusted deaths figure is based on the exposure of the study and must be converted to extra deaths per thousand in order to secure an approximate net temporary extra premium (see Appendix II).

Table IX(a). (G 2) *Carcinoma, with operation, once, within 6—10 years of application*
Substandard. Total entrants 327.* Experience by duration.

Policy year durations	Exposed to risk	Actual deaths Policies	Actual deaths Lives	Expected deaths	Mortality ratio
1— 2	609	1	1	1.84	54%
3— 5	610	11	10	3.28	335%
6—10	486	8	8	4.26	188%
11—15	127	2	2	2.01	100%

Table IX(b).

Duration years	Actual deaths	Expected deaths	Mortality ratio	Confidence interval
3— 5	11	3.28	335%	+94 to —72
6—10	8	4.26	188%	+66 to —47

* 1951 Impairment Study.

These figures are derived from a risk exposure between the years 1935 and 1950, and this report indicates some progress in cancer control has been made in the past decade and more is to be anticipated in the next. Therefore, these potential extra deaths per thousand should be regarded in an optimistic as well as a pessimistic light and perhaps some combination of the two may be made to fit carefully classified groups of cancer cases. To illustrate this point, Table X was prepared to show the extra deaths per thousand in terms of both the higher — pessimistic, and lower — optimistic, mortality ratios.

Table X.*

Duration years	Mortality ratio	Confidence interval	Mortality range
3— 5	335%	+94 to —72	429% to 263%
6—10	188%	+66 to —47	254% to 141%

Higher: Pessimistic			Lower: Optimistic		
Mortality ratio	Adjusted deaths	Extra deaths per M	Mortality ratio	Adjusted deaths	Extra deaths per M
429%	14	17.6	263%	9	9.4
254%	11	13.9	141%	6	3.6

* 1951 Impairment Study.

Mr. WEBSTER took the 17.6 extra deaths per thousand from these calculations and said: "The conservative approach indicates that the net temporary extra premium must be at least $18.00 per thousand." Based on study and consideration of the elements of the cancer problem outlined in this report, it is our conclusion that we know enough to make a controlled, intelligent move into more selective and optimistic tables of cancer extra mortality premiums.

As already indicated, the number of applicants with a history of cancer will continue to increase for the incidence of cancer is increasing along with enlargement of the population in the older age groups. More applicants with the history of cancer will be seen and, naturally, more of the unusual types will be scattered among them. It will be to our advantage to become familiar with cancer pathology so that the physician's report with histologic diagnosis will have exact significance. Of great value, too, is general background knowledge such as the conclusions drawn in the "Cancer in Connecticut" study, i.e., a more hopeful prognosis is justified in cancer of the colon, rectum, prostate, uterus — both cervix and corpus; while cancer of the lung, stomach, esophagus, ovary and soft tissues continues to present a more discouraging picture. The treacherous metastatic potential of the malignant melanoma must be countered by an adequate waiting period or a very specific detailed physician's statement. The definite diagnosis of thyroid papillary adenocarcinoma warrants a more favorable action than would be given to thyroid alveolar or follicular adenocarcinoma.

The Medical Director must be prepared to correspond with the surgeon or the pathologist in an effort to secure specific statements concerning the type of cancer removed, whether it was localized or showed signs of blood vessel invasion or regional lymph node involvement, whether clinical examination or x-ray study showed any evidence of metastases. A knowledge of which cancer types have bone and lung metastatic tendencies can lead to a request for a chest x-ray which will help provide a sound basis for mortality evaluation. The applicant's concern to keep in follow-up touch with his physician is a favorable factor and an effort to learn if he is doing so can be very helpful.

Having secured these facts we can then proceed to classify the individual problem and fit it to a reasonable and stable pattern which should give optimum selection results. Underwriting action is based on the conviction that cancer is not just a simple entity. It is a complex pattern of many types, degrees and classifications. It is certain that factors such as site, duration, histologic structure, lymphatic spread, blood vessel invasion — *all* are involved and interrelated in their influence on the life expectancy of the individual concerned. For that reason, practically no hard and fast rules can be established which are applicable to every case. This is true even though our rate revision is the result of much study, research and consultation with cancer experts. Future changes in these rating classifications will be entirely justifiable and are to be expected.

We have continued at the North American Reassurance Company to underwrite cancer along the lines of the procedures developed as a result of our 1956 study and, so far, have not been aware of any need to change the rating schedule used. We must admit the number of cancer cases we receive is not staggering and it will be quite some time more before they can be the basis for a worthwhile study. Therefore, just as the 1951 Impairment Study gave us only a suggestion as to our underwriting experience, we still cannot do more than think around this problem in prognosis from as many available clinical and statistical viewpoints as possible.

It has been calculated that if cancer could be eliminated as a cause of death in men between the ages of 0 to 60, the average length of life would be increased only by approximately 1.8 years. To express this fact in another way, in possibly more insurance applicable terms, the present expectation of life in a standard male risk under age 60 is 1.8 years less than it should be because of cancer mortality. Our current expectation of life table shows:

Age	*Standard life expectancy*	*Substandard B, 150%*
20	52 years	47 years
40	33 years	29 years
60	18 years	15 years

Thus, a five, four and three year loss in life expectancy is covered by as slight an extra rate as +50. It would appear reasonable in view of these figures to believe that if the long sought and sincerely desired cure for cancer were to be announced tomorrow, the change in average life expectation would not warrant much change in our insurance mortality tables. We realize very well that our concern in insurance mortality is the death rate, not the life expectancy, but the two have certainly an intimate relationship and we find a consideration of both viewpoints helpful in medical prognostic thinking.

This basic evaluation of cancer in its influence on the mortality of a so-called standard group is worth knowing and assessing in terms of the many factors — progress in medicine, public health, nutrition, housing, economic well-being, etc., — which have functioned so effectively to lengthen life expectancy over the past few decades. Obviously such knowledge is not the answer to underwriting the applicant with a cancer history but, for some of us at least, it may put such underwriting in a better perspective and cause us to feel more secure in making an effort to apply what appears to be a reasonable rating on selected applicants who have undergone cancer therapy regarded as curative.

The complexity of cancer underwriting is known to all of us. We are dealing with a frightening disease, an entity usually inexplicable as to origin, often unpredictable in its response to therapy and without any completely valid basis for prognosis. No matter how much study is given to individual cases in an effort to classify them in mortality terms, many of them will remain potentially explosive and our action in approving an issue can be subjected to quite critical review by both our claim departments and ourselves in the event of an early death. It's an old story, how easy prognosis and underwriting generally become when subjected to analysis under the "retrospectoscope"!

However, when we remember that the doctor in his work with patients will always, with no exceptions, have to accept ultimate defeat, we, as Medical Directors, can certainly continue our efforts to underwrite the hazardous risk with all the skill our knowledge of the problem permits.

In the practice of Life Insurance Medicine we must combine scientific classical underwriting as based on statistical group prognosis with the art of modern underwriting as based on clinical statistics and individual case evaluation. Neither can do a completely satisfactory job alone, in their union there is strength and growth. We believe any reasonable investigator or student of Life Insurance Medicine will recognize the limitations, as well as the value of statistics, in the study of medical problems.

The placebo demonstrates one of these limitations quite conclusively. The placebo is an essential tool in the clinical evaluation of medical drugs. This is so because the study of the pharmaceutical potency of a medication is subject to many variables — two of the most potent being the patient's susceptibility to suggestion and the doctor's susceptibility to bias. We all recall the observation made by Dr. William Osler: "One should treat as many patients as possible with a new drug while it still has the power to heal!" The unquestionable healing effect of the placebo is real and has been demonstrated thousands of times in such diverse impairments as headaches, arthritis, post-operative pain, gastric dysfunction, motion sickness, nausea and the common cold. How and why it works can't be explained, for the nature of the nervous system response that, in a particular man or woman, changes illusion into fact, is not understood.

Another difficulty arises from the fact that in many medical problems too few reports exist for group classification. In these cases and, indeed, even in the more common impairments well reported on statistically, it is the subjective judgment of medical directors or medically trained lay underwriters that has assigned the risk to a group classification which becomes in time the predecessor of more statistical guides for future underwriters. Recalling the varied rate classifications which underwriters in the same company, as well as in different, competitive companies, have assessed on the same set of facts, it becomes simply a clear-cut fact that what we are doing and pretty much have been doing for ten or fifteen years past is blending group and individual underwriting.

In underwriting cancer it is obvious much of our prognostic problem is solved by the high death rate in the early years when cancer identified as far advanced, inoperable, disseminated, metastatic, recurrent, palliatively treated by chemotherapy or radiation therapy, etc., takes its vicious toll. Putting these cases aside as beyond our practical concern, our postponement action for a period of two to four years after what is regarded as curative treatment brings us to the point where our clinical and statistical judgment must be applied to the case under consideration.

This judgment is strictly the Medical Director's responsibility and he is entitled to all the available information his study of the situation leads him to regard as necessary. With these facts, he should come to a conclusion as to the acceptability of the case and assess an extra premium in accord with the time since treatment, the nature of the cancer and the current status of the applicant.

At North American Reasurance Company we normally have a discussion of any cancer case among the members of our medical staff before a final decision is made. We would advise the Medical Directors of direct writing companies, particularly the smaller ones with only one doctor, to use the consultation facilities available to them with the medical staff of their reassurance company.

In support of our belief that we can and must underwrite the selected cancer history applicant, we present a report, Table XI, from the End-Results Group of the Fourth National Cancer Conference, September 1960: "Survival Experience of Patients with Malignant Neoplasms" from the Public Health Service of the United States Department of Health, Education and Welfare. In this report the survival figures for the period after 1950 show a definite improvement over those from before 1950. This appears to warrant the conclusion that significant progress in cancer control has occurred since 1950.

Table XI. *Percentage of patients surviving five years after surgical or radiation treatment for localized cancer*

	Before 1950		After 1950	
	Male	Female	Male	Female
Stomach	40%	34%	50%	48%
Large intestine	56	43	70	77
Rectum	51	59	72	73
Breast	—	83	—	85
Cervix	—	85	—	92
Corpus uteri	—	87	—	91
Ovary	—	64	—	68
Prostate	49	—	60	—
Testis	64	—	70	—
Melanoma	65	72	65	76
Thyroid	80	87	88	98
Lymphosarcoma	41	48	49	47
Hodgkins	28	37	25	40

End-Results Group of the Fourth National Cancer Conference, September 1960: "Survival Experience of Patients with Malignant Neoplasms" from the Public Health Service of the United States Department of Health, Education and Welfare.

There is no doubt that a five year survival is, per se, not enough for our insurance experience needs. However, cancer mortality beyond that period tends to reduce and its curve flattens out to parallel reasonably well that of general population mortality. I conclude from the above data that the pressure to educate the public and doctors, and particularly medical students, to realize that of all cancers roughly 20% are visible, 30% are palpable, and 30% can be seen with the aid of diagnostic instruments, is producing successful results. The deeply burned in fact that 80% of all cancer is susceptible to early diagnosis and thereby a far greater chance of curative treatment is going to continue to reduce our cancer mortality.

Another element which is very impressive and influences my judgment is the success cancer research has had in transplanting human cancer into animals. This recent development has provided new understanding of the immunologic processes involved in the growth and control of cancer. Some of these transplanted tumors show a growth or proliferative potential in the laboratory animal which is never seen in the human host. This fact seems to confirm the presence of a restraining control which functions in the human cancer victim. Studies on human volunteers and laboratory experiments directed toward finding the key to these apparently immunologic processes are intensively under way. Basic concepts are being established and details fitted together which will go far to clarify our hazy understanding of the whys and hows of immunity as it applies to cancer in the human.

Recent research indicates the reinforcement of surgery with the application of radiation therapy and chemotherapy directed toward improving over-all survival experience, is practical and successful within limits. Current reports forecast continued progress in this field of combined therapies as better control of local application, distribution and dosage measurement gradually reduces the dangerous side-effects and produces improved end-results. The progress in the last few years in the effective use of chemotherapy as a surface application, as an intra-arterial injection, as a perfusion, and an interstitial injection, has been phenomenal. What is being learned will be basic building material for further successful control of cancer. We know there is still no cure for disseminated cancer, but we must agree that real progress toward that end has been made in the field of chemical and hormone therapy.

The major means of cancer treatment, surgical excision, has undergone tremendous improvement in the past ten to fifteen years. The preoperative evaluation and preparation of the patient is much more exact and thorough. The knowledge that cancer cells are present in the blood stream due to an expanding tumor invading blood and lymph vessels, due to pressure on or manipulation of the tumor, or as a result of biopsy or major surgery, has caused great changes in diagnostic studies, in means of therapy, in surgical techniques. We have learned that the presence of these circulating cancer cells does not guarantee metastases, but we do not have the answer to why successful invasion, i.e., the beginning of a distant metastatic lesion, occurs. It appears partly due to the nature of the cells, i.e., their ability to form clots, and to the number of free cancer cells circulating. Surgical procedures have been steadily refined to reduce the possibility of this source of metastases. Artery, vein and lymphatic ligation has been stressed as an essential preliminary to extirpation of the tumor. Careful protection of the operative field from tumor content contamination is routine. The use of post-operative x-ray irradiation, the instillation of radioactive solutions into the body cavities from which tumors have been removed, the local infusion of various chemotherapeutic agents (nitrogen mustard, nitromin, mercury perchloride, etc.), all are methods used alone or in combination with what appear to be effective results in limiting or preventing the incidence of metastatic recurrence.

We believe we have outlined enough of the thinking which brings us to the conviction that we can and must continue to make an honest, courageous effort to underwrite and issue many cancer history applicants. We are confident that our success will be at least of a degree to satisfy our own professional pride and secure our companies' investment.

In no field of medical prognosis more than in that of cancer will Medical Directors, acting as medical underwriters, in their day to day weighing of imponderables, evaluating intangibles and assessing those factors which influence mortality ever fear the unhappy fate described by ALBERT EINSTEIN: "The fairest thing we can experience is the mysterious. He who knows it not and can no longer wonder, no longer feels amazement, is as good as dead, a snuffed out candle."

We would do well to remember a quote attributed to Hippocrates centuries ago: "Physicians should bow low before the gods, because their art is not provided in abundance with means of cure." There are several possible interpretations of that thought, but it appears to us we should take the hint at face value and as cancer underwriters keep it in mind — it can certainly do us no harm. From an entirely different viewpoint, we present another suggestion concerning our efforts in this field of medical prognosis. The experienced wise man will seek to handle cancer underwriting as he handles his alcohol — striving to know when to take it, how much to take, and when to leave it alone!

Appendix I. *Numerical data from which graphs in Fig. 1 and 2 were prepared:*
"Cancer in Connecticut 1935—1951"
"U.S. Life Tables 1949—1951"

Years	General population % surviving	Cancer % surviving	% Surviving: Cancer classified by stage at diagnosis		
			Localized	Regional	Remote
			Males		
1.	96	45	63	35	11.5
3.	87.9	29	46	17	2.9
5.	79.7	22	37	11	1.4
8.	67.8	17	28	7	0.8
10.	60.2	14	24	5.7	0.5
13.	49.8	10	18	4.1	0.5
15.	43.6	9	16	3.5	0.0
			Females		
1.	97.8	61	77	61	14.1
3.	93.1	42	61	36	3.7
5.	88.0	34	52	26	1.6
8.	80.1	27	43	19	0.8
10.	74.6	23	38	16	0.5
13.	66.3	20	32	13.5	0.1
15.	60.9	17	28	9.8	0.0

Appendix II. *Calculations used in analysis of section G-2, 1951 Impairment Study*
G-2 Carcinoma, with operation, once, within 6—10 years of application.

Duration	Exposed to risk	Actual deaths	Expected deaths	Mortality ratio
3— 5	610	11	3.28	335%
6—10	486	8	4.26	188%

Actual deaths ÷ Expected deaths = Mortality ratio

I. Group 3—5

11 ÷ 3.28 = 335%

335% has a confidence interval of + 94 to — 72

1. Pessimistic, i.e. higher mortality ratio.

335 + 94 = 429

x ÷ 3.28 = 429

x = 14 adjusted actual deaths

Actual deaths — Expected deaths = Extra deaths per number exposed

14 — 3.28 = 10.72 extra deaths in 610

Extra deaths per # exp. : # exp. : : Extra deaths per M : M

10.72 : 610 : : x : M

x = 17.6 extra deaths per M

2. Optimistic, i.e. lower mortality ratio.

335 — 72 = 263

x ÷ 3.28 = 263

x = 9 adjusted actual deaths

9 — 3.28 = 5.72 extra deaths in 610

5.72 : 610 : : x : M

x = 9.4 extra deaths per M

II. Group 6 to 10

$8 \div 4.26 = 188\%$
188% has a confidence interval of $+ 66$ to $- 47$

1. Pessimistic, i.e. higher mortality ratio.

$188 + 66 = 254$
$x \div 4.26 = 254$
$x = 11$ adjusted actual deaths
$11 - 4.26 = 6.74$ extra deaths in 486
$6.74 : 486 :: x : M$
$x = 13.9$ extra deaths per M

2. Optimistic, i.e. lower mortality ratio.

$188 - 47 = 141$
$x \div 4.26 = 141$
$x = 6$ adjusted actual deaths
$6 - 4.26 = 1.74$ extra deaths in 486
$1.74 : 486 :: x : M$
$x = 3.6$ extra deaths per M

References

American Cancer Society. Annual Report, 1955; and 1960.

Cancer. Journal of the American Cancer Society, New York, N. Y.

Cancer at Mid-Century. MICHAEL B. SHIMKIN, M. D. Presented at National Cancer Conference, June, 1956.

Cancer Bulletin. University of Texas, May and June, 1956. University of Texas, March and April, 1961.

Cancer — Diagnosis, Treatment, Prognosis. L. V. ACKERMAN, M. D., and J. A. DEL REGATO, M. D., 1954, C. V. Mosby Co.

Cancer — Diagnosis and Treatment. JOHN B. FIELD, M. D., et al., 1959, Little, Brown & Co.

Cancer in Connecticut, 1935—1951. MATTHEW H. GRISWOLD, M. D., et al., 1955.

Cancer in Iowa, 1956. EDMUND G. ZIMMERER, M. D., et al. Public Health Service Publication #466, 1956.

Cancer in Midlife. Statistical Bulletin, Metropolitan Life Insurance Co., June, 1956.

Cancer Mortality. N. E. MCKINNON, M. B., Transactions of Association of Life Insurance Medical Directors, 1954.

Cancer of the Colon and Rectum. N. W. SWINTON, M. D., et al., J.A.M.A., July 21, **161**, 12, 1139 (1956).

Cancer of the Ovary. L. A. EMGE, M. D., Reports of the International Congress of Gynecology and Obstetrics, **1**, 1—8 (1954).

Cancer Prognosis Manual. ARTHUR G. JAMES, M. D. American Cancer Society, 1961.

Cancer Statistics. CHARLES S. CAMERON, M. D. Medical Clinics of North America, May, 1956.

Chemotherapy of Cancer. Symposium, N. Y. Medicine, April 5, 1956.

Comments on the 1951 Impairment Study. A. C. WEBSTER, Transactions of Association of Life Insurance Medical Directors, 1955.

Diagnosis and Treatment of Lung Cancer. FOSTER MURRAY, M. D., Geriatrics, March 1956, 118.

Epidemiological and Vital Statistics Report. World Health Organization, **9**, 5 (1956), and **12**, 10 (1959).

Evaluation of Annual Examinations in the Detection of Cancer. C. B. JENSON, M. D., et al. J.A.M.A., December **3**, 174—14 (1960).

Evaluation of the Cancer Problem. PAUL E. STEINER, M. D. Presidential address at 1952 meeting of the American Association for Cancer Research.

Extent of Cancer Illness in the United States. Public Health Service, Publication #547, 1958.

Importance of the General Practitioner in Cancer Detection. J. R. HELLER, M. D., J. Ch. Dis., September, **2**, 3, 345 (1955).

Improvements in Cancer Survival Rates. MATTHEW H. GRISWOLD, M. D., et al. New England J. Med., June 7, **254**, 23, 1062 (1956).
Lung Cancer. J. R. HELLER, M. D., J. Ch. Dis., January, **1**, 1, 96 (1955).
Minnesota Cancer Detection Research Center. J. B. AUST, M. D., et al. Geriatrics, March 1955, 105.
Morbidity from Cancer in the United States. Public Health Service Publication #418, 1955. Public Health Service Publication #56, 1959.
Outlook in Cancer. Statistical Bulletin, Metropolitan Life Insurance Company, December, 1960.
Postwar Cancer Record. Statistical Bulletin, Metropolitan Life Insurance Company, May, 1951.
Pulmonary Nodule. D. L. PAULSON, M. D. Minn. Med. **39**, 127 (1956).
Recent Advances in Treatment of the Cancer Patient. WARREN H. COLE, M. D. J.A.M.A., November 5, 174—10 (1960).
Relationship of Nucleic Acid Anabolism to the Treatment of Cancer. C. P. RHOADS, M. D., Medical Clinics of North America, May, 1956.
Role of the General Practitioner in Cancer Detection. R. S. BOLES, M. D., et al. J.A.M.A., March 17, **160**, 923 (1956).
Screening for Cancer. J. E. DUNN, JR., M. D. J. Ch. Dis., October, **2**, 4, 450 (1955).
Sloan-Kettering Institute for Cancer Research. Report XIV, 1960, New York, N. Y.
Some Observations on the Epidemiology of Cancer in the United States. J. R. HELLER, M. D., et al. J.A.M.A., December 24, **156**, 1628 (1955).
Statistical Facts about Cancer. J. Mich. State Med. Soc., December, 1955.
Survival Experience of Patients with Malignant Neoplasms. Public Health Service, Publication #FS 2.22:SU7, 1960.
Survival in Breast Cancer Cases in Relation to the Structure of the Primary Tumor and Regional Lymph Nodes. MAURICE M. BLACK, M. D., et al. Surg., Gyn. & Ob., **100**, 543 (1955).
Survivorship of Reported Cancer Cases in Northern New York State. PAUL R. GERHARDT, M. D., et al. A.J.P.H., July, **46**, 7, 836 (1956).
The Meaning of Early. Cancer Research, May, 1956; **16**, 277.
Treatment of Early Mammary Cancer. ROBERT ELMAN, M. D. J.A.M.A., July 7, **161**, 10, 972 (1956).
Tumors of the Breast. Symposium: N. Y. Medicine, March 20, 1956.
1951 Impairment Study. Section G. Tumors, page 211.

The demonstration of anti-hypertensive substances in the urine

E. Tanner · H. Suter · J. Conti · J. Wanner

Introduction

Medical research constantly gives Man new medicaments which have the capacity to influence anatomical functions and controls in a way previously unsuspected.

We know of certain important groups of agents which are capable of suppressing all symptoms of diesase to such an extent that physical examination of the patient simulates a normal picture. However, the basic affliction need be influenced only to an insignificant degree if at all. Consequently the "normal condition" only persists whilst the agent is regularly administered. It is quite feasible that the actual disease which is concealed may even become worse whereas the psycho-visual image, that is the result of medical examination, gives no ground for suspicion. Such substances thus result not only in normalization of the symptomatology but also in a form of camouflage. This masking effect is of very special interest to us as insurance medical advisers.

From this viewpoint particular importance is attached, in an insurance medical examination, to two groups of medicaments: the modern antidiabetic drugs (sulphonyl-ureas and biguanides) and anti-hypertensive substances. Anti-convulsant and psychotherapeutic drugs may also be included in this category but are of less importance. In insurance medicine anti-hypertensive substances are of outstanding interest.

For these there are two principal considerations:

a) What are the effects of anti-hypertensive substances on long-term prognosis of sufferers from high blood pressure?
and
b) How can we recognize hypertension which has been normalized by the use of medicaments?

The very important prognostic problems will not be considered here, but only the indirectly connected second question as to how the examining doctor can ascertain whether an insurance candidate has been taking anti-hypertensive drugs.

Without doubt, there is a very great temptation for insurance candidates with high blood pressure to take anti-hypertensive substances before medical examination, with the intention of producing a blood pressure indication lower than their actual blood pressure. Every insurance medical adviser to-day knows that it does not stop at being a temptation but that in fact anti-hypertensive substances are used ever more frequently with intent to mislead.

What opportunities does the insurer have of ascertaining whether a candidate has used anti-hypertensive drugs?

1. The application form can include the question: "Have you ever taken, or are you at present taking, any medicaments which will reduce blood pressure?"
   Whoever intends to mislead the insurer will, of course, be undeterred by this harmless question.
2. Clinical examination.
   The examining doctor must look for the typical side-effects and signs associated with the use of anti-hypertensive drugs.

A strong suspicion of a drug-induced reduction in blood pressure arises when the blood pressure is normal but the heart shows left preponderance or the ECG indicates left ventricular hypertrophy or even left heart strain. Marked postural changes in blood pressure are even more suspect. It should therefore be a principle to measure the blood pressure in both the upright and the recumbent position.

In the case of the ganglion-blocking agents (Ecolid etc.) and Guanethidine (Ismelin) the blood pressure often falls in the upright position only. If there is a tendency to an orthostatic collapsing pulse, accompanied by bradycardia, Guanethidine (Ismelin), may well be the cause. Orthostasis with side-effects akin to those of atropine, suggests ganglion-blocking agents.

Single doses of Reserpine produce only slight side-effects, such as a swelling of the nasal mucuous membrane. Extrapyramidal disturbances are not an early symptom.

Hydrazinophthalazine can produce nausea, giddiness, vomiting, headaches and tachycardia.

Saliuretics are also of practical importance. However, apart from a striking diuresis, their clinical side-effects are of little significance.

Unfortunately all clinical side-effects represent, at most, circumstantial evidence. Conclusive indication, however, requires unequivocal proof. We are helped here by the observation that anti-hypertensive substances principally leave the body through the kidneys. It is therefore necessary to prove the use of such substances by demonstrating their presence in the urine.

The demonstration of anti-hypertensive substances in the urine

We have set ourselves a twofold task:

1. The method should be technically simple.
2. The indication must be unequivocal and characteristic of the substance concerned.

These requirements are not easily satisfied, since the quantity of the substances necessary to reduce hypertension is very small and consequently the urine concentration of these substances must be very weak.

Moreover, the indication of substances in the urine by their specific characteristics is difficult, due to the great number and variety of typical excretion products, including products of metabolism.

In recent years several writers [*2—16*] have discussed the indication and quantitative determination of anti-hypertensive substances in biological matter. Methods used are based on:

Extraction of substance to be indicated [*2, 3, 4, 5, 6, 7*]

Extraction of colour complex compounds of the substance [*11, 12*]

Precipitation of colour complex compounds [*8, 9, 10*]

from the biological matter, followed by paper-chromatographic indication [*5, 6, 10, 13*], determination with the photo-spectrometer [*2, 3, 4, 7, 8, 9, 11, 12, 13, 14*], the spectro-fluorophotometer [*15, 16*] or a scintillation counter [2].

The Ion-exchange method is also used for concentration of weak solutions [*13, 14*].

All of these methods are primarily concentration processes.

In order to find a method which would satisfy the particular requirements of insurance medicine, we investigated each of the above processes. Most of the methods demanded special measuring apparatus, were time-consuming or were not considered to be sufficiently sensitive for our purpose. Such observations were made, for example, in the case of the concentration of Guanethidine by ion-exchange resin [*13*] and further concentration of the effluent by subsequent thin-layer chromatography. The extraction of the bromo-cresol-green complex [2] of Guanethidine from urine also gave difficulties, particularly in chromatographic separation.

For this reason the methods indicated were not found by us to be satisfactory. They did not sufficiently meet our basic requirements of simplicity and unambiguity. We therefore sought another method and found an answer by developing the thin-layer chromatography method of Stahl, a new method of trace analysis in biological liquids [*19*].

The thin-layer chromatography method of Stahl [*17*]

This method is finding increasing application in modern analysis and has important advantages over paper-chromatography from which it has been developed; the developing times are shorter, there is greater sensitivity and it permits the use of a large selection of spray reagents.

The principle involves the uniform coating on a glass slide of a thin, even layer (thickness of layer about ¼ mm) of a watery slurry of an adsorption substance, for example kiesel gel or aluminium oxide, which is then dried. Adhesion of the coating is ensured by the addition of a small quantity of gypsum to the glass slide and the coating can then be used for chromatographic separation.

The practical procedure is as follows:

At a starting point at the lower edge of the slide is applied a small spot of 1—100 mm^3 of the solution to be analysed. Comparative substances are then applied to the slide at horizontal intervals of 2 cm.

After drying, the slide is placed in a sealable glass tank and a mixture of a solvent, described as the elution agent, is poured in, to a depth of about 1—2 cm. The elution agent, for example water-saturated butanol, is then sucked up by capillary action, dissolving and carrying away the test substance at the starting point of the slide. As the solvent moves upwards the various other control substances now in solution move, each at its own specific velocity, behind the front of the solvent. If the chromatographic process is interrupted at the right time the various substances will be deposited as more or less round spots at various points along the path of the solvent, that is they are chromatographically separated, and can be made visible with the aid of suitable spray reagents. The ratio of the distance from starting point to centre of spot and the distance from starting point to front of solvent, is a characteristic constant known as the Rf-value. In practice Rf-values range from 0—1.

Our investigations

With the aid of the thin-layer chromatography method of STAHL, we investigated the urinary excretion of the following four groups of anti-hypertensive agents:

Hydrochlorothiazide, Guanethidine, Chlorisondamine and Reserpine.

It was first of all necessary to seek the optimum indication method for the four substances chosen.

1. The determination of optimum conditions of detectability

In practice we proceeded as follows:

We first found for each substance a sensitive dye reagent and the most suitable elution agent (solvent), determining also the smallest detectable amount of each substance. For this purpose various concentrations of solutions of the substances in urine were spotted on to the starting point of the slide and developed with various elution agents. We obtained the best results with the following conditions:

Hydrochlorothiazide

Solvent:	13 g Morpholine dissolved in 150 ml n-butanol
Rf-value:	0.83—0.87
Period of development:	about 3 hours for 10 cm
Spray reagent:	sprayed with 2 n H_2SO_4, kept at 105° C. for $\frac{3}{4}$ hour, then sprayed with a 0.1% $NaNO_2$ solution followed by a 0.1% N (Naphthyl)-ethylene-diamine-chlorohydrate solution. A red azo-dye colour appears on the spot of the Hydrochlorothiazide chromatograph.
Smallest detectable quantity:	spots which contain at least 0.1—0.2 γ (millionths of a gram) are clearly detectable.

Guanethidine

Solvent:	n-butanol, shaken up with a 20% watery solution of CCl_3COOH. Clear butanol is used.
Rf-value:	approximately 0.40
Period of development:	about 3 hours for 10 cm
Spray reagent:	Equal parts by volume of a 1.1% potassium iodide solution and 0.135% chloroplatinic acid are mixed before use. Alternate spraying 2 or 3 times with the above solution and with a 0.5% solution of iodine in chloroform gives a colour indication of Guanethidine as greyish-blue spots on a pinkish-red background.
Smallest detectable quantity:	5—10 γ Guanethidine per spot.

Chlorisondamine

Solvent:	37.5 g of trichloroacetic acid dissolved in 20 ml water and 150 ml of n-propanol.
Rf-value:	0.1—0.2
Period of development:	about 3 hours for 10 cm
Spray reagent:	Equal parts by volume of a 1.1% potassium iodide solution and 0.135% chloroplatinic acid are mixed before use. Chlorisondamine gives bluish-grey spots on a pinkish-red background.
Smallest detectable quantity:	0.05 γ Chlorisondamine per spot.

Reserpine

Solvent:	15 ml of 25% watery ammonia + 150 ml of pure ethyl alcohol.
Rf-value:	0.90—0.93
Period of development:	about 1½ hours for 10 cm
Spray reagent:	5% trichloroacetic acid and 0.025% sodium nitroprusside in methanol. After spraying, Reserpine is shown as a greenish fluorescent spot under filtered UV light.
Smallest detectable quantity:	0.01—0.02 γ Reserpine per spot.

2. *Results of preliminary experiments*

The conditions are extremely favourable with *Hydrochlorothiazide* as the urea concentrations of excreted Hydrochlorothiazide, even after oral ingestion of only 20 mg, are above the limit of detectability which we found using the thin-layer chromatography method. It was therefore to be expected that positive results would be obtained from direct application of urine at the chromatogram starting point.

DOLLERY, EMSLIE-SMITH and MILNE [2] and also TOMPSETT and colleagues [*13*] report exhaustively on the excreted condition of *Guanethidine*. DOLLERY and colleagues found that the concentration in the urinary excretion is at the highest during the first 12 hours after oral ingestion and that during this time, on average, about 19% of the dose administered is excreted.

Our tests confirmed that these concentrations are not sufficient, however, to give a direct indication by the thin-layer chromatography method. In favourable circumstance there are 0.5—2.0 γ Guanethidine in 50 mm³ of urine. It was therefore considered that concentration of the urine to a 40th of the volume would certainly bring Guanethidine within the sphere of detectability. However, this high concentration was not found to be satisfactory since the typical substances contained in the urine upset the method of Guanethidine determination. A specially selective extraction method subsequently resulted in sufficient concentrations for a definite indication.

According to SHEPPARD and colleagues [*12*] 73% of unchanged *Chlorisondamine* is excreted in urine within 24 hours of injection into dogs.

With oral ingestion in man, if one supposes a urinary excretion of 10% with an individual dose of 25 mg of Chlorisondamine, then the concentration excreted (0.25 g in 50 mm³) would be many times higher than the minimum of detectability (0.05 g in 50 mm³) as determined by us.

Nevertheless, the first trial with 25 mg Chlorisondamine (oral administration) gave no positive indication results in the morning urine. It is necessary to carry out further more precise investigation of the excretory processes.

None of the works of reference examined by us reports on the excretion of *Reserpine*. However, its low degree of stability [*18*] gives no cause for expectation of sufficient urinary secretion in an unchanged form.

After oral administration of 0.1—0.25 mg Reserpine, we were therefore not able to indicate its presence in urinary excretion even though the limit of detectability which we had earlier found was in fact very low at 0.01—0.02 γ Reserpine in 50 mm³ of urine. Thus, detection would have to be based on further investigation work into the metabolites formed.

3. *Clinical tests*

a) *Hydrochlorothiazide* (Esidrex). After oral ingestion of 10—25 mg Hydrochlorothiazide in the evening, the urine was chromatographically tested the following morning without concentration of the liquid. In case F the dose was administered after the midday meal and the evening urine was tested. In every chromatogram parallel tests were also made with control urine without Hydrochlorothiazide and also with pure Hydrochlorothiazide.

Table I.

Individual dose of Hydrochlorothiazide (Esidrex)	Test case	Number of hours after urinary excretion before examination carried out	Result
20 mg	A	3 hours	pos.
10 mg	B	27 hours	neg.
25 mg	C	27 hours	pos.
25 mg	D	27 hours	pos.
25 mg	E	27 hours	pos.
25 mg	F	16 hours	pos.

After oral ingestion of 25 mg Hydrochlorothiazide the indication was positive in every case.

b) *Guanethidine* (Ismelin). In a series of tests following oral administration of 10 mg Guanethidine, investigations were carried out on the morning urine as well as the urine 24 and 36 hours after ingestion. Tests were also made of the stability of the urine samples and the urine extractions.

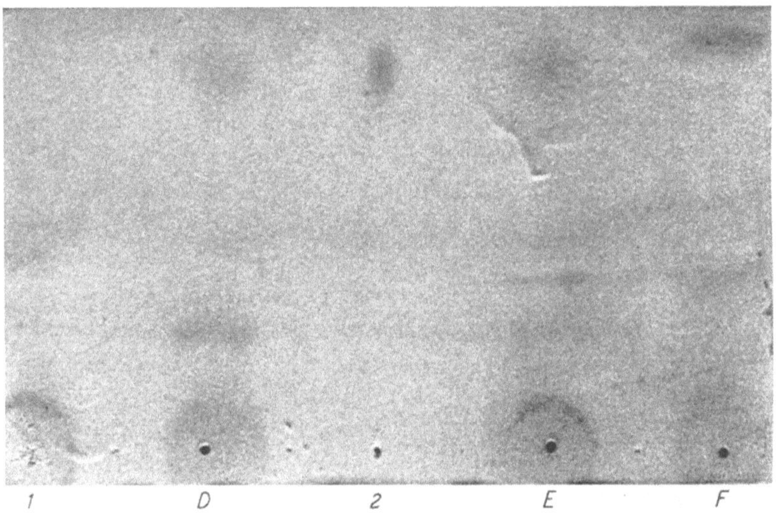

Fig. 1. *Series of Hydrochlorothiazide tests (Esidrex).* The figure represents a thin-layer chromatogram. At starting point No. *1* was dropped a test of control urine without Hydrochlorothiazide, at starting point No. *2* one gamma of pure Hydrochlorothiazide and at the other starting points 50 mm³ of urine from each of the test cases *D*, *E*, and *F*

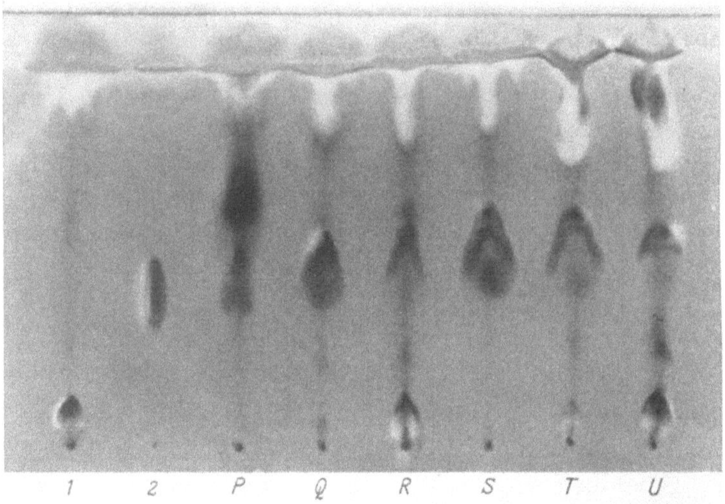

Fig. 2. *Series of Guanethidine tests (Ismelin).* The figure represents a thin layer chromatogram. At the first starting point were dropped 50 mm³ of Reinecke extract of normal urine, at starting point 2, 10 γ Guanethidine (as Reinecke), and at the remaining starting points *P*—*U* 90—100 mm³ in each case of Reinecke extract of the urines of test persons who had previously each taken a single dose of 10 mg Guanethidine

Above the Guanethidine chromatograph spot of test case *P*, appears another spot. This might indicate the presence of another substance foreign to the urine, e.g. another medicament

Method. 100 cm³ of the urine to be tested was placed in a separating funnel with 10 ml of 8% caustic soda and 0.2 ml of a 1% watery solution of Reinecke salts. This was shaken for a short while and left to stand for half an hour. After being shaken up twice more, each time with 10 ml methylisobutyl-ketone, and clarification of the combined ketone layers by centrifugation and filtration, all liquid was evaporated in a vacuum. The residue was dissolved in 0.2 ml acetone and 10—100 mm³ of this solution were chromatographed. Each chromatogram also had a test Reinecke extract of control urine as well as a test of pure Guanethidine. The method may also be used with only 30 cm³ instead of 100 cm³ of urine.

Table II.

Individual dose of Guanethidine (Ismelin)	Test case	Urinary excretion ... hrs. after ingestion	Analysis of test ... hrs. after last urinary excretion	Result
10 mg	A	0—12	3 hrs./Room temp.	positive
			Extract 24 hrs./Room temperature	negative
10 mg	B	0—12	3 hrs./Room temp.	positive
		12—24	15 hrs./Room temp.	positive
10 mg	C	0—12	3 hrs./Room temp.	positive
10 mg	D	0—10	3 hrs./Room temp.	positive
10 mg	E	0—12	3 hrs./Room temp.	positive
10 mg	F	0—11	3 hrs./Room temp.	positive
10 mg	G	0—12	3 hrs./Room temp.	positive
10 mg	H	0—12	24 hrs./Room temp.	positive
		12—24	15 hrs./Room temp.	positive
		24—36	3 hrs./Room temp.	negative
10 mg	J	0—12	24 hrs./Room temp.	positive
		12—24	15 hrs./Room temp.	positive
		24—36	3 hrs./Room temp.	negative
10 mg	K	0—12	3 hrs./Room temp.	positive
10 mg	L	0—12	3 hrs./Room temp.	positive
10 mg	M	0—12	3 hrs./Room temp.	positive
10 mg	N	0—12	3 hrs./Room temp.	positive
10 mg	O	0— 7	3 hrs./Room temp.	positive
			4 days/6° C	positive
			Extract 4 days/6° C	positive
10 mg	P	approx. 12	7 hrs./Room temp. + 20 hrs. 6° C	positive
10 mg	Q	approx. 12	7 hrs./Room temp. + 20 hrs. 6° C	positive
10 mg	R	approx. 12	7 hrs./Room temp. + 20 hrs. 6° C	positive
10 mg	S	approx. 12	7 hrs./Room temp. + 20 hrs. 6° C	positive
10 mg	T	approx. 12	7 hrs./Room temp. + 20 hrs. 6° C	positive
10 mg	U	approx. 12	7 hrs./Room temp. + 20 hrs. 6° C	positive

A summary of the results in Table II gives the following picture:

By administration of an individual dose of 10 mg orally it was possible to detect Guanethedine in the urine within a period of 0—12 hours; 24—36 hours after taking this drug it was no longer detectable. The Guanethidine indication works also with urine samples and urine extractions which are kept for four days at 6° C before testing, and also with urine samples which have been left to stand for 24 hours at room temperature. On the other hand an originally positive urine extract gave a negative result after standing for 24 hours at room temperature. These degrees of stability must be taken into consideration in practice.

c) *Chlorisondamine (Ecolid) and Reserpine (Serpasil).* We attempted to find a similar method for Chlorisondamine (Ecolid) and Reserpine (Serpasil) as was found for Hydrochlorothiazide and Guanethidine.

With oral doses of 25 mg Ecolid we could obtain no indication of the unchanged substance in the urinary excretion. We had a similar lack of success with oral doses of Serpasil of 0.25 mg. We were in fact only able to show that the corresponding urine tests contained less than 0.1 γ Ecolid and 0.01—0.02 γ unchanged Serpasil, respectively. Moreover, tests with extractions and concentrations of 40 and 100 times respectively, showed that even in such concentrated samples the unchanged agent was not detectable.

We are inclined to assume that metabolites were formed. Should this be the case, then these must first be identified before there is any prospect of indicating their presence in the urine. We must furthermore ascertain when and with what dosage one may expect excretion of a detectable quantity. The sensitivity and exactitude of the chromatographic method offers every possibility of further work resulting in unambiguous determination of these drugs and of other medicines in the urine.

Discussion of our results

The aim of our investigation, namely the demonstration of anti-hypertensive substances in the urine, was achieved in the cases of 2 of the 4 substances under discussion.

Preliminary experiments to determine the optimum conditions of detectability showed that the thin-layer chromatography method of Stahl is well suited to all 4 substances. The substances in question could also be detected in minimal concentrations in mixtures of liquids, as also after addition to urine.

However, in clinical tests it was shown that, following therapeutically suitable doses, only Hydrochlorothiazide (Esidrex) is contained in the urine in a sufficiently concentrated form, that is in concentrations which are within the range of detectability by thin-layer chromatography.

These concentrations were not reached with the drug Guanethidine (Ismelin), which is relatively more important both clinically and, above all, from the viewpoint of insurance medicine. A suitable extraction process had to be, and was in fact, devised.

We think we may assume that, as for Hydrochlorothiazide and Guanethidine, it might also well be possible to find a way of demonstrating the presence of other substances in the urine. CAMPBELL has also shown in the case of antidiabetic drugs that thin-layer chromatography is a good way of demonstrating the presence of medicaments in the urine.

Thin-layer chromatography is all the more valuable by virtue of its technical simplicity, which permits it to be practised in any suitably equipped laboratory. It gives no difficulties as regards interpretation, which fact could be of particular importance from the legal standpoint.

Summary

Certain large groups of diseases in which long-term prognosis is important, may to-day be influenced by medicaments to such an extent that these diseases give a misleading appearance of being cured. Routine medical examination is no longer able to discover these diseases, or at least not with any certainty.

Diabetes mellitus and high blood pressure are among such afflictions mentioned above.

This successful masking by the use of medicines, especially in the case of high blood pressure, creates an entirely new problem in medical prognosis for insurance.

It is significant that more and more candidates for insurance take anti-hypertensive substances before the medical examination, with intent to mislead.

In order to recognize hypertension masked by medicines, we have sought an objective method of demonstrating the presence of anti-hypertensive substances as such.

By a technically perfect, unequivocal method we have succeeded regularly and with certainty in detecting by thin-layer chromatography the presence in the urine of 2 of the 4 substances under investigation, namely Guanethidine (one of the group of ganglion-blocking agents) and Esidrex (one of the chlorothiazides).

It may be concluded that there is a logical possibility of finding a method to determine clearly by thin-layer chromatography the presence of other anti-hypertensive medicaments and also other agents.

It also seems probable that thin-layer chromatography will be further improved and simplified in the future.

References

[1] BÄUMELER und RIPPSTEIN: Pharm. Acta Helv. **36**, 382 (1961).
LIEBICH: Dtsch. Apoth.-Ztg. **99**, 1246 (1959); **100**, 393 (1960).
NÜRNBERG: Arch. Pharm. **292/64**, 610 (1959).
GÄNSHIRT: Arch. Pharm. **293/65**, 925 (1960).

[2] DOLLERY, EMSLIE-SMITH and MILNE: Lancet (1960), No. 7147, 381.
[3] Experientia **14**, 159—160 (1958).
[4] HAYCOCK, SHETH, CONOLLY and MADER: Journal of the association of official agricultural chemists Vol. **42**, No. 3, 613 (1959).
[5] KORZUM, ANDRÉ and ULSHAFER: J. Amer. pharm. Ass., sci. Ed. Vol. **XLVI**, No. 12, 720 (1957).
[6] ANDRÉ, KORZUM and WEINFELDT: J. org. Chemistry **21**, 480 (1956).
[7] BAER, PAULSON, RUSSO and BEYER: Amer. J. Physiol. **186**, 180—186 (1956).
[8] ZEIMIS: Brit. J. Pharmacol. **5**, 424—430 (1950).
[9] HARINGTON: Clin. Sci. **12**, 185—198 (1953).
[10] SHEPPARD, SACHS D'ASARO: Nature **177**, 1089 (1956).
[11] PERRY: J. Lab. clin. Med. **41**, 566—573 (1953).
[12] SHEPPARD, PLUMMER and SABBAGH: Fed. Proc. **15**, 483 (1956).
[13] TOMPSETT, FORSHALL and SMITH: Acta pharmacol. (Kbh.) **18**, 75—79 (1961).
[14] ROSENHEIM et al.: Lancet No. 7089, 17 (1959).
[15] HAYCOCK, SHETH and MADER: J. Amer. pharm. Ass., sci. Ed. Vol. **XLVIII**, No. 8, 479 (1959).
[16] SHEPPARD, WAGLE and PLUMMER: Fed. Proc. **13**, 404 (1954).
[17] STAHL: Pharmazie **11**, 633 (1956); Chemiker-Ztg. **82**, 323 (1958); Parfümerie u. Kosmet. **9**, 564 (1958).
[18] CUZZONI: Pharmaco, ed. pract. **12**, 204 (1957).
BAYER: Pharmazie **13**, 468 (1958).
KREBS: Dtsch. Apoth.-Ztg. **98**, 1341 (1958).
[19] TANNER, SUTER, CONTI und WANNER: Lebensversicher.-Med. **13**, 69—71 (1961).

Author index

MIX
Papier aus verantwortungsvollen Quellen
Paper from responsible sources
FSC® C105338

If you have any concerns about our products,
you can contact us on
ProductSafety@springernature.com

In case Publisher is established outside the EU,
the EU authorized representative is:
Springer Nature Customer Service Center GmbH
Europaplatz 3, 69115 Heidelberg, Germany

Printed by Libri Plureos GmbH
in Hamburg, Germany